SENIOR FEMALE INTERNATIONAL MANAGERS

To my husband, mother, and the memory of my father

Senior Female International Managers
Why so few?

MARGARET LINEHAN

Ashgate

Aldershot • Brookfield USA • Singapore • Sydney

Published by
Ashgate Publishing Ltd
Gower House
Croft Road
Aldershot
Hants GU11 3HR
England

Ashgate Publishing Company
Old Post Road
Brookfield
Vermont 05036
USA

Ashgate website: http://www.ashgate.com

British Library Cataloguing in Publication Data
Linehan, Margaret
    Senior female international managers: why so few?
    1. Women executives 2. International business enterprises -
    Management 3. Sex discrimination in employment 4. Executive
    ability
    I. Title
    658.4'09'082

Library of Congress Catalog Card Number: 99-75558

ISBN 0 7546 1200 7

Printed in Great Britain by
Antony Rowe Ltd, Chippenham, Wiltshire

Contents

List of Tables and Figures

Acknowledgements

As this book developed from research which I carried out for the completion of a PhD thesis, I extend my heartfelt thanks to my PhD research supervisor and friend, Dr James S. Walsh, Department of Management and Marketing, University College, Cork. Jim provided superb mentoring, encouragement, support, and networking opportunities during our many projects together. This book is a result of his 'Go for it!' advice.

I am very grateful to the fifty managers who contributed a rich source of research data for this study, by giving their time to be interviewed and sharing their experiences of their international career moves in an enjoyable, humorous, interesting, and forthright manner.

Special thanks to the best female manager I know, my mother, Joan Linehan, who does her best to manage me! Thanks for your support, friendship, and for always spoiling me. Thanks also to my uncle, Fr Michael Kelleher, MSC, for his continuing interest in my everyday concerns.

Sincere thanks to my best female friend, Frances O'Gorman, an expatriate trailing spouse, for your continued interest in all my ventures and 'for always being there'. Perhaps, I will take your advice and publish my next book on coffee shops!

Finally, and especially, my love and thanks to my husband and best friend, John Mullins, for your love, patience, and support always, and for your 'high-tech' expertise and copy-editing in preparing this text.

1 Introduction

1.1 Introduction

This study is an assessment of the international career move made by senior female managers in Europe. The perspective explored is that of currently employed senior female managers in a wide range of organisations, who have made at least one international career move. The study is based on data collected from interviews with fifty senior female international managers. The voices of the female managers illustrate difficulties they encounter in 'a man's world' and remind us that there is still much to be changed. The study, for the first time, assesses an exclusively *senior* sample of female international managers. Previous studies have established that, throughout Europe, women's advance into senior *domestic* management positions has been very slow, despite legislative changes, including the European Union's social protocol, to enforce issues related to equal opportunity such as equal pay and sex discrimination (Davidson and Cooper, 1993; Hammond and Holton, 1991). The number of female managers pursuing international management careers, however, remains considerably lower than the number in domestic management. Harris (1995b) and Adler (1993b) estimate that only three per cent of expatriate managers are women. This study examines a number of explanations from the relevant literature and analyses the empirical data collected from the fifty interviewees in order to develop a more complete model of the senior female international career move in Europe. This research is particularly relevant, as existing European studies have not specifically addressed issues pertaining to the *senior* female expatriate manager.

This chapter provides an overview of the study. First, the changing role of women in management is discussed. Second, recent findings and trends in international human resource management and European management are outlined. Various gaps in the international human resource management literature are identified which help to justify the rationale for the study. Finally, the research focus of the study together with details of the interviewees and the methodological choices made are presented.

1

1.2   The Role of Women in Management

One of the most significant features of the global labour market in the last half of the twentieth century has been the increasing labour-force participation rate of women. In recent years, in particular, there has been an increase in the number of women pursuing managerial careers (Harris, 1995; Davidson and Cooper, 1993; 1992; Gordon and Whelan, 1998). According to Alimo-Metcalfe and Wedderburn-Tate (1993), however, in terms of the managerial population, it is difficult to establish accurate figures for the proportions of women in management since definitions of management used by different studies may vary. Despite these definitional difficulties, however, it is evident from the extant research that women are not progressing to senior management positions at comparable rates to their male counterparts (Harris, 1995; Smith and Hutchinson, 1995; Burke and Davidson, 1994; Izraeli and Adler 1994; Berthoin-Antal and Izraeli, 1993; Davidson and Cooper, 1992).

Berthoin-Antal and Izraeli (1993) noted that, until the late 1970s, women managers were virtually invisible in most countries. In the mid 1980s, Ho (1984, p. 7) observed that:

> Statistics show that women represent one third of the world's workforce, do two-thirds of the world's working hours, but they earn only one-tenth of the world's income and own one-hundredth of the world's goods . . . they hold less than one per cent of the world's executive positions.

Berthoin-Antal and Izraeli (1993) reported that, during the 1980s, the under-representation of women in positions of power emerged as a 'problem', and became an item of high priority on the agenda of industrialised countries. Adler and Izraeli (1988) highlighted globalisation, skill shortage, labour-force participation, and women's resources and commitment as the forces that contributed to this change. Adler and Izraeli believed that, first, the globalisation of competition created the need to encourage excellence and maximise the human potential in the workforce. Second, demographic forecasts indicated a shortage of qualified white men for top-level jobs. Third, the increased participation of women in the labour force contributed to the perception of women as an underused source of human resources. Finally, the continuing investment in education and training made by women themselves, and their active searches for promotion, made it more difficult to overlook women in recruitment and promotion decisions (Adler and Izraeli, 1988).

Despite the awareness of the under-representation of women in management in the 1980s, however, studies have indicated that the situation has not yet greatly improved. Research from the USA, Australia and Europe reports similar trends in the position of women in management, for example, statistics from the USA have established that women constitute nearly half of the labour force and occupy a significant and growing proportion of entry and mid-level managerial positions, but less than five per cent of executive positions are held by women (USA: Department of Labor, 1996). A 1995 USA census further revealed that while women accounted for ten per cent of corporate officers, they represented just 2.4 per cent of the highest ranks of corporate leadership, and held only 1.9 per cent of the most highly compensated officer positions in *Fortune 500* companies, and only four of the *Fortune 1000* CEO positions are held by women (Catalyst, 1996).

Research from Australia established that women constitute 42.3 per cent of the Australian workforce (Australian Bureau of Statistics, 1994). Women, however, are still under-represented in middle and senior managerial positions, occupying an estimated 21.1 per cent of all management positions (Australian Bureau of Statistics, 1993). According to Korn/Ferry International (1993), women are moving into middle management positions in industries such as banking and finance, but, only three per cent reach senior executive positions.

Statistics from Europe indicate that females make up 41 per cent of the working population (Eurostat, 1996). Throughout all the European Union countries, however, there is still job segregation based on gender, and over half of women are employed in the service sector which includes trade, education, retail, health-care and clerical duties (Davidson and Cooper, 1992). Women in corporate environments tend to be at the lower end of the managerial hierarchy, even after being employed for a decade or more in management jobs, with fewer than five per cent in *senior* management positions (Davidson and Cooper, 1993). Research by Davidson and Cooper (1992) concluded that, overall, women employed in European Union countries do not enjoy the same job conditions, pay, status and career opportunities as their male counterparts.

As outlined, the figures given for women in senior *domestic* management positions in most industrialised countries remain negligible. The figures for the number of women pursuing *international* managerial careers, i.e., who relocate to a different country to work for an extended period, are even lower, remaining at between two and five per cent (Reynolds and Bennett, 1991; Adler, 1984). Very little research has been carried out concerning female international managers, mainly due to their relative scarcity (Harris, 1995b). The available research, however, on women international managers in the USA, Britain and some Asian countries such as Japan, indicates that, of those organisations which promote women through their domestic managerial hierarchy, few are prepared to allow women to expand their career horizons via international placements (Adler, 1993; Adler and Izraeli, 1988).

Adler's extensive research conducted in North America with female expatriate managers shows that none of the participants in her studies occupied her company's most senior position in North America or in any country. The majority were employed in *junior* managerial positions supervising from zero to twenty-five subordinates, with the average falling just below five. Interestingly, research conducted by Izraeli et al. (1980) concluded that only exceptional expatriate women could succeed as heads of multinational corporations, as outstanding competence was necessary to overcome the additional barriers.

Harris (1995) conducted research with female British expatriates, but only 20.5 per cent of the participants were in the *managerial* category and only ten per cent were based in western Europe. Harris suggested that further research might be conducted with female expatriates who are employed in cultures similar to those in their home countries, rather than concentrating on females assigned to traditionally male dominated countries. This research agenda, therefore, extends previous work by examining the experiences of female managers moving to countries with cultures similar to those in their home countries.

McGee-Calvert and Ramsey (1992, p. 80) suggested that the study of women in management has not experienced 'any dramatic leaps forward in quite a while', because using men as a standard of comparison and 'adding' females to the sample has not really changed the nature of the research. This research has taken as its starting point the unique perspectives and experiences of *senior* female international managers. From these different perspectives and experiences, different assumptions about women in international management and female lifestyle choices are arrived at. McGee-Calvert and Ramsey also suggested that women's collective voice has been silenced in the field of management, because of pressures placed on women to conform to the existing norms of organisations and because of the rejection by women themselves of the notion that they are different, as difference has most often been defined as inferiority. This research has given women an opportunity to break the silence in the field of international human resource management. The findings from the research resonate with the description of women's voice put forward by Aptheker (1989, p. 83):

> Women have a distinct way of seeing and interpreting the world. This is not to say that all women have the same consciousness or share the same beliefs. It is to say that women of each particular culture or group have a consciousness, a way of seeing, which is common to themselves as women in that it is distinct from the way the men of their culture or group see things.

Arising from the lack of empirical data which details the role and career moves of the *senior* female international manager, a number of largely untested assumptions have been used in an attempt to explain the low participation rate of females in international management. This study (i) highlights a number of these assumptions, (ii) discusses and analyses both the covert and overt barriers faced by women in their progression to senior managerial positions, and (iii) empirically tests the reasons which have been given in the literature in an attempt to explain the relative scarcity of female international managers.

1.3   International Human Resource Management

> Successful international managers, whether mobile, or non-mobile, must be able to act locally, but to plan and think strategically and globally (Barham and Rassam, 1989, p. 149).

According to Torrington (1994), in order to examine what international human resource management is, it is important to first of all consider two things that it is not. First, international human resource management is *not* copying the practices from the Americans, the Germans, the Taiwanese, the Koreans, or the Japanese. Torrington suggests that whereas technical and financial operations may transfer across all countries, people-management methods do not necessarily transfer from one culture to another. Second, international human resource management is not a matter of managers learning the cultures of every country in which they have to deal with and modifying their own behaviour when dealing with those nationals. Torrington (1994, p. 4) cautions that cultures are both robust and subtle and 'we have great difficulty in achieving more than a modest level of behaviour adaptation'. Torrington (1994, p. 6) suggests that:

> In many ways international human resource management is human resource management on a larger scale; the strategic considerations are more complex and the operational units are more varied, needing co-ordination across more barriers.

Dowling (1988) similarly summarises that the difference between domestic and international human resource management is that international human resource management is more complex than domestic human resource management. He further adds that in practice many organisations are still coming to terms with the human resources issues associated with international operations. Scullion (1995, p. 352) defines international human resource management as:

> The human resource management issues and problems arising from the internationalisation of business, and the human resource management strategies, policies and practices which firms pursue in response to the internationalisation process.

Tung (1984) argues that, in the international arena, the quality of management seems to be even more critical than in domestic operations. The effective management of human resources has increasingly been recognised as a major determinant of success or failure in international business. This is primarily because the nature of international business operations involves the complexities of operating in different countries and employing different national categories of workers.

Most of international human resource management research has been conducted by American researchers, has been primarily concerned with American expatriates, and was written from an American rather than an international perspective. Scullion (1995) suggests that the research on international human resource management has focused on two general areas. The first is international staffing, which primarily deals with the problems of selecting and managing expatriate managers. The second is international management development. The reasons research has focused on these two areas are because, in all countries, organisations have to address the same human resource management issues: how to obtain and keep people to perform relevant tasks; how to develop them to be able to fulfil such tasks; how to resolve the dilemma of control and commitment. Brewster and Tyson (1991) suggest, however, that the means found in each country to resolve these issues will be based on and be part of the culture of that country. Studies have shown that national cultures affect organisation structures and policies as well as the work-related values and attitudes of employees. National cultures also influence the process of organisation decision-making and the relationships between people in organisations. Laurent (1986, p. 93) suggests that corporate cultures may also have a profound behavioural effect and points out that 'international human resource management may only be international in the eyes of the designers'.

1.4   European Human Resource Management

Several comparative analyses of European and international human resource management have been carried out in order to identify the most significant influences that have shaped human resource management. According to Brewster and Bournois (1991, p. 4-13), however, these studies have tended to describe the general national practices of human resource management and have focused on differences and similarities, thus providing 'a glimpse of the uneven way in which concepts of human resource management have been applied across Europe'.

Given its largely North American origins, Sparrow and Hiltrop (1994) suggest that it is important to first of all develop an understanding of what human resource management is in a *European* context. Brewster and Hegewisch (1994) suggest that, in a global perspective, Europe has a coherence of its own and a distinctiveness from other major blocs. Remer (1986, p. 363) similarly suggests that, although there are differences in human resource management conditions and circumstances within western Europe, taken as a whole 'they stand out as being distinct from other economic areas like the USA, USSR or Japan'. According to Brewster and Tyson (1991), throughout the late 1980s and early 1990s a process of 'Europeanisation' has taken place and this provides an opportunity to re-evaluate human resource management in a regional context, by examining and interpreting differences in labour markets, participation structures, legislation, rewards, recruitment patterns and the harmonisation of qualifications. Sparrow and Hiltrop (1994), however, make the point that the need for the re-evaluation of what is meant by human resource management in a European context is not just driven by international developments. Such a requirement is also driven by the growing academic criticism of many studies on European human resource management. This criticism suggests that these studies simply provide descriptions of best practice in traditional personnel management areas such as recruitment and selection, performance appraisal, pay, training and development, without providing any credible framework for what is meant by European human resource management.

Thurley and Wirdenius (1991, p. 128) point out the need to 'distinguish European Management as a possible alternative approach' because of the predominant focus of American and Japanese conceptions of management. They consider this as necessary to reflect the different cultural values and legal–institutional practices that are dominant in Europe. They suggest that a European approach is emerging, but cannot be said to exist except in limited circumstances. Brewster and Hegewisch (1994) suggest that a model of European human resource management is required that re-emphasises the influence of such factors as culture, ownership structures, the role of the state and trade-union organisation. In European management practices, for example, trade unions are recognised as social partners with a positive role to play, whereas the culture of American management appears to be anti-union.

In the 1980s, when theories and models of human resource management were first being developed, underlying cultural assumptions became apparent. By this time, American organisations in particular were under severe competitive threat from Japan. Management writers began to draw attention to low levels of commitment in Anglo-Saxon organisations and the need for major restructuring and reorganisation in order to meet the challenge of new competition. According to Peters and Waterman (1982), the role of quality, and the need to tie people in the organisation deeper into the heart of the business, should be seen as central to achieving this restructuring. It was argued that restructuring was to be achieved by linking 'people management' and strategic planning processes and this linkage was seen to differentiate human resource management from traditional personnel management. The concept of human resource management was initially taken up by countries like Britain and Australia whose cultures most resembled that of the USA. The language, theoretical concepts and the practice of human resource management, therefore, moved into continental Europe from America through Britain (Sparrow and Hiltrop, 1994). Pieper

(1990), however, argues that, although it is widely acknowledged that much of the human resource management literature within Europe is rooted in America and human resource management is largely seen as an American invention, paternalistic personnel management and human resource management concepts have a long history over the course of European industrialisation.

Lawrence (1993) argues that human resource management is essentially an Anglo-Saxon construct that has been 'grafted on' — rather than having 'taken root' — in continental Europe. According to Legge (1995), the shift in language from 'personnel management' to 'human resource management' in the 1980s in America and Britain signifies that some changes in some sectors of industry have taken place in the management of the labour process and in employment relationships. Legge's 1989 review of British and American literature of human resource management notes that there are three main areas that distinguish human resource management from personnel management. First, human resource management gives greater emphasis to the development of the management team than personnel management. Second, it differs from personnel management as an activity for line managers because it is more firmly integrated in the general co-ordinating activity for line managers. Third, it emphasises the management of corporate culture as a senior management activity. Legge (1995, p. 34), however, suggests that the development of such language is a pragmatic response to opportunities and constraints in the economic environment, rather than 'constituting expressions of a coherent new employment philosophy'.

Throughout Europe different political, economic, social and cultural considerations lead to a reinterpretation of management agendas at a local level. Every European country has a different historical and legal inheritance and 'so European human resource management must remain an ambiguous concept' (Sparrow and Hiltrop, 1994, p. 30). Brewster et al. (1991) comment that until recently there has been little empirical evidence and that few quantitative data exist to allow a systematic analysis of international and European trends in human resource management. Thurley (1990) suggested that, although there is no clear model for European human resource management, many European multinationals and some medium-sized cross-border organisations display some pan-European human resource management principles in a distinct form. Sparrow and Hiltrop (1994), however, suggest that there are still some marked differences across Europe, and between Europe and America, in terms of human resource management practices and policies. Albert (1989, p. 75) has argued that, regarding human resource management practices in Europe, 'we are in culturally different contexts and, rather than copy solutions which result from other cultural traditions, we should consider the state of mind that presided in the search for responses adapted to culture'. Forster (1992) indicates that for a human resource management strategy to succeed in a European context it has to be highly responsive to local cultures; national, legal, and institutional frameworks; business practices; and ownership structures, which are the major determinants of local human resource management practice. Similarly, Whitley (1992) notes that despite increasing internationalisation within many European industries, national institutions remain quite distinct.

Interview research conducted by Calori et al (1994) with fifty-one top managers of forty large international companies with headquarters or major operating units in Europe asked 'Is there something like a European model of management?'. The research team's original hypothesis was that management in Europe is diverse, but, when compared to America and Japan, some common characteristics appear across Europe which together form the components of an evolving management model. Data from their interviews reveal that a typical remark was 'Europe is in between'; if there is a European style of management, it is 'halfway' between the USA model of management and the Japanese model. Calori et al. conclude that a simplified but reliable image of the diversity of management in Europe would be to view management philosophies, structures, and practices in Europe as if they were stretched between three poles, with (i) Anglo-Saxon management to the west, (ii) the German model to the east, and Japan to the far east, and (iii) the Latin model to the south. This research by Calori et al. highlights the cultural diversities in Europe and should help to explain some of the difficulties experienced by the largely European sample of participants in this research, when moving to cultures which are considered similar to those of their home countries.

Overall, it can be seen that cultural differences in Europe are considered to be both deeply ingrained and to persist over time. As Evans (1990, in Utley, p. 7) stated, 'There are profound differences between European countries, not just in markets and competencies, but in basic concepts of management'. In Europe, management philosophies, structures, and practices are diverse and share some common characteristics when countries are compared with each other and with America and Japan. According to de Woot (1994, p. 261), European national management systems 'will doubtless remain strong, and this is no bad thing, since diversity is Europe's greatest strength'. He argues that in the past we have tended to believe too strongly in a universal model of management and have attempted to imitate the American or the Japanese model, 'but culture is stronger than methods' (1994, p. 262).

1.5   Rationale for the Study

> The option of limiting international management to one gender is an arm-chair 'luxury' that no company can afford (Adler, 1993b, p. 55).

Recent years have seen a rapid increase in global activity and global competition in all industrialised countries, which has resulted in more women entering lower-level managerial positions (Izraeli and Adler, 1994). Despite women's increased investment in higher education, their greater commitment to management as a career, the shortages of international managers, and equal opportunity legislation, female managers in every country remain 'only a tiny fraction of those in senior positions' (Adler and Izraeli, 1994). Scullion's (1995) study of forty-five British and Irish international firms revealed that, despite the shortages of international managers, there was no evidence that British multinationals were taking serious steps to increase the proportion of women in international management. Adler's (1987) North American research illustrated the success of women as expatriates, but home-country senior male managers continue to be concerned about a woman's ability to function effectively in countries where her activities may be curtailed because of local customs and regulations. According to Davison and Punnett (1995), gender, race, religion and other distinguishing personal characteristics frequently arise in expatriate decisions, but, these issues are seldom specified by managers or researchers. These issues have been highlighted from research conducted in North America in an attempt to explain the low proportion of females partaking in international management. Empirical work with *senior* female expatriate managers in Europe is now necessary in order to explain why international management is still generally reserved for the male manager.
From the limited research available on female international managers, primarily from North America, a number of explanations have been put forward in attempting to explain the very low proportion of female managers who partake in overseas assignments. European empirical research,

however, has not been conducted with *senior* female international managers, presumably because of their relative scarcity. Adler (1993b) argued that home-country senior managers tend to question if women can succeed in international assignments, as it is estimated that only three per cent of expatriates are women. An examination of the literature for the explanation of the low participation rate of women in international management by Harris (1995) revealed that (i) stereotypical assumptions by home-country managers which equates good management with characteristics associated with male managers, and (ii) assumptions regarding female managers' availability, suitability and their wishes to partake in international management have been cited frequently.

This study will empirically test these assumptions and investigate the difficulties female managers face in attempting to break into this male preserve.   Burke and Davidson (1994), however, cautioned that in attempting to identify specific reasons for women's lack of advancement to senior management positions, it is important to remember that managerial and professional women live and work in a larger society that is patriarchal, a society in which men have historically had greater access to power, privilege and wealth than women. Burke and Davidson also noted that, because the field of women in management has gained research attention only since the 1980s, many research questions remain unanswered or have been only partially addressed. In the international management field, however, the position of female managers has received far less attention than female managers in *domestic* organisations, which also means that many research questions remain unanswered. This study, therefore, proposes to address a number of questions and issues, which can broadly be divided in three main literature categories, namely, women in management, career theory, and women in international management, which should be important in furthering our knowledge of the senior female international career move.

First, in the women in management domain, the study proposes to investigate the overt and covert barriers which prevent female managers from progressing to senior management positions. According to Vinnicombe and Colwill (1995), women occupy only about ten per cent of management positions in Europe and women managers remain concentrated in junior and middle management positions. As there is a dearth of empirical research with *senior* female international managers in Europe, the findings should highlight the significant barriers and biases that women managers have to cope with in comparison to their male counterparts in their home and host countries.

Most of the research on women in management has concentrated on women in *domestic* organisations. The sample studied for this research consisted of fifty successful managers who have broken through the glass ceiling and glass border. These women were senior executives and directors in industrial and service industries, and senior members of high-status professions, such as lawyers, accountants and medical consultants. As these fifty managers have overcome obstacles and biases in their careers, both in their home and host organisations, it is necessary to examine the strategies that successful female managers use to reach senior managerial positions, in an attempt to further the progression of future female managers.

Second, the findings of the study will contribute to literature in the career theory domain, by addressing a number of pertinent questions in relation to career planning. The study will investigate whether female managers engage in career planning and examine the respondent viewpoints in relation to planning careers. Because female managers face more overt and covert barriers than their male counterparts, the career planning process for women is different from that of men and far more complex in terms of frequent shifts between home and work. The findings should help understand the additional complexities for women in planning their careers in comparison to their male colleagues.

Career development is closely linked with career planning, therefore, the study proposes to investigate whether there is a model of career development which fits the experiences of female managers. Men have generally served as standards by which others, including women, are compared. Women are often studied to see how they depart from the male standard, both in choice of a career and in career development. In relation to women's career development, Perun and Bielby (1981) stated that research on adulthood in women has focused on the family cycle at the expense of the work cycle. In their view, the outcome was that no formal theory of women's occupational behaviour existed. The findings should illustrate the difficulties experienced by female managers when they depart from the male linear model of career progression, the model which is generally considered the norm in organisations. The findings should also provide answers to the implications for female managers of non-adherence to the traditional career development model which does not consider career breaks and time out for child-bearing and child rearing and the level of responsibilities female managers have in relation to home and family members.

Third, a number of questions remain unanswered in the women in international management domain, due to the lack of available empirical

European research. The study will attempt to establish whether the 'glass ceiling' still exists in Europe, and if the variables which constitute this ceiling are similar across national boundaries. Previous research studies have established that numerous barriers exist for female managers in their home organisations in comparison to their male counterparts. This study investigates whether there are additional barriers for female managers when they partake in international management. As research on European women's international career moves is relatively new, the study attempts to establish whether there are additional difficulties for female international managers when the male partner is 'the trailing spouse'. Previous research studies have established that the majority of expatriate managers are male and are usually accompanied abroad by a non-working trailing spouse.

Given the largely pioneering role of European female international managers, it is necessary to address whether mentors have an influence on the careers of these managers. Mentors have been recognised as a source of organisational support for managers in their home organisations. The gender of the mentor also merits further investigation, as previous research regarding mentors with female managers in their home organisations is inconclusive. Another form of organisational support is that of network groups, and this study will assess the role networking groups have on the career of the senior female international manager. The study will investigate differences in men's and women's access to informal networks at work, and highlight the differences between male and female networks. Because of the relative scarcity of women in international management, the study will examine whether additional difficulties exist for the female international manager as part of a minority group. The study will also address how women cope with this situation. Closely related to the low participation rates of women in international management is the lack of female role models. The study highlights the role-model function these fifty successful managers now provide in an attempt to increase the number of female international managers.

Tung (1984) argued that, in the international arena, the quality of management seems to be even more critical than in domestic operations. The effective management of human resources has increasingly been recognised as a major determinant of success or failure in international business. There is no profile of the ideal expatriate, but the majority of managers (approximately 97 per cent) are male, which means that the research to date has typically focused on the *male* international career move. It is, therefore, necessary to examine the characteristics which female managers require in order to make an international career move and the managerial style senior female international managers adopt. According to Feldman and Tompson (1993), the empirical research on international career moves in general has 'lagged far behind' the descriptive and theoretical models of the process. Brewster and Scullion (1997) suggest that, in general, the study of expatriation has followed the traditional male expatriate 'cycle' — selection, training, relocation and adjustment, pay and performance, and return. The transfer cycle for female international managers in comparison with their male counterparts now needs to be investigated, for example, whether the female transfer cycle is based on the male model, or if a separate female transfer cycle exists.

Additional difficulties are experienced by female managers because of the stereotypical image of the international male manager created by home-country senior management. These assumptions typically cast women in a relatively disadvantaged position in the corporate structure. Because of these additional difficulties faced by women expatriate managers, and in particular married female managers, a widely held view by senior home-country male managers is that these women do not want to be international managers. This study investigates whether female managers want international management careers, and finally assesses the overall impact gender has on the international career of female managers. This study proposes to address these questions to senior female international managers, whose practical experience should contribute to our understanding of the senior female international managerial career move, and also to report, discuss, and analyse other relevant issues which arise from the fieldwork to be conducted.

1.6 Research Focus of the Study

This study is exploratory as there is little previous research specifically addressing the issue of *senior* female international managers employed in Europe. Woodall and Winstanley (1998, p. 70) have defined a *senior* manager as one of those managers who is 'responsible for the overall direction and operation of an organisation, developing appropriate policies and strategy, and setting objectives for the rest of the organisation'. For the purpose of this study and following Woodall and Winstanley, a *senior* manager is defined as a manager with executive decision-making functions.

A semi-structured interview format was used to ensure that the interviews covered the same main questions, but allowed respondents to reply in a variety of ways and raise issues which were pertinent to the topics being investigated. In order to get a number of potentially different perspectives, interviews were conducted with fifty senior female international managers across a wide range of industry sectors. The general conclusions of the study are reported, based on a summary of the interviews.

None of the managers selected for inclusion in the study refused to be interviewed. The interviewees were all eager to participate, indicating that, because there were relatively few women expatriate managers, topics and issues which were specifically relevant to their situations had received very little attention in the international human resource management literature. They believed that it was timely for organisations to face and address the difficulties female managers encounter in their progression to senior managerial positions, because of the paucity of women expatriates. They expected this imbalance to change in the future. The findings suggest that taking a proactive approach to female expatriate managers should give organisations a competitive advantage in the international environment. As all fifty participants had been employed in senior management positions, both in their home and host organisations, 76 per cent of participants believed that articulating their concerns and highlighting their successes might provide other European female managers with role models.

The study takes as its unique focus, therefore, the perceptions of *senior* expatriate managers in relation to the female international managerial career move. In order to support these perspectives, an interview guide was developed by the author and used for conducting all fifty semi-structured interviews.   In summary, the study extends work primarily in the international human resource management literature, while also contributing to the research literatures on women in management and career theory, focusing on senior female expatriate managers in Europe and assessing in particular their perceptions of the difficulties and opportunities in relation to their international career moves.

1.7   The Interview Pool

A key difficulty in qualitative research utilising the interview technique is to determine the precise number of interviewees (Mintzberg, 1979).   The approach adopted in selecting the number of interview participants for this study was based on a strategy called 'theoretical sampling' where the actual number of cases studied is relatively unimportant (Glaser and Strauss, 1967). McCracken (1988, p. 17), for instance, endorses the use of small samples, and states that 'for many research projects, eight respondents will be perfectly sufficient'. According to Siedman (1991), there are two criteria for 'enough'. The first is sufficiency. This determines if there are sufficient numbers to reflect the range of participants and sites that make up the population so that others outside the sample might have a chance to connect to the experiences of those in it. The other criterion is saturation of information, when the interviewer begins to hear the same information reported and she is no longer learning anything new (Siedman, 1991). Mason (1996) suggests that qualitative samples are usually small for practical reasons relating to the costs, especially in terms of time as well as money, and for generating and analysing qualitative data.

1.8   The Sample

Fifty senior, female managers were selected for inclusion in this study. A listing from *Fortune 500* top companies provided the starting point for targeting interviewees. Initially, an introductory letter was sent to the Chief Executive Officers of these companies in England, Belgium, France and Germany (for practical reasons, such as time and travel), detailing the criteria for inclusion in the study. These were that, first, the women had to be part of the *senior management* team and second, they had to have made at least one *international* career move. Another source used for targeting interviewees in Ireland was the Dun & Bradstreet *Marketing Guide to Ireland 1997* . One-hundred and eighty letters were sent in total. One hundred and twelve responses were received and, of these, fifty-eight replied that they did not have female managers with international experience in their organisations. The responses from both of these listings ensured that the original target of fifty was drawn up quite speedily. Table 1.1 presents employment details of the fifty senior managers interviewed:

Table 1.1 Nationality, Prior Employment Locations, Present Location and Current Organisation of the Fifty Managers Interviewed

Manager No.	Nationality	Prior Employment Locations	Present Location	Current Organisation
Manager 1	German	Germany England Japan	Germany	Deutsche Morgan Grenfell
Manager 2	Scottish	Scotland England USA	England	Sainsburys
Manager 3	Irish	Ireland USA	Ireland	Department of Foreign Affairs
Manager 4	German	Germany South Africa	Germany	BMW
Manager 5	American	USA	Belgium	Ernst & Young
Manager 6	Irish	Ireland Switzerland Britain USA Cayman Islands	Ireland	Irish Tourist Board
Manager 7	American	Unites States	Ireland	Aughinish Alumina
Manager 8	Belgian	Belgium USA Asia	Belgium	Solvay
Manager 9	Irish	Ireland Germany	Ireland	Helsin Birex
Manager 10	American	USA	Ireland	Digital
Manager 11	English	England France	England	NCR

Table 1.1 (contd) Nationality, Prior Employment Locations, Present Location and Current Organisation of the Fifty Managers Interviewed

Manager No.	*Nationality*	*Prior Employment Locations*	*Present Location*	*Current Organisation*
Manager 12	French	France	England	Thomson Training & Simulation
Manager 13	English	England Singapore Japan	England	British Telecom
Manager 14	Irish	Ireland USA	Ireland	Sensormatic
Manager 15	Irish	Ireland Germany USA Switzerland Spain Mexico Brazil	Ireland	Sandoz
Manager 16	Irish	Ireland England	Ireland	Kodak Ireland
Manager 17	English	England France	England	Thomson Training & Simulation
Manager 18	Canadian	Canada	Belgium	Federal Express
Manager 19	American	USA	Belgium	AirTouch Europe
Manager 20	Swedish	Sweden	Belgium	European Commission
Manager 21	French	France USA	Ireland	GSI
Manager 22	English	England USA Hungary	England	Thomson Training & Simulation

Table 1.1 (contd) Nationality, Prior Employment Locations, Present Location and Current Organisation of the Fifty Managers Interviewed

Manager No.	*Nationality*	*Prior Employment Locations*	*Present Location*	*Current Organisation*
Manager 23	Irish	Ireland USA	Ireland	Beaumont Hospital
Manager 24	English	England Australia Japan	England	British Telecom
Manager 25	Canadian	Canada USA	Belgium	Federal Express
Manager 26	Scottish	Scotland	Belgium	Ingram Micro
Manager 27	Irish	Ireland France	Ireland	IBM
Manager 28	Irish	Ireland France Belgium	Ireland	IBM
Manager 29	Irish	Ireland England Canada	Ireland	APC
Manager 30	Irish	Ireland Holland Singapore Germany	Ireland	Sensormatic
Manager 31	Dutch	Holland	Ireland	Gateway 2000
Manager 32	Irish	Ireland Scotland England USA	Ireland	Novell
Manager 33	American	USA England	Ireland	Sandoz
Manager 34	American	USA	Ireland	Digital

Table 1.1 (contd) Nationality, Prior Employment Locations, Present Location and Current Organisation of the Fifty Managers Interviewed

Manager No.	*Nationality*	*Prior Employment Locations*	*Present Location*	*Current Organisation*
Manager 35	American	USA	Ireland	Bupa
Manager 36	Canadian	Canada USA	Ireland	Microsoft
Manager 37	French	France Czech Republic Japan	Ireland	Banque Nationale de Paris
Manager 38	Irish	Ireland USA	Ireland	Motorola
Manager 39	Canadian	Canada	England	BAT Industries
Manager 40	Swedish	Sweden	Belgium	European Commission
Manager 41	English	England Germany	Belgium	Zimmer Europe
Manager 42	Scottish	Scotland France	England	Shell UK Limited
Manager 43	German	Germany USA France	Germany	Landeszentralbank in Hessen
Manager 44	Scottish	Scotland England	Ireland	Motorola
Manager 45	German	USA Holland	Belgium	Bristol-Myers Squibb Int. Corporation
Manager 46	English	England Germany	Belgium	CEN

Table 1.1 (contd) Nationality, Prior Employment Locations, Present Location and Current Organisation of the Fifty Managers Interviewed

Manager No.	Nationality	Prior Employment Locations	Present Location	Current Organisation
Manager 47	Belgian	Belgium Africa Asia China	Belgium	Generale de Banque
Manager 48	Belgian	Belgium Portugal	Belgium	Generale de Banque
Manager 49	English	New Zealand England	Ireland	Esat Telecom
Manager 50	Scottish	USA England	Ireland	Irish Life Ireland & UK

The fifty senior managers who participated in this study were representative of a broad spectrum of industries including: mining, software engineering, pharmaceutical/chemical manufacturing, financial services, car manufacturing, tourism, electronic components manufacturing, management consultancy, international retailing, telecommunications, mobile telephone manufacturing and distributing, oil refining, computer manufacturing, and medical and state-owned enterprises. At the time of the interviewing (January to June 1997), twenty-five of the participants were based in Ireland, thirteen in Belgium, nine in England and three in Germany. All interviews were conducted in the countries where the participating managers were then based. Different profiles of age, marital status, length of marriage, number and ages of children, and choice of occupation caused subtle differences in the issues each female manager faced. For example, a female manager with pre-school children may have valued child-care support more than those with school-aged or older children. The research, however, focused on commonalities among the senior female international managers rather than on variations, as a way of highlighting major themes and issues. Quantitative statements of the number of managers maintaining views on the major themes and issues are presented, thus clarifying where minority views are also represented. Table 1.2 categorises the number of interviewees by marital status, number of children and career status relative to their partners.

Table 1.2 Interviewees' Marital Status, Number of Children, and Career Status Relative to Partners' Career Status

Marital Status	*No. of Children*	*Relative Career Status*
10 Single	None	–
31 Married	11 with no children	18 main careerists (incl. 2 sole careerists)
	7 with one child	11 'equal' careerists
	10 with two children	2 secondary careerists
	3 with three children	
8 Divorced or Separated	3 with no children	–
	3 with two children	–
	2 with three children	–
1 Widow	1 with two children	–

All fifty interviews for this study were recorded on tape. The use of interviews was particularly advantageous in the context of this research study, as interviews provide depth; information from non-verbal behaviour; opportunity to probe; greater sensitivity to misunderstandings; and, more spontaneity in the answers given — all required, given the complexity of the research question addressed in this study.

2   Barriers to Women in Management

As women occupy only about ten per cent of management positions in Europe and women managers remain concentrated in junior and middle management positions, this chapter focuses on the barriers which prevent women from reaching top-level managerial positions. It is difficult, however, to put an accurate figure on the numbers of women in management in Europe, because different countries have a different definition of a 'manager', and in many countries there are no regularised systems of gathering statistics in this area. According to The European Commission (1999), however, ten per cent of men hold top-level managerial jobs in comparison with only six per cent of women (1999a, p. 17). The major focus of research on women in management has generally been on women themselves as they arrived in and advanced through organisations. The emphasis has not been on gender aspects per se, but on the implications of gender *for* the organisation. According to Marshall (1995), the term 'gender' is gaining breadth of usage. The original connotation referred to the social expectations and roles attributed to or experienced by people based on their biological sex. Gender is now taking on a much broader and more diffuse set of meanings. Marshall suggests that it has become a general label for talking about women, men, the relationships between them, related aspects of organising, processes through which gender-differentiated behaviour patterns are enacted, and associated issues of power in various guises. Marshall maintained that the gender aspect of management is not a particularly coherent field, but a highly diverse field.

Scase and Goffee (1990) observed that, despite our increasing knowledge of the problems and experiences which are directly related to gender and affect women in management, many issues remain unexplored and, as yet, have not been the subject of detailed *empirical* research. As more women enter the workforce, their failure to reach the highest management positions has become the cause for considerable research and debate both in their home countries and in international management. European women, like their American and Australian counterparts, are confronted by a 'glass ceiling' and 'glass wall'. Women face barriers to progression within organisations, barriers which are not faced by their male counterparts. Despite the recognition of these additional problems, however, there is a lack of empirically-based European studies. As a result, much discussion relies on untested assumptions rather than rigorously conducted social investigation.

In a number of countries, while women are gaining managerial experience, they still encounter a *glass ceiling* — a term used to describe 'a barrier so subtle that it is transparent, yet so strong that it prevents women and minorities from moving up the managerial hierarchy' (Morrison and Von Glinow, 1990, p. 200). According to Morrison and Von Glinow, the glass ceiling is not simply a barrier based on the person's inability to handle a higher-level job, it 'applies to women as a group who are kept from advancing higher because they are women'. In the case of the *glass wall* lateral movement is also prevented. According to Davidson and Cooper (1992, p. 13):

> While it seems relatively easy for women to gain employment at the lower levels of organisations, it is still proving very difficult for them to reach upper, middle and senior management positions, even in the more enlightened USA.

Similarly, research by Smith and Still (1996) revealed that women in senior management positions in Australia constitute less than three per cent. Australian female expatriate managers are concentrated at middle, rather than senior management levels. There are major organisational barriers which constitute the glass ceiling. These include: a lonely and non-supportive working environment; treating differences as weaknesses; excluding people from group activities because of their differences; and failure to help individuals to prepare to balance work and personal life issues. According to Schwartz (1989), however, the metaphor of the glass ceiling is misleading as it suggests an invisible barrier created by corporate leaders to hinder the promotion of women managers. Schwartz (1989, p. 68) believes that:

> A more appropriate metaphor would be the kind of a cross-sectional diagram used in geology. The barriers to women gaining senior management

positions occur when potentially counterproductive layers of influence on women — maternity, tradition, socialisation — meet management strata pervaded by the largely unconscious preconceptions, stereotypes, and expectations of men. Such interfaces do not exist for men and tend to be impermeable for women.

There is now an extensive literature on this topic, with evidence from Australia, America, and Europe, which indicates that women face obstacles in their careers that are not faced by their male counterparts. Overcoming 'hidden' or less obvious organisational barriers to managerial equity may be difficult for women to achieve in the near future. According to one estimate, attaining full economic integration for women at every organisational level would take seventy-five to one hundred years at the current rate of change.

Cross-cultural studies and reviews which have been undertaken in order to compare male and female managers in terms of managerial efficiency and performance have produced results which reveal that there are far more similarities than differences in terms of managerial efficiency and performance. Where differences do occur, they tend to be found not so much in the way each sex 'manages', but stem from factors associated with the low proportion of female managers, attitudinal differences, prejudices, discrimination, and different life circumstances and stressors of female managers in comparison to male managers. Many of these differences are regarded as negative and, therefore, hamper the career advancements of women in management.

The specific problems and pressures which have been identified as unique to female managers include: burdens of coping with the role of the 'token' woman; being a test case for future women; lack of role models and feelings of isolation; strains of coping with prejudice and sex stereotyping; and overt and indirect discrimination from fellow employees, employers and the organisational structure and climate. Women managers in token positions are subjected to isolation imposed by males at work, which in itself can restrict social and business life. For a woman in management, the task of breaking into this male-dominated 'club' can prove difficult, and she can be denied policy information, opportunities, contacts, and social support. It has been estimated that over 50 per cent of all jobs in management come about through personal contacts (Davidson and Cooper, 1992). These difficulties, on top of trying to maintain a family and home, are creating enormous pressures on women in management, which may manifest themselves in a variety of undesirable ways, for example, facing greater pressures and stress than working men.

2.1 Cultural, Legislative, Educational, Work–Family, Corporate, and Attitudinal Barriers

Many of the constraints which often hinder women in attaining senior managerial positions are quite similar in most countries. There are, for example, cultural, educational, legislative, attitudinal and corporate constraints in most countries. The relative importance of each constraint varies from society to society. Research by Izraeli and Adler (1994, p. 13) suggests that the specific image of an ideal manager varies across cultures, 'yet everywhere it privileges those characteristics that the culture associates primarily with men'. They point out from their research that this belief is widely supported by male managers, and that successful management is associated with masculinity. The requirements for effective managerial performance are not 'culture free' but are influenced by the national culture in which the behaviour is performed, and that effective performance requires managers to adapt their behaviours accordingly.

According to Adler (1987), almost all cultures differentiate between male and female roles. Societies expect women to behave in certain ways, and men in others. In many cultures the traditional female role maintains attitudes and behaviours that fail to support those attributes associated with that of traditional managers. This is evident, for example, in Italy where there are only three per cent of women are employed in upper management positions. This is a lower percentage than in other European countries. This low percentage of senior female managers can be attributed to the sociological context of Italian society and, in particular, the historical role of the Catholic church which has played an important aspect in cultural values, and to the fact that only 30 per cent of Italian women work outside the home. The representative value of marriage and motherhood for women is still very strong, and may help explain why many women stop working after the birth of children (Olivares, 1993). The European Commission (1999b) reported that in Italy, marriage is still the main determinant of women withdrawing from the labour market.

A similar situation pertains in Portugal, where, if equal opportunities for men and women in managerial careers are to occur, major cultural and social changes would be required. Women in Portugal are still expected to fulfil their maternal role, which includes not only childbirth, but also child rearing responsibilities, and at the same time are expected to pursue a serious professional career. Portugal also has the lowest rate of childcare facilities in the European Union for children between the ages of three months and six years.

In Spain, the proportion of women in senior management positions is still less than five per cent, and these women are usually employed in service-sector firms, small- and medium-sized firms and newly created businesses. The social role of women in Spain, however, is still linked to their role in the family, while for men, time spent at work is of prime importance. Stereotypes still exist about women who hold responsible posts, for example, that they are incapable of accepting responsibility or risks, that they have little interest in promotion, and that they are excessively concerned with the running of their home (Fernadnez, 1993). Spain still remains below the EU average in employment rates of prime age women (European Commission, 1999b).

Similarly, in *northern* Europe, for example, in Switzerland there is a cultural norm that if a Swiss man's wife works it must be because the man is not able to provide adequately for her and for his family. This creates a strong cultural norm for Swiss men not to encourage or allow their wives to work or pursue managerial careers. Women's progress in management is further inhibited by some of the key concepts of family law, for example, a wife can have a profession only if the husband consents. The wife is responsible for taking care of the household and can represent the household only on items of housekeeping, but the husband can withdraw that right (Black et al. 1992).

It is apparent, therefore, that cultural barriers still exist for women managers. Cultural traditions and norms are formed slowly, and change even more slowly. The persistent stereotype that associates management with being male is still a major obstacle for women managers in most countries. The implications of these cultural barriers are significant for this research as (i) domestic cultural barriers limit the numbers of senior female managers which, in turn, reduces the availability of female managers for international assignments, and (ii) female managers have to contend with a new set of domestic barriers in the culture of their host countries.

In addition to cultural barriers, female managers also experience difficulties with the various and complex laws pertaining to the employment of women, which still exist throughout Europe, despite the attempts of the European Union to standardise employment legislation. Legislation on matters such as equality, equal pay and maternity leave still form barriers to women achieving senior managerial positions. Analysis of statistics on the structure of earnings in the fifteen EU states reveal a continuing difference in earnings between women and men (European Commission, 1997). According to *The Economist*, women all over the world, on average, are paid less than men — typically about 20-30% less — for similar kinds of work (1998, p. 5). In 1974, the European Community established a Social Action Programme. The promotion of women's rights has been a central aim of this programme. Article 119 of the EC Convention, as well as Directives 75/117, 76/207 and 79/9 impose additional measures in all European Union countries which abolish the distinction between men and women in the field of employment, professional education, promotion and social security schemes. Various explanations have been suggested for the introduction of this legislation, an economic motive being to the fore. The economic recession of the 1970s created an opportunity in the European Community for greater economic planning to combat unemployment in member states. During the same decade, most countries in the European Community had introduced some form of equality legislation as a response to the increased participation of women in the labour market. According to O'Donovan and Szyszczak (1988, p. 195), 'the notion of a social action programme was perhaps an attempt to paint a human face over bare economic priorities'.

The shift in emphasis from economic priorities to social priorities, however, has not always occurred in various member states. This can be seen in the attitude of some the member-states towards new social policy proposals. In Britain, the government has frequently blocked new proposals, for example, when it opposed the draft directive on parental leave. Nielsen (1983) and Hoskyns (1985) were critical of the European Community decision-making process suggesting that the equality laws are neither mobilised for nor implemented by women. Hoskyns (1985, p. 72), further argues, that 'The European legislation . . . was not fought for in any direct sense by women, and remains virtually unknown to those who are supposed to be its beneficiaries'.

Maternity leave legislation throughout Europe can be regarded as complex. Parental leave provisions are difficult to compare meaningfully because of the varying levels of statutory regulations across Europe. Only a sixth of employers in Sweden, for example, provide enhanced maternity leave, but legislation on maternity leave in Sweden entitles women to fifteen months leave, twelve months of which will be paid at the statutory benefit rates (about 90 per cent of average earnings). In contrast to Sweden, British statutory maternity leave provisions are restricted according to length of service and provide low levels of pay.

In Ireland, legislation is derived from the Constitution which came into effect in 1937. Despite amendments over the years, the Constitution has not adequately addressed many social changes over the intervening years. The Irish Constitution specifically mentions the role of women in the home and as mothers (Articles 40.3.3 and 41.2.1). There is no mention of the word 'father' in the Constitution, and there is no mention of men in their domestic context. According to Connelly (1993, p. 5), it is clear from the constitutional provisions 'that it is in their role as wives and mothers that women are especially valued'.

Dutch legislation shows that the focus has been on equal rights, but the legislation took a long time to enforce. It was not until 1957 that the law dating back to 1935 which prohibited married women from employment in the civil service was removed. The Dutch government did not ratify the Equal Pay Act until 1975. It took another five years for the Equal Opportunities Act to be passed. In 1985, a few full-time childcare facilities were subsidised, which catered for only one per cent of all children between birth and five years, and supply did not meet demand in any way (Tijdens, 1993).

In Germany, although there has been some equalisation in pay, there is still a large income gap between men and women. The income gap exists across all spheres — female blue-collar workers, female white-collar workers and women in management. Women in management are rare, and their salaries are 23 per cent lower than those of male managers (Eurostat, 1995). There is no specific anti-discrimination law in Germany, although a proposal for such a law was officially discussed at a hearing of the German Parliament (Bundestag) in 1982 and again in the late 1980s, but no political majority could be obtained to pass it. A number of laws in the Code of Civil Law impose equality into working life, and compliance with these laws was and still is officially regarded as sufficient to achieve equal opportunity in working life.

In France, an equality law was passed in 1983. The main purpose of this law was to provide businesses with tools to evaluate the work situation of women and to promote equal opportunity, through comparative employment status reports and positive action schemes. Each year companies must draw up a report on the comparative status of women and men in relation to recruitment, training, promotion, qualifications, working conditions and pay. Under the positive action schemes, companies are encouraged to negotiate with unions to improve the status of women in areas such as recruitment, training, promotion or working conditions. Since the 1983 law has been passed, however, only about thirty-five firms in the private sector and only four public sector companies have implemented positive action schemes. These relatively low figures would indicate that most companies do not feel it necessary to include equality of opportunity among their objectives, or do not wish to promote policies regarding the promotion of equal opportunities in the workplace (Laufer, 1993).

Throughout Europe, when mothers take additional leave beyond statutory maternity provisions — a frequent occurrence particularly in countries with low childcare provision and short leave arrangements — they will often break their employment contracts. This often leads to a loss of seniority and other benefits related to continuity of employment. In Germany and Britain, for example, the concept of a career break, of providing extended unpaid leave, has gained prominence. The career break scheme involves some continued professional contact and arrangement for periodic attendance at training courses or holiday cover to ensure that professionals' skills are kept up to date. The concept of a career break is much less common in other European countries, being virtually unknown, for example, in the Scandinavian countries.

Hegewisch and Mayne (1994) observed that throughout Europe there are strong country differences on employers' equality measures. These authors, however, doubt if European equality legislation has had any positive impact on women's actual position in the workforce, given the continued inequality of women in employment, as demonstrated in terms of their low share of managerial positions, persistent pay gaps, and the rigid occupational segregation between men and women's work across Europe.

Despite the efforts of European Union legislators over recent years, it is clear that many legislative barriers still exist and cause difficulties for women in achieving senior management positions in various European countries. In order for the position of women in management to improve there may be a need for stronger legislative programmes to bring about change regarding the principles and realities of equal opportunities.

The concept of equal opportunities in education is another factor to be considered when discussing career achievement of women. This can be traced back to the early school-going years where male and female students are treated differently. A United Nations Study (1993) found that among those countries where gender-based statistics are collected no country treats its women as well as its men:

> Researchers in 33 countries including the USA admit . . . that they haven't found a place where women have education, employment and health opportunities equal to those available to men.

The trend towards higher levels of educational achievement shows a faster rate of growth in university students for women than for men in all industrialised countries.   As more women gain the necessary educational qualifications, however, a United States Department of Labor report found that men all over the world hold the highest management positions, with greater inequalities occurring between men and women the closer they get to the top of organisational hierarchies (International Labor Office, 1993). Despite a gradual upward trend in most industrialised countries, women are still severely under-represented in the natural sciences and technological faculties of universities.   Roobeek (1989) suggests that it is generally assumed that managers employed in technological firms, almost regardless of their function, must have technological training, even though once in the job they may never be required to use their training.   Roobeek's study of women, management, and technology in Europe showed that the presumption of male technological competence combined with the stereotype of female technological incompetence, may keep new technological firms out of reach for female managers.   Roobeek (1989, p. 12) concluded that 'the traditional view of technology as a male domain is used to exclude women'.

Educational barriers for women still exist in most European countries, for example, in France, managers are typically recruited from among the graduates of a small number of élite universities, such as the Grandes Écoles which, until recently, were male dominated.   According to Serdjénian (1988), these institutions functioned to filter women out of the paths to power.   The difference in positions held by men and women in France reflects the traditional division in male and female roles.   Women are generally at the lower of the scale in each profession (Laufer, 1993).

In Switzerland, the army serves as a special kind of 'school' and represents a major recruitment pool, especially for more senior managers. Swiss corporations, and especially banks, have a strong preference for promoting men who are army officers.   Both the military training and the social networks of army officers are considered to be important assets for managers (Berthoin-Antal and Izraeli, 1993).

In universities and business schools in England, the Master of Business Administration (MBA) degree programme has increased in widespread acceptance as the top management qualification. Leeming (1994), however, suggests that doubts exist on the accessibility and overall success of the course for women managers. Women form approximately only 14 per cent of students on MBA programmes, despite the fact that the numbers of men and women undergraduates are at equal levels. Simpson (1995) conducted a research project in Britain which sought to make a comparison of the potential returns of an MBA for men and women. Participants from twelve business schools took part in her study, and of the responses she received, 128 were male and 55 were female. Simpson cautions that it is difficult to attribute the managerial changes that have occurred following an MBA course solely to the MBA itself. The research, however, reveals that the careers of both men and women have improved considerably since completing the course — but with men gaining greater advancement than women. The proportions of both men and women rose from junior and middle management roles to senior management, however, there was more than a 100 per cent increase for men, in comparison with a 50 per cent increase for women (Simpson, 1995).

Similarly, Australian research conducted by Sinclair (1995) argued that an explanation for the MBA being less successful for women is that the culture of MBA programmes is constructed on gendered understandings of who managers are, what they should do, and how they should learn. Sinclair further suggested that the MBA culture may be diagnosed as a microcosm of a broader management masculine culture which may provide insights into why women are not making greater progress in the ranks of management in general.

A study of women MBAs carried out by Dix (1990) revealed that the desire for a major career change emerged as an important reason for women undertaking the programme. Simpson, in agreement with Dix, noted that the MBA could be an important device for women in achieving career change. According to Simpson, career change would seem to see women in management moving from the traditionally female support functions of administration, education and personnel to specialist areas such as production and information technology which have largely been the preserve of male managers. Simpson states that, overall, the MBA does not seem to be as successful for women in terms of career advancement and salary levels as it is for men. Simpson (1995, p. 8), however, concludes that, the MBA could be the appropriate programme for women managers, but that more women will need to enrol for this qualification 'if the full effects of their talents and capabilities are to be felt in organisational life, and if the dynamics of gendered power in the workplace are to be fully challenged'.

It can be seen, therefore, that educational barriers exist for women throughout Europe, beginning with their early school days and continuing into their second level education — a pattern which governs their choice of courses at university and ultimately their career choice in organisations. Men's and to a lesser extent women's negative attitudes and behaviours towards women in management combine to serve as barriers to women's entry both at the educational level and for promotion in management careers. At the initial stages of career choice these attitudes and behaviours can discourage women from pursuing careers in management.

Another barrier which women in management have to overcome is the stress and pressure resulting from work–family conflict. This is experienced when pressures from the work and family roles are mutually incompatible, such that participation in one role makes it more difficult to participate in the other. According to Hochschild (1989), because of the uneven distribution of household work, women are said to work a 'second shift' at home in addition to their first shift at work. Hochschild believes that women continue to work this second shift because their jobs are considered to be less important than those of their husbands. According to Hochschild (1989, p. 254):

> Because men put more of their 'male' identity into work, their work time is worth more than female work time — to the man and to the family. The greater worth of male work time makes his leisure more valuable, because it is his leisure that enables him to refuel his energy, strengthen his ambition, and move ahead at work. By doing less at home, he can work longer hours, prove his loyalty to his company, and get promoted faster. His aspirations expand. So does his pay. So does his exemption from the second shift.

In Britain, Cooper and Lewis (1993) found that 73 per cent of women still do 'nearly all the housework' and that men with working partners have an average of six hours more spare time at weekends than their partners do. Because of this, female managers are much more likely to experience higher pressures and stress in relation to the demands of their career and home responsibilities. Similarly, in Spain, research conducted by Fernandez (1993) showed that the social role of women is linked to their role in the family; whereas for men, time spent at work is deemed to be of prime importance. Women's family ties are seen as obstacles to promotion because these ties stand in the way of their availability for work, and being available is seen as essential for promotion. It is women who are mainly responsible for organising the household, and it is women who take time off from their professional lives to devote time to their children.

Vinnicombe and Sturges (1995) suggest that some organisations operate a double standard for marriage, they view the married male manager as an asset, with a stable support network at home which allows him to give his undivided attention to his work, but they view the married female manager as a liability, likely to neglect her career at the expense of her family at every possible opportunity. Because of the double standard for marriage, many women managers have had little choice but to take this into consideration, and avoid the responsibility of family commitments wherever possible. The profile that emerges is that a majority of women managers in Europe are not married (i.e., single, divorced or widowed) or, if married, have no children.

According to Davidson and Cooper (1992), if women managers decide not to marry, they are likely to experience pressure from colleagues who perceive them as an 'oddity', as the stereotype of the 'old maid' still exists. Other potential stressors which are associated with the unattached woman manager are the pressures and strains linked with having to take care of elderly parents and dependants, particularly if they are the 'only' daughter. Davidson and Cooper further suggest that single women 'get the rawest deal' in caring for relatives because it often means giving up their social life, having large financial commitments and in some cases having to retire early. Davidson and Cooper add that a further possible stressor for the unattached female manager is entertaining and socialising. This is seen as an important aspect of managerial life as a great deal of business goes on in these social settings — usually where the wife has to prepare a meal. The social ethic, however, is that 'you have to be one of a pair'.

The work functions and duties performed by managers in all industrialised countries appear to be based on total commitment measured in terms of time spent at the workplace. Career breaks for women managers for child-bearing and child-rearing show incompatibilities with the job of management, which is presumed to be a full-time and continuous job. Career breaks are seen to indicate a lack of commitment and re-entry is also problematic. Despite women's increased involvement in the work-force, research over time and across cultures continues to document the persistence of inequality in the allocation of household work and family responsibilities, even among couples with 'modern' ideologies and in countries with commitment to gender equality at home and at work.   Women's extra domestic responsibilities can create role conflict and over-load and can reduce the potential for achievement in their careers.   Most women feel that promotion in their careers has been achieved at the expense of time with their children and of the quality of family life.   Family responsibilities, therefore, involving marriage, childcare, and household activities, can hinder women managers' career achievements.   These family responsibilities produce work–family conflicts to which women may respond by reducing their employment involvement, which, in turn, restricts career opportunities and advancement.   However apparent these restrictions are on female managerial careers in home-country organisations, women in international management have to overcome additional difficulties — such as mobility, spousal adjustment and balancing dual careers.

In an attempt to explain the under-representation of women in management, and in particular in senior management, it is necessary to examine the corporate barriers which exist.   Among the most cited barriers are recruitment and selection barriers and organisational polices and structural barriers.   In addition to encountering barriers to advancement towards senior-level positions, women also face barriers associated with industry-sector and managerial functions.   Fisher (1987) notes that opportunities for women in management may be greater in industries like computers and telecommunications that are experiencing a rapid pace of change.   Fisher suggests that these emergent industries simply have not been in existence long enough to have established rules about who is or should be a manager, relying more on managerial ability than on gender to make employment decisions.   According to an American survey on women in corporate management, women are more likely to hold senior management positions in human resources and communications, and are far less likely to hold senior positions in production or plant facilities functions (Catalyst, 1990).

Other corporate barriers which prevent women managers from reaching senior level positions include: recruitment methods; selection and assessment methods; and organisational policies and structures which may cause problems for those who care for other family members.   According to Rothwell (1984), many jobs are still seen as 'men's' or 'women's' jobs and this influences the initial intake of a particular gender to organisations. Rothwell points out that if the initial intake for particular career routes are unbalanced, it is unlikely that the pattern will improve later, particularly in organisations which have a policy of 'promotion from within' where possible.

The subjective selection interview is still used in almost all selection circumstances, despite all the evidence which shows it to be unreliable and more likely to facilitate bias against minority candidates. According to Alimo-Metcalfe (1995), interviews are frequently poorly conducted and are open to potential prejudices and personal bias. These effects are even stronger when the post in question is male-dominated. Sources of bias include the interviewers' perceptions of 'feminine' dress, physical attractiveness and a female candidate's suitability for a 'masculine' job. Alimo-Metcalfe (1994, p. 96) suggests that, 'interviews can be regarded as a social judgement process which is highly subjective and therefore easily susceptible to bias and prejudices'. Conclusions from a study by Glick et al. (1988) showed that male applicants were still preferred for the traditionally 'male' job, and female applicants were favoured for the traditional 'female' job.

Because of the weaknesses of the selection interview, management in organisations have become interested in more 'scientific' techniques of assessment, such as psychometrics. According to recent studies, British organisations are increasingly using psychometric instruments for selection and assessment, with critical reasoning and personality measures being the most commonly used. These tests are used because of their non-gender bias and the tests are regarded as offering reliable and 'objective' information of an individual's ability or potential. The difficulty with these tests, however, according to Webb (1987, p. 4), is that the sources of bias are developed gradually and are so subtle that the bias becomes difficult to challenge. Webb notes:

> It is well established, but worth restating, that measures of individual abilities are not neutral with respect to all social categories, but are normative. They contain evaluative judgements about what should count as 'skills' and 'abilities' and what test items measure these. They are likely to be modelled on the perceived traits of current job occupants, which means that atypical applicants are disadvantaged.

Women in management are such a group. The psychometric tests used are based on items which are identified within a particular population sample and then piloted on a similar population. From this, norms are established which again are based on the sample population. Alimo-Metcalfe (1994) warns that with regard to the managerial population there is likely to be a male bias, as the norms would be derived from a male population. Ability tests and intelligence tests are also used by some organisations as selection procedures. Psychologists, however, have also outlined problems associated with the design and norms of intelligence tests. According to Webb (1987, p. 5):

> The construction of test items can be manipulated so as to favour one group over another and this has long been known in the sphere of intelligence testing . . . The IQ debate continues, but there is adequate work to substantiate the argument that the construction of such tests can be manipulated to reproduce, or to undermine, socially approved results for the distribution of intelligence according to class, gender and ethnicity.

Alimo-Metcalfe (1995) suggests that many of the popular intelligence tests used by organisations as part of the selection process of managers appear to favour the way in which men tend to think. She notes that there is evidence of women scoring higher on verbal tests of intelligence than men, while men generally score higher on numerical tests. From these results, Alimo-Metcalfe asks if verbal ability has a lower status than numerical ability for managers.

Another development in assessing the potential of managers is the assessment centre. This provides for a particular method of assessment, based on the notion of 'if we want to see if someone can do a job, let's observe them trying to do it'. With this method, candidates who may be considered for a particular job are brought together and asked to undertake group and individual exercises that are designed to assume important activities of a job. The candidates are observed in these and other roles and are assessed by senior managers in the same organisation who have been trained to assess their behaviours. In Britain, assessment centres have increased in usage, despite the high expenses involved. Such expenses include the cost of the consultants who design the centre and who train the managers, and the cost of individuals' absence from work, which typically takes two or three days and usually involves additional high accommodation costs. A reason for the increased popularity of assessment centres is that they provide the most accurate assessments of individual potential, and are used for senior management selection and to identify high flyers for fast-track career development programmes.

Despite the increased accuracy of assessment centres, concerns about possible sources of sex bias have been raised. As mentioned above, senior managers from the organisation assess the behaviour of the candidates. These senior managers would have been given 'behavioural frameworks' or 'guidelines' which contain specific examples of 'above average', 'average' and 'below average' behavioural indicators. If these indicators have been developed from a totally male management group, however, and if there is evidence of gender differences in management style, then these indicators can offer potential sources of sex bias (Alimo-Metcalfe, 1995).

The various approaches to recruitment and selection outlined above show that organisations attempt to increase the 'fairness' of selection and assessment by adopting more scientific forms of assessment. They may, however, be increasing the effect of gender bias. Alimo-Metcalfe concludes that 'as the techniques of assessment become more complex, sources of bias are far less obvious and hence less likely to be challenged' (Alimo-Metcalfe, 1994).

Other corporate barriers which female managers have to overcome relate to discrimination and career development. For women, gender is generally considered to be a disadvantage for job promotion or career prospects. Women are more prone to sex discrimination, prejudice and inadequate job training experience in comparison to men, and men are generally treated more favourably by management. According to Rothwell (1984), the ethos of an organisation and especially the style and personalities of top managers are likely to have a major impact on the scope and pattern of women's career development. Rothwell suggests that a very positive attitude can ensure the career development of some women and a very negative attitude will mean that no women advance beyond a certain low level, except in an occasional specialist sideline 'suitable' for women.

According to Storey (1989, p. 8), much depends on the organisation's view of women; whether they are viewed as a cost or investment, or as he expresses it, 'valued asset rather than variable cost'. Management perception of women in an organisation and the level of understanding of their specific problems will to a large extent determine the nature of the employers' 'women-friendly' policies and the employers' levels of commitment to them. Research by Dickens (1992), however, cautions that various 'flexibility' initiatives such as home-working or part-time working for women, which are often cited as evidence of an equal opportunities approach, may be double edged in that they are seen as 'atypical' because they differ from the male norm. Developments such as career breaks and part-time work, while recognising the current reality of women's lives attempting to juggle salaried work and domestic work, can be seen as initiatives which in practice take women out of competition for jobs and thus 'save' full-time jobs for men.   Similarly, Cockburn (1991) suggests that flexibility initiatives also help to perpetuate the assumption that women bear the primary responsibility for caring for and raising children. Cockburn also suggests that the more that women are granted various kinds of work flexibility to enable them to cope with motherhood and other domestic responsibilities the more they can be dismissed as 'different', and less serious than male employees.   Dickens (1994) suggests that even if career breaks are open to, and taken by, both men and women they are likely to be taken for different reasons and to be regarded differently by the organisation. Time out taken to study is considered as career enhancing, but time out if used for childcare is considered career detracting, reflecting the low value placed on women's experience in household and family management despite the organisational, managerial, and interpersonal skills involved.

Another serious corporate barrier that women in management face is the attitude of senior male managers towards them. In addition to employer practices, deep-seated attitudes remain towards working women, in particular those who work part-time. Employers often see women as being less ambitious, not worth training or promoting (because they may leave to have children), less reliable (because of domestic responsibilities), and generally less committed to work than male counterparts.   According to Davidson and Cooper (1992), the typical employer attitude that women are 'poor training and promotional investments' — who leave work on marrying and/or starting a family — is particularly detrimental to those who work continually after marriage and to single women who do not marry, a profile which fits the majority of women in management.

Other attitudes by employers are that women are far less committed to work and far less able to undertake a full-time career than men. When promotion arises and when an employer is given the choice between a man and a woman with equal qualifications, the woman is frequently viewed as the greater risk.   Flanders (1994, p. 5) suggests that typical employer attitudes are:

> When it comes to promotion and career development, women are judged not so much on their abilities and achievements, but on assumptions about their family life, responsibilities, and future intentions.

Cross-cultural studies and reviews which have made comparisons of male and female managers in terms of managerial efficiency and performance have concluded that there are far more similarities than differences. According to Cooper and Davidson (1984, p. 160), where differences occur, however, 'the differences tend to stem from factors associated with the low proportion of female managers, and attitudinal differences — especially prejudice and discrimination, stressors, and different life circumstances of women managers compared to men managers'. Antal and Izraeli (1993, p. 63), in a worldwide overview of women in management, state that 'probably the single most important hurdle for women in management in all industrialised countries is the persistent stereotype that associates management with being male'.

A study by Hunt (1975) of management attitudes and practices towards women at work discovered that managers in Britain thought that all the qualities needed for managerial jobs were more likely to be found in men than in women. A follow-up study by Hunt (1981) on women and under-achievement at work found that although attitudes had become slightly more favourable, women were still regarded as inferior. Schein (1989) and Schein and Mueller's (1990) survey of male and female middle managers in America, and of young business students in America, Germany and Britain, however, found that the attitudes regarding the characteristics of effective managers are still associated with males, or as Schein says 'think manager equals think male'. In a follow-up study, Schein et al. (1994, p. 13) suggest that the strength of male business-student perceptions are somewhat disquieting: 'As they become managers and decision makers of the future, these stereotypical attitudes are apt to limit women's access to and promotions within management internationally'. Schwartz (1989, p. 67) similarly notes:

> Men continue to perceive women as the rearers of their children so they find it understandable, indeed appropriate, that women should renounce their careers to raise families . . . Not only do they see parenting as fundamentally female, they see a career as fundamentally male . . . This attitude serves to legitimise a woman's choice to extend maternity leave and even, for those who can afford it, to leave employment altogether for several years.

In conclusion, according to Schein et al. (1994), male attitudes to managerial women are strong, consistent and pervasive and appear to be a global phenomenon. Schein (1994, p. 50) predicts that the progression of women to senior management positions will be kept low if the attitudes of male decision-makers, influenced strongly by managerial sex typing, are allowed to go unchecked. Finally, she suggests that while laws and corporate practices focusing on objective criteria and removing structural barriers are important, it seems 'time to address ways to change stereotypical attitudes as well'.

2.2   Mentoring, Tokenism, and Networking

It is clear that female managers are currently faced with overt barriers in achieving upward mobility, as outlined above. In addition to these barriers, however, covert barriers such as lack of mentors, being members of minority groups in organisations and lack of networking also hinder female managers in their progression to senior managerial positions. Mentoring relationships, while important for men, may be *essential* for women, as female managers face greater organisational, interpersonal, and individual barriers to advancement. Although mentors may be essential for advancement in organisations, female managers may be further hindered in their attempts to obtain mentors because of interpersonal and organisational barriers. Generally, a mentor provides information, training, advice, direction, achievement of social and professional integration in organisations and psychosocial support for a junior person in a relationship lasting over an extended period of time.

Much of the literature on mentoring comes from the USA, where the main focus has been on the male experience of mentoring. Individuals who were mentored were found to have better career outcomes than individuals who were not mentored, regardless of their gender or level, and were found to have more organisational policy influence and access to important people and resources (Fagenson, 1989; Ragins, 1989).

Although mentoring relationships may be particularly important for the advancement of women in organisations, there is a smaller supply of mentors available to women than to men, and women may be less likely than men to develop these relationships. There are many possible explanations for the infrequency of mentoring relationships among women in organisations. Generally, these explanations are that (i) women may not seek mentors, and (ii) mentors may not select protégées (i.e., female protégés). According to Ragins (1989, p. 6), one reason why women may be less likely than men to seek mentors is that they may fail to recognise the importance of gaining a sponsor, and may 'naively assume that competence is the only requisite for advancement in the organisation'. Other difficulties in approaching male mentors may be compounded by the female's fear that her attempts to initiate a relationship may be misconstrued as a sexual approach by either the mentor or others in the organisation.

Another explanation put forward for the under-representation of women in mentoring relationships is that mentors may be unwilling to select female protégés. The selection process may therefore be biased by the tendency of male mentors to choose male over female protégés. Even if women are considered as suitable candidates for the protégée role, male mentors may choose male protégés because they may be more comfortable developing a professional and personal relationship with another male (Ragins, 1989). An issue which deserves more investigation, therefore, is whether a mentor's gender influences the effectiveness of the mentoring relationship.

From the limited research that has been conducted, however, contradictory findings emerge. Noe (1988), for example, revealed that protégés in mixed gender relationships use mentors more effectively than protégés in same-gender relationships, and the research also showed that women receive more psychosocial benefits than men from their mentoring relationships. In contrast, however, Gibb and Megginson (1995) identified problems with cross-gender mentoring and found that men mentors are less sensitive to the feelings and perceptions of women protégés.

Women may seek to avoid the difficulties associated with obtaining a male mentor by seeking a female mentor. This, however, can lead to another difficulty, namely, that of finding a female mentor, as there are still comparatively very few senior female managers. The relatively few females in mentoring positions may, therefore, receive an overload of requests from the larger block of women in lower levels of an organisation. This may result in a reduction of access to mentors. Factors other than gender which play a more important role in the pairing of mentor and protégé are the similarity in the personal traits of mentors and protégés. Vinnicombe and Colwill's (1995, p. 84) research revealed that when asked to describe the characteristics of their ideal mentors and protégés, both men and women choose people who are similar to themselves rather than people who are stereotypically masculine or feminine. As Vinnicombe and Colwill note that 'there are few top-level executives whose mirror reflects a woman', which suggests that most male and female junior managers will be mentored by men.

Closely linked with the lack of female mentors is the difficulty of belonging to a minority group. Additional strains and pressures are experienced by female managers which are not felt by dominant members of the same organisational status. Kanter was one of the first to suggest that if women comprise less than 15 per cent of a total category in an organisation they can be labelled 'tokens', as they could be viewed as symbols of their group rather than as individuals. She observed that token women in a large organisation were highly visible and subject to greater performance pressures than their male counterparts (Kanter, 1977b). She suggests that the smaller the minority that women find themselves in an organisation, the greater their chances of being isolated and evaluated on the basis of sex-role stereotypes. The behaviour of one token is generally perceived as representative of all tokens. These women have difficulty gaining the trust of their male co-workers, and are excluded from informal networks.

Other disadvantages which have been associated with the token woman include increased performance pressure, increased visibility, being a test case for future women, isolation, lack of female role models, exclusion from male groups, and distortion of women's behaviour by others in order to fit them into pre-existing sex stereotypes. In addition, negative attitudes toward female managers, particularly if they are token managers, may restrict the range of acceptable behaviour for them and limit their approaches to managerial situations, thereby harming their ultimate effectiveness.

According to Freeman (1990), being a token woman not only means having no female peer support but working in an environment which provides no role models of women in senior positions. Female role models in higher managerial positions act as important influences in terms of career aspirations for other women. But, as in the case of female mentors cited above, the relative scarcity of women in senior managerial positions makes it difficult for junior women to find both female role models and female mentors.

Given the difficulties associated with the 'token woman' how do women cope with this situation? Interviews conducted by Davidson and Cooper (1992) with female managers revealed that the majority of their respondents reported having being pressurised into adopting certain sex-stereotype roles at work, for example, the mother, the confidante, the seductress, or the pet. Davidson and Cooper's research established that the 'mother-earth role' was by far the most common role reported by female managers.   They described the 'mother-earth' role as a function of an individual from whom others can seek personal counselling about work as well as other problems.   This role can be both time consuming and exhausting.

Peer relationships and interpersonal networks should provide a source of organisational support for female managers, particularly in the absence of mentors and because of their additional difficulties as members of a minority group.   Networking and mentoring suggest some similarities.   Both mentor and peer relationships can facilitate career and personal development. Networking can be useful at all stages in career development, while mentors are particularly useful at the early stages of career development.   Peer relationships are different from mentoring relationships in that they often last longer, are not hierarchical, and involve a two-way helping.   Peer relationships have advantages, particularly since a significant number of both women and men may not have had mentors.   Burke and McKeen (1994, p. 75) suggest that 'it seems clear, however, that managerial women are still less integrated with important organisational networks, and it is these internal networks that influence critical human resource decisions such as promotion and acceptance'.

Women have been largely excluded from 'old boy networks' which traditionally are composed of individuals who hold power in an organisation. In Denmark, for example, there are many established networks, clubs, and groups — both inside and outside companies — 'in which women are not even allowed to participate' (Albertsen and Christensen, 1993).   An important characteristic of networking and the old boy system is that it is dependent upon informal interactions involving favours, persuasion, and connections to people who already have influence.   Networks also provide essential information on office policies and actual requirements of work situations not found in formal publications.

Scase and Goffee's research (1989) established that attempts by male managers to exclude females from joining old boy networks merely reinforces existing stereotypes of negative male attitudes towards female managers.   Davidson and Cooper (1992, p. 89) also suggested that certain established traditional male institutions have developed exclusively male customs and traditions, which perpetuate the 'old boy network and safeguard it from female intrusion'.   If women are not allowed to participate in existing networks, clubs, or groups, they must form their own organisations.   From the late 1970s, women managers began organising support groups in a number of countries in western Europe, sometimes affiliated to a management centre. The first international association of women in management was founded in 1984 with the creation of the European Women's Management Development Network (EWMD), with its headquarters in Brussels. While primarily European in orientation and membership, the EWMD maintains informal ties with leading figures in management organisations worldwide. The EWMD, in turn, serves as a catalyst for the establishment of networks for women in management in countries where networks had not previously existed. By providing opportunities for women in management to share information, views, and experiences, the EWMD encourages experimentation with new approaches tried in other countries. In this way, EWMD helps to deconstruct myths about 'impossible' ideas or 'natural' ways of doing things. Membership is open to men and women who share a commitment to three key objectives: (i) to promote and further develop the knowledge and performance of women in management; (ii) to encourage women to move into powerful positions in the workplace and the community; (iii) to work towards a more evenly balanced mix of men and women in senior management roles and thereby help to improve the quality of management internationally.

Overall, it appears that, while networking with female contemporaries is a useful support system, until more women gain senior positions in management, women will have to learn how to successfully break into the male-dominated networking system, particularly at senior levels. Davidson and Cooper (1992, p. 129) believe that breaking into the male-dominated networking system is important because 'politics and networking are bound up with power, and unfortunately the power is still held predominantly by men'.

2.3   Sexual Harassment

Sexual harassment is the term given to unwanted sexual attention, requests for sexual favours, and other conduct of a sexual nature, expressed or implied. It may consist of physical gestures or touching, it may be verbal, including sexual innuendoes and jokes (O'Donovan and Szyszvzak, 1988). The Trades Union Congress in Britain has defined sexual harassment as:

> Repeated and unwanted verbal or sexual advances, sexually explicit derogatory statements or sexually explicit remarks made by someone in the workplace which are offensive to the worker involved, which cause the

worker to feel threatened, humiliated, patronised or harassed, or which interfere with the worker's job performance, undermine job security, or create a threatening or intimidating work environment (in Davidson and Earnshaw, 1990, p. 23-27).

Until 1976, in the United States, there was no legal definition of sexual harassment. Since then, however, sexual harassment has been defined in two ways. The first is *quid pro quo* which involves demands for sexual favours in return for a job-related outcome. This involves an unwanted imposition of sexual requirements in the context of unequal power, and has been defined by MacKinnon (1979, p. 1) as:

Sexual harassment . . . refers to the unwanted imposition of sexual requirements in the context of a relationship of unequal power. Central to the concept is the use of power derived from one social sphere to lower benefits or impose deprivations in another . . .

The second aspect of sexual harassment involves a hostile work environment 'where sexual attention is persistent and unwelcome, although the threat of actual loss of job or job benefits is not necessarily present' (Cleveland, 1994, p. 169). According to Cleveland, however, a hostile work environment is difficult to define. The principal victims are women, while men are the most frequent harassers or perpetrators. Single or divorced women and women with a higher level of education report more sexual harassment experiences. Women in non-traditional jobs, including male-dominated management jobs, experience more sexual harassment which includes hostile and threatening sexual comments, which are designed to let the women know they are outsiders. In a detailed study of sixty female managers in Britain, Davidson and Cooper (1992) found that 52 per cent of the sample reported that they had experienced sexual harassment at work. In addition, Davidson and Cooper found that women occupying middle- and junior-level management positions, in particular, were more likely to have been victims compared to senior female executives. According to Lach and Gwartney-Gibbs (1993), an interpretation of these findings is that sexual harassment appears to be a form of retaliation against women for threatening male economic and social power.

In Britain, the Equal Opportunities Commission received 151 complaints of sexual harassment in 1988, but most complainants felt unable to pursue the matter in a tribunal. The Equal Opportunities Commission in

Britain suggested that this may represent only a small proportion of sexual harassment, as in many cases the victims will not report what has happened. Davidson and Earnshaw (1990) suggest that some of the reasons for the lack of reporting of sexual harassment include: the seniority of the harasser, the fear of reprisals, the fear of the victim being blamed rather than the harassers, and the fear of not being taken seriously. In 1997, the European Commission reported that the EU social partners acknowledged that 'sexual harassment is a widespread problem, but they did not conclude an agreement on this subject' (1998, p. 23).

The concept of power is central to understanding sexual harassment. From an organisational perspective, sexual harassment is the improper use of power to obtain sexual gratification — it is coercive, exploitative, and women are treated as sex objects (DiTomaso, 1989). From a legal perspective, as mentioned above, sexual harassment reflects an exploitative use of power (e.g., *quid pro quo*). A feminist perspective on sexual harassment also includes a power relationship, male over female, and 'the potential for economic coercion that threatens women's economic livelihood' (Cleveland, 1994, p. 175). Cleveland and Kerst (1993) suggest that three levels of power come together at work to provide the conditions for sexual harassment: societal, organisational and interpersonal or personal power. Kanter (1977) noted that in organisations men normally hold positions of higher status or power, and individuals who occupy higher-status positions are believed to be within their rights to make demands of those in lower-status positions. Sexual harassment may be viewed by those in high power positions as simply an extension of that right. In the informal work situation, as outlined above, there is evidence that managers acquire power through networking and through mentors which are central to the organisation. These informal power structures exclude females and strengthen males organisational power. The societal and organisational bases of power set the conditions of the work environment, which in turn interacts with the interpersonal or personal power of men and women. As outlined above, women are less likely to occupy positions where they have the opportunity to exercise power, which can lead to the reinforcement of the perceptions of their powerlessness. Societal, organisational and personal factors, therefore, combine to affect the perceptions of women as relatively powerless in the workplace, which increases the likelihood of sexual harassment. Power differences, however, cannot be used to fully explain sexual harassment.

Tangri et al. (1982) have proposed three models for the explanation of sexual harassment, and have assessed them using a sample of 20,083 federal employees in the United States. These include the natural/biological model, the organisational model, and the sociocultural model. The natural/biological model suggests that sexual harassment is a natural outcome of stronger male sex drives, and therefore men will more frequently initiate sexual contact. According to Tangri et al., an explanation arising from this model is that sexual harassment may be an outcome of a natural process, and that men do not intend to harass. Little empirical evidence, however, has been found to support this model.

The second model is the organisational model. This model states that sexual harassment results from the 'opportunity structures created by organisational climate, hierarchy, and specific authority relations' (Tangri et al., 1982, p. 35). This suggests that men and women have different positions in the organisation, with men in positions of greater power. Tangri et al. found from their empirical work that this division of power appeared to be true at all levels of the organisation and across virtually all functional units. Partial support has been found for this model.

The third model is the sociocultural model. This model suggests that power differences between men and women, supported by society at large, lead to sexual harassment. Men are rewarded for being assertive sexually while women are rewarded, both socially and economically, for being more compliant and passive. Partial support was found for the explanations put forward in this model. Tangri et al. concluded that each model provides some useful information about the reasons for sexual harassment but none of them provides a full explanation.

As noted above, power does not fully explain sexual harassment, but informal power differences among men and women occupying the same jobs can create conditions for harassment. Co-workers can exercise power by providing or withholding information, co-operation, and support. Pryor (1987) found that co-workers are the most frequent perpetrators of sexual harassment, but according to Cleveland and Kerst (1993) they tend to engage in less severe forms. According to DiTomaso (1989), men threatened by female co-workers may believe that an increase in power for women means a decrease in power for men. Cleveland (1994) suggests that a strategy used to increase power is to highlight a woman's sex role or sexuality over her gender role, which reminds her and others in the work group that she is a member of an out-group. Over time, Cleveland (1994, 177) suggests that 'the out-group member receives less challenging work assignments and may be less well informed than co-workers in the supervisor's in-group'. Cleveland and Kerst (1993, p. 269) suggest that, because working well with one's co-workers is a requirement in many managerial positions, 'co-workers can accumulate formal power bases and demand sexual favours from a woman in return for co-worker support and peer feedback to the supervisor'.

Personal outcomes of sexual harassment include general tension, anger, stress, disgust, anxiety, hurt, depression, sadness or guilt, fear and self-blame. Physical ailments often accompany psychological problems, which include nausea, headaches, tiredness, teeth grinding, binge eating, inability to sleep, loss of appetite, weight loss and crying spells. According to Cleveland and Kerst (1993), sexual harassment may have an indirect effect on job performance. Harassment denies women access to informal social networks and to necessary feedback for job performance, and these may be important for managerial women who rely on such information.

Much of the research cited here on sexual harassment is from studies in the United States and Britain. Future research might deal with sexual harassment issues in other countries. In Davidson and Cooper's (1993) study of women in management in eleven European countries, Britain was the only country to mention sexual harassment as an issue for female managers. Future research might investigate if European women encounter problems similar to women in the United States after gaining access to senior management positions.

2.4 Career Development

As outlined above, female managers face more overt and covert barriers to career advancement than their male counterparts. Because of these barriers the career development process for women is different from that of men, and far more complex in terms of frequent shifts between home and work. Research on adulthood in women has focused on the family cycle at the expense of the work cycle, which means that no formal theory of women's occupational behaviour exists. According to White et al. (1992), theoretical advances have been made since 1982, although most have received some criticism as career-development theorists have generally based their models on studies of men. Three main theoretical trends, have guided research on women's career development, (i) the classic model; (ii) the neoclassic model; and (iii) the dual-development model. Traditional career-development theorists such as Super (1957) and Ginzberg et al. (1951) originally based their theories almost exclusively on studies of male subjects. The result is what has been termed the *classic model* in which career patterns are typified by the careers expected of successful males.

Gilligan (1979, p. 432) argued that theories of the life cycle, that take the lives of men as their model, fail to account for the experiences of women, 'implicitly adopting the male life as the norm, psychological theorists have tried to fashion women out of a masculine cloth'. Gilligan further stated that woman's place in man's life cycle 'has been that of nurturer, caretaker, and helpmate, the weaver of those networks of relationships on which she in turn relies' (1979, p. 440). Women, she contended, are socialised to give primacy to nurturing roles, and career or achieving roles assume secondary or negligible priority. According to White et al. (1992, p. 16), the classic model ignores the family situation of women and places no significance on demands on women in the external work environment, and 'as such, it cannot accommodate female experience'.

The *neoclassic model* does acknowledge that competing family demands and individual preferences may interact with organisational needs, and thereby affect careers. Super (1984) claims that the career patterns of men are essentially applicable to women if they are modified to take marriage and childbearing into account.

The *dual-development model* suggests that the understanding of women's careers requires an acknowledgement that women have fundamentally different situations in developing careers than men have (White et al., 1992). Family and competing demands which are external to the work environment need to be considered together with phenomena within the workplace which may distinguish men from women. Larwood and Gattiker (1986) proposed that women's career development does not merely lag behind that of men, but, that it may proceed in a different manner. Career gains and professional accomplishments are for women complements, not substitutes, for strong inter-dependent relationships. While work may be central to men's sense of identity, the ongoing process of attachment to significant others is an important source of identity, maturity and personal power for women.

Fitzgerald and Crites (1980) believed that career development for women is more complex because of the differences in socialisation and in the combination of attitudes, role expectations, behaviours and sanctions that constitute it. The socialisation of women to give primacy to nurturing roles, and secondary or negligible priority to career or achieving roles, leads to home–career conflict, lack of serious career planning, and restriction of options to sex-stereotypical occupations. Astin (1984) also highlighted the importance of early socialisation experiences for women regarding career development. Her proposition stated that basic work motivation is the same for men and women, but that they make different choices because of their differing early socialisation experiences and structural opportunities. Ginzberg (1984) found that, for women, the tentative period of career development corresponded closely to the same period for men, occurring at approximately ages 11 to 18 and consisting of four stages: interests, capacity, value, and transition to the reality period. Following the capacity stage, however, in which the balance between interests and capacities begins to be considered, gender differences began to be apparent. By the transition stage the women were strongly oriented towards marriage. Many men were also oriented towards marriage, but for them traditionally there has been no conflict between marriage and career. It is clear, therefore, that the male model of career preparation and choice did not fit the female prototype as many women interrupted their educational preparation for marriage and experienced frequent shifts between home and work.

Gutek and Larwood complained that, although it was likely that women's careers would be different from those of men, this did not mean that every study of women's career development should involve a comparison with men. Gutek and Larwood (1989, p. 10) reported that as more women entered the labour force, some theorists suggested that 'women will behave more and more like men in the development of their careers'. Gutek and Larwood, however, believed that women's careers were different and are likely to remain different in the future for at least four reasons:

(i) There are differential expectations for men and women regarding the appropriateness of jobs for each sex that affect the kinds of jobs young men and women prepare for and select.

(ii) Husbands and wives are differentially willing to accommodate themselves to each other's careers, with wives generally more willing to move or otherwise adapt to a husband's career needs than vice versa. To the extent that husbands receive more attractive job offers and their careers progress faster, this is a generally rational strategy to maximise total family career progress.

(iii) The parent role is differentially defined for men and women; the mother role requires substantially more time and effort than the father role.

(iv) Compared to men, women are faced with more constraints in the workplace, including discrimination and various stereotypes detrimental to career advancement (Gutek and Larwood, 1989, p. 10).

Diamond (1989), coinciding with Gutek and Larwood, points out that a variety of attitudes and behaviours still set up barriers to women's optimal career development, and particularly to their participation in non-traditional occupations. Women are often discouraged from entry into non-traditional professions, and for those who do enter, they are subjected to harassment and hostile behaviour.

Bardwick (1980) and Gilligan (1982) believed in a distinct theory of female adult development. These researchers noted that women emphasise the importance of relationships and attachments and that, even for the accomplished professional and career women, traditional roles and interpersonal commitments remain a core part of female identity. Bardwick (1980) argued that there is a distinctly different phase of adult life for men and women between the ages of thirty and forty. For men, she argues, this is a period of enhanced investment in career, while women require much more than career and professional success.

It is evident that a clear picture of the career-developmental process for women has not yet emerged. Diamond (1989) and Larwood and Gutek (1989), however, suggested that there is a need to develop a theory of women's career development. Larwood and Gutek suggested that if a comprehensive theory of women's career development were to be developed, particular attention should be given to (i) career preparation, (ii) opportunities available in society, (iii) the influence of marriage, (iv) pregnancy and children, and (v) timing and age. Diamond (1989, p. 25) also suggested that more research is needed in this field. Such research, however, 'must not be based on the male model but must be relevant to the many unique aspects of women's experience and involve broad enough samples of women to embrace all the pertinent variables — socio-economic, demographic, educational, environmental, biological and psychological'. Diamond suggested that the research should be tested empirically and longitudinally. Only then can the process of career development for women, and its similarities to and differences from the career development process for men, be more fully understood.

2.5 Additional Barriers for Female International Managers

Given the significant barriers and biases that women managers have to cope with in their home countries, as outlined above, it is necessary to examine the additional difficulties experienced by women in developing their international careers. The evidence of greater barriers existing for women in expatriate management is reflected in the comparative number of female managers, for example, in the United States approximately 40 per cent, and in Britain approximately 27 per cent — with the number of female expatriate managers from both of these countries between only 3 and 5 per cent. According to Smith and Still (1996, p. 2), the international human resource management literature has given very little attention to women as expatriates, 'probably because international assignments have long remained a male preserve'.

This research strand began in the United States in the 1970s, in western Europe in the early 1980s, in Asia towards the mid-1980s, in the former Communist countries of eastern Europe, and in the People's Republic of China towards the end of the 1980s. Up to the early 1980s, research on women in international management was primarily restricted to the role of the expatriate wife, especially the wife of a western manager in facilitating or hindering her husband's performance overseas. Research conducted in North America by Adler (1994; 1987; 1986; 1984) has provided the most comprehensive examination of the role of women in international management to date.

Adler argues that as a result of a historical scarcity of local female managers in most countries, organisations have often enquired if women could function successfully in cross-border managerial assignments. According to Brewster (1991), another negative reason for not appointing women in international management positions may result from a tendency of organisations to confuse the role of female expatriate managers with that of the female expatriate partner, whose frequent failure to adapt has been one of the most commonly cited reasons for premature expatriate returns.

According to Berthoin-Antal and Izraeli (1993, p. 85), the structure of the expatriate managerial role may allow senior home-country management to discriminate against women. The role of the expatriate involves even more uncertainties than that of the domestic manager, and as uncertainty increases the need for trust, this is perceived as having further implications for limiting women expatriate managers. The need for certainty motivates managers to select others who are most similar to themselves, and presumably more likely to be trustworthy and predictable. Situations of uncertainty also increase the likely use of stereotypes and, in the absence of reliable knowledge about future performance or in situations where past experience is limited, stereotypical beliefs about the characteristics and abilities of men and women are employed by home-country senior managers. These stereotypical beliefs result in women's deselection for more senior managerial international positions (Izraeli and Izraeli, 1985). It is suggested that the greater the uncertainty, the smaller the probability that a multinational will assign a woman to an expatriate role, and under conditions of high uncertainty, headquarters will prefer men as expatriates.

According to Dallalfar and Movahedi (1996), much is assumed by home-country senior managers about the requirements of international managers and the abilities needed for fulfilling such roles. These assumptions typically cast women in a relatively disadvantaged position in the corporate structure. In particular, assumptions and perceptions by home-country managers are reinforced by the traditional profile of the typical male international executive, who is approximately thirty-one years old when he first goes abroad, is married with a trailing spouse who is mobile and committed, spends at least three years on each foreign assignment, and has three such assignments during his career (Harris, 1995a). Similarly, interviews conducted by Adler (1988) with fifty-two female expatriate managers, while on assignment in Asia or after returning from Asia to North America, showed that perceived disadvantages of being female in these cases had more to do with the attitudes of their own companies than with the international assignments themselves.

While organisations may be prepared to promote women through their domestic managerial hierarchy, few women are given opportunities to expand their career horizons through access to international careers. Mandelker's (1994, p. 16) term the 'glass border' describes stereotypical assumptions by home-country senior management about women as managers and about their availability, suitability and preferences for international appointments. Women may also miss out on international appointments because they lack mentors, sponsorship, role models and access to appropriate networks, all of which are commonly available to men.

According to Harris (1995), research shows that senior management chooses managers who have 'high potential' in their home organisations as future international managers. Initial assessment of 'high potential' takes place at an early stage in an employee's career (1995b). Given the problems and biases women managers have to contend with in their home countries, and the different models of career development which exist for men and women, outlined above, it can be seen that women face additional barriers before being picked for having 'high potential'. Other strategies used by home-country senior management to reduce risk under conditions of uncertainty include the limiting of the woman's expatriate assignment to internal rather that to external client contacts and to a short-term rather than to an extended stay, or even to define her assignment as temporary. These strategies are designed by organisations to reduce uncertainty for the woman expatriate manager, even though uncertainty may actually be increased by the adoption of these strategies thus increasing the likelihood of failure (Berthoin-Antal and Izraeli, 1993).

According to Izraeli et al. (1980), expatriate managers generally rotate every four to five years, and this however, raises special difficulties for women. Gaining recognition for personal authority for the male and female manager requires time; a male manager must confirm expectations of his success, whereas a female manager must often disconfirm expectations for her failure as perceived by senior home-country managers. Adler (1984c) surveyed human resource vice presidents and managers from sixty of the largest North American multinationals, and over half of the respondents reported that they hesitate to send women abroad because (i) their commitments to husbands and children limit their mobility and (ii) they believe that foreigners would not accept them. Almost four times as many reported being reluctant to select women for international assignments than for domestic management positions. Eighty per cent of surveyed managers of United States firms reported that they believed that women would face disadvantages if sent abroad. Adler further suggests that because only three per cent of expatriate managers are women, many home-country senior managers question whether women can succeed in international assignments (Adler, 1993a).

The research evidence on the impact of senior home-country managers' perceptions regarding the suitability of women in international management is inconclusive. The available literature does, however, draw attention to the potentially negative effect that such perceptions can have on women's opportunities in international management. It has also been argued that the tendency for management styles to be equated with masculine qualities will negatively affect managers' perceptions of the ability of women to hold international management positions.

The belief of policy makers in corporate headquarters that women expatriates will be hindered by cultural prejudice in the host country creates a further obstacle to women's progress in international assignments. Adler (1994) suggested that one of the major reasons cited by managers of North American multinationals for the low participation rates in international assignments by women was that host-country nationals are prejudiced against female managers. Harris (1995) noted that research on the issue of host-country cultural prejudices as a major barrier to female expatriate managers appears to have been conducted solely where women have been assigned to traditionally male-dominated cultures. Little research has been carried out on the experiences of women in countries with ostensibly similar cultural values, for example, British women expatriates in North America or Europe.

It seems that concerns about women being accepted as expatriate managers arise more from male managers in the home-country organisation blaming other cultures for their own prejudices. Further research needs to be undertaken to clarify the argument put forward by many home-country senior managers that women will not perform successfully in expatriate management positions as a result of host-country cultural prejudices. Research could also investigate whether the restrictions encountered by North American females working in Asia are unique to Asia or if similar restrictions are imposed in other overseas countries.

An assumption often made by senior home-country managers, that women in dual-career marriages do not want an international posting is another problem for female international managers. As more women move into management positions, the 'trailing spouse' is increasingly likely to be the male partner, that has to put his own career on hold, and some organisations expect dual-career status to generate greater employee hostility to geographical relocation. As the majority of expatriate managers is still male, the non-working expatriate spouse group is largely female, and the non-working husband may find himself the lone man in a group of wives. In addition to these concerns, work-permit restrictions by some host countries make it difficult for a spouse to work, for example, the United States, Australia and Switzerland, seldom grant work permits to both spouses. In other countries it may be socially unacceptable for the male partner to be the homemaker and the traditional volunteer activities that wives have been encouraged to undertake may not be available or appropriate for males in some countries. Currently most dual-career couples' problems are left up to the couple to resolve, with no help from the parent corporation. This is problematic because multinationals who ignore policy-making on dual-career issues may find it difficult to recruit and maintain high standard expatriate managers. Dual-career couple issues should be highlighted as a major expatriate concern and the management of dual-career couples should receive greater organisational support in the future. Organisations may no longer be able to assume that the male partner's career will always take precedence, and conversely that the female partner will always subordinate her career aspirations to those of her partner.

It would seem, therefore, that home-country management is not supportive of dual-career couples. Senior home-country managers are apprehensive about sending married women abroad because they presume that married women, rather than married men, will have greater spouse-related problems. The management of dual-career couples is increasingly becoming a challenge for home-country senior managers. While home-country senior management may recognise the conflicts and stresses of dual-career couples, few managers attempt to provide job-placement assistance for the trailing spouse, or relocation and repatriation counselling for all family members. The low participation rate of women in international assignments who are in dual-career marriages, therefore, may result as much from the attitudes and perceptions of home-country managers rather than issues arising from dual-career marriages.

When women's suitability for international assignments is being discussed marital status becomes an issue. Stereotypical thinking and the double standard towards married managers are evident, whether single or married, the female expatriate's family status is presumed to be problematic. It has been suggested that male managers tend to believe that a single woman, away from the social influence of her home country, is more vulnerable, than a man is, to harassment and other dangers. In contrast, if a married woman accepts an international assignment, home-country senior managers may be concerned with potential tensions in the family, and with the problems associated with dual-career issues. In the case of single women in international management, some human resource executives have expressed concerns about women's physical safety and the hazards involved in travelling in underdeveloped countries. Additionally, concerns have been expressed by senior home-country management regarding single women's loneliness, isolation and physical safety, which excludes them from working in remote and underdeveloped countries. Historically, therefore, it seems that one of the most difficult aspects of an international assignment for women, either married or single, is obtaining the assignment in the first place.

As outlined above, it has been widely argued that organisations select managers, firstly for domestic assignments by methods which appear to have distinctive male biases. As men hold most upper level management positions, they do most hiring, including sending individuals on overseas assignments, and they may not be willing to offer career advancement opportunities to women subordinates. Potential international managers are often identified at early stages in their careers, where separation of work from family and chronological career timetables are seen as important for career development. According to White et al. (1992), the concept of career has traditionally been reserved for men. If women worked, it was expected that this would be a secondary activity, as they would have a 'job' rather than a 'career'. Some women have difficulties adhering to progressive, linear career models, which are designed for traditional male career paths, due to their interrupted career patterns, for example, for childbearing and child rearing. This may lead to occupational segregation in organisations which allow senior management to assume that women have difficulty in partaking in international assignments.

A number of attributes are considered to be universally desirable in an international manager. These attributes are shown to privilege the lifestyle that societies most frequently reserve for men. Beliefs, such as, that successful managers must prove their worth by their early thirties, that career breaks to care for family members indicate a lack of organisational commitment, and that being the last person to leave at night demonstrates organisational commitment, 'all advantage a lifestyle more easily pursued by men than by women' (Izraeli and Adler, 1994, p. 12). The managerial role in the West for most of the twentieth century has 'a masculine ethic':

> This 'masculine ethic' elevates the traits assumed to belong to some men to necessities for effective management: a tough-minded approach to problems; analytic ability to abstract and plan; a capacity to set aside personal emotional considerations in the interests of task accomplishment and a cognitive superiority in problem-solving and decision-making (Korabik, 1988, p. 20).

The assumptions of these traits cause problems for female managers, for example, when senior managers assume that men, rather than women, have a tougher-minded approach to problem solving, they tend to hire mostly men for managerial positions, which they believe require tough-mindedness. They then interpret women's absence from such positions as evidence of an inherent shortcoming among women, that is, that women lack a sufficiently tough-minded approach to problem solving. This segregation of men and women into different categories of appointments is considered to be institutionalised discrimination (Izraeli and Adler, 1994). When this segregation pattern is established, senior managers use women's absence from certain managerial positions, including international assignments, to justify women's continued exclusion from such positions. Women may also experience further organisational discrimination as a result of the considerable uncertainty surrounding: (i) what an international manager should do, (ii) the qualifications required for getting the job, and (iii) the skills required for the job. As outlined above, there is a tendency for managers to promote people who most resemble themselves. According to Izraeli and Adler (1994, p. 14), senior male executives perceive women as being different and not being completely like them, so they tend not to select women for international positions, as 'only similarity can form a basis for trusting new managers, rather than any form of more precise performance measurement'. Selecting international managers on the basis of similarity secures the status quo regarding the distribution of rights, privileges and rewards for the primarily male cohort of managers.

Formal organisational policies are formed by wider gender-based societal assumptions regarding the suitability of men or women for international managerial assignments. Formal organisational policies also influence informal processes such as networking and mentoring, which may effect the participation of female managers in international management. Female international managers may be disadvantaged when accessing informal career networks — which provide important aspects of the informal socialisation process by sharing between members of a group who are similar to each other and who have similar backgrounds. In this regard, women are seen as 'non-typical, and therefore risky' by men who comprise the majority of informal networks (Harris, 1995a). It is evident, therefore, that the informal networking facilities which are available to male international managers are not equally available to female managers. If women are excluded from informal networks they may lack information, advice, influence, and power, which are important for international career success. Networking may be particularly important for career and personal development for female managers as a significant number of women may not have had mentors. Although the impact of informal networking processes remains an under-researched area, it is clear that managerial women are still less integrated in organisational networks, and it is these networks which can influence promotion and acceptance.

The second informal process which may effect women's participation in international management is mentoring. As discussed earlier, women may be disadvantaged in setting up informal mentoring relationships because of gender related issues, such as male mentors not selecting female protégées because of the difficulties associated with cross-sex relationships. It appears, however, that mentoring relationships are more important in international management than in domestic management. The importance of having a mentor in home organisations, who supports expatriate managers' interests while they are overseas, helps them to avoid the feeling of 'out of sight, out of mind' by their home organisations.

A further problem which female managers face is that senior management in home-country organisations believe that entry into a new job abroad requires total involvement and longer than usual hours of work. The expatriate woman is, therefore, likely to be even less available to her family while abroad than during her home-country employment. Home-country senior managers may assume that because of these barriers women may not want to partake in international assignments. Table 2.1 highlights some of the difficulties that women experience in advancement to senior positions. It is evident that female international managers encounter additional difficulties in comparison to those experienced by domestic managers, as the number of senior female international managers remains considerably lower than for those in domestic management.

Table 2.1 Summary of Research Findings on Career Experiences of Women Managers

Experiences	Representative Findings
Career advancement	Women progress more slowly up the managerial hierarchy than men do.
Barriers to career advancement	The existence of a glass ceiling indicates that women face obstacles in their careers, which are not faced by their male counterparts.
Salary	Women managers earn lower salaries than those of men. Despite similar starting salaries, the salaries of female MBA graduates, throughout a career, averages about 80% of the salaries of men with MBA degrees.
Marital status	Women managers are less likely to be married than men managers Married male managers are viewed as assets, but female married managers are viewed as liabilities.
Housework and childcare	Women managers spend longer hours each week on housework and childcare than employed men do.
Stress	Women managers face greater pressures than men managers.
Efficiency and Performance	More similarities than differences in terms of managerial efficiency and performance of male and female managers.
Mentoring	Lack of mentors available to women, as male mentors tend to choose those most similar to themselves.

3 Working at Senior Management Level: Empirical Evidence

This study assesses new developments in the international senior managerial career move, by conducting empirical research with fifty female *senior* international managers in Europe. This research contributes to filling an empirical gap in the international human resource management literature, where researchers such as Scase and Goffee (1990, p. 124) noted that 'without empirical research, such discussions [about the international career move] are often sterile and do not contribute to policy formulation and action-setting agendas'.

From the empirical interviews conducted, twelve main themes emerged. From these, six thematic areas are selected for this chapter. The six themes of this chapter apply both to female managers in their home-country organisations as well as to females in international management. The discussion shows how this research confirms, challenges, or adds to previous studies in the fields of international human resource management, women in management, and career-theory literature. Due to the dearth of empirical research with senior female international managers, the results from this work are frequently compared and contrasted with the extant data from prior research conducted with junior female international managers and male international managers.

3.1 Breaking the Glass Ceiling

In the first chapter, a number of topics were identified to promote an understanding of the senior female international career move in Europe. This section is the first of the dominant themes to emerge from an analysis of the data. Each interviewee was asked if she believed the glass ceiling still exists in Europe, and if she had personal experience of the glass ceiling. The findings reveal that all fifty managers were very aware of 'hitting the glass ceiling' in their home organisations at the early stages of their careers, the selected quotations in this section are representative of the sentiments of all the interviewees:

> Let me tell you the glass ceiling is there and it is harder than glass. As far as the term is concerned, every time I hear it I think you've got to be kidding; we're talking concrete here. Sometimes we are talking plywood, but don't minimise it, it is not glass, it is not just a 'glass' ceiling (Manager, Software Company).

> The glass ceiling is still there, in the sense that there are so few women in global terms that have gone to real positions of seniority in companies (Manager, Oil Company).

> I don't think I have broken through the glass ceiling. As I moved up the ceiling has moved up, and I would not say that I have broken through the glass ceiling at all. It is definitely still present   (Managing Director, Telephone Company).

The research results confirm that career blockages for women appear at much earlier stages than for men, with the respondents observing that as they moved up the managerial hierarchy, they repeatedly encountered the glass ceiling. The interviewees spoke of the ceiling being harder than glass, and asserted that it was 'firmly, firmly in place'. These sentiments resonate with Schwartz (1989) who suggested that the metaphor of the glass ceiling is misleading, as 'counterproductive layers of influence on women' such as tradition, socialisation, and negative stereotypes, hinder their progression to senior managerial positions. The interviewees also suggested that, it was most difficult for them to be taken seriously at the initial stage of their respective managerial careers when, they believed, they were generally judged on their appearances — unlike the case of their male counterparts. The respondents reported from their experiences that they believe the glass ceiling still exists throughout Europe, the United States, South America, Australia, New Zealand, Africa, China, Singapore, and Japan.

> The glass ceiling is still in place for women, and not a glass one, but absolutely a concrete one. There is no question in my mind but it is firmly, firmly there, and not just here in Ireland, but in America too. There is no question about that (Director, Health Insurance Company).

The glass ceiling is still there for women today. I think here in Belgium it is significant, it is not cracking here (Partner, Management Consultancy Firm).

The glass ceiling is still in place here in this company because of top management. It is what they promote and it goes right down through the organisation. Women have to be better than men. The men in this organisation are very, very critical. They would tear you to pieces at the least opportunity, even when you get into more senior positions than theirs (Vice President, Computer Company).

Twelve of the respondents believed that they could break through the glass ceiling and make it to the top of their professions, but that this would mean sacrificing much of their personal lives. This finding is similar to a view expressed by Fuchs (1989), who commented that women's progress in the labour market has been offset by the loss of leisure time and the decline of marriage, with employed women more likely to divorce than non-employed women. Morrison et al. (1987) and Marshall (1984) also suggested that women, in comparison with their male counterparts, need to choose among different lifestyle options. Such lifestyle choices include decisions about the importance of a career relative to other areas of life; whether or when to marry; whether or when to have children; arrangements for managing housework and childcare; managing relationships with spouses, relatives, and friends; as well as managing competing demands from various life roles. This research, however, has identified that for female *international* managers lifestyle choices are even more difficult than for domestic female managers. For example, managing relationships with spouses while partaking in international assignments was identified by twenty-two of the fifty respondents as the most difficult obstacle to be overcome. In this regard, the respondents spoke of additional strains placed on personal relationships where the male partner became a trailing spouse, or how their quality of life suffered where the couple decided to have a commuter marriage. The interviewees with children added that while on foreign assignments childcare was a major concern for them, and one interviewee stressed that unless she was completely satisfied with childcare arrangements she would not take an international management position. The managers believed that when their male counterparts move internationally they do not have to take the responsibilities for housework and childcare. The interviewees with children also believed that they missed out on family support for childcare, which would have been available to them in their home countries.

Parasuraman and Greenhaus (1993) noted that women managers are less likely to be married and more likely to be childless than their male counterparts, suggesting that women who are strongly committed to their managerial careers have chosen not to marry or, in the event of marriage, not to have children.   The situation of the ten unmarried interviewees concurs with the findings of Parasuraman and Greenhaus, as these ten managers chose not to marry in order to commit themselves to their careers.   These interviewees believe that it is more beneficial to their careers to remain unmarried, especially when partaking in international management, as they have only themselves to think about when moving abroad.   Thirty-one of the fifty interviewees are married and believe that there are additional sacrifices to be made by female managers who partake in international management, as they assert that balancing a career, marriage and childcare from a distance is much more difficult.   Twenty-six of the interviewees have children.   The quotations below indicate some of the additional barriers which prevent female managers from progressing to senior management positions:

> Balancing home life is difficult if you have children.   I must say that I have done more homework for the children around the world by e-mail than most people.   It has never been unusual for faxes to arrive at my hotel room wherever I am, as well as e-mails from my son to ask if I can read his assignment, or sometimes saying that he cannot understand what he has to do for his homework.   So you have to allow an extra amount of time for that type of thing (Human Resources Manager, Manufacturing Company).

> It is definitely more difficult for women to have a senior career position and to have children also.   That is another obstacle for women to overcome. Women have to sacrifice more.   In the case of myself and my partner, for example, when I first met him I was the one in a more senior position; then our son came along, life did not change for my partner, but life totally changed for me.   My whole life was turned upside down.   I did hire a nanny for the first two years, and I continued on as though I didn't have a child, but that was not satisfying for me personally.   I felt that I couldn't leave the child with a nanny because the sacrifice was too great in the formative years. I wanted to give my kids every chance.   I had watched my friends who had kids before me not being able to talk to their kids in their teenage years, and I did not want that to happen to me, so I had a big issue with that.   I believed that a balance was needed: I would either give fifty per cent to the job and fifty per cent to the kids, or I would give it all to the job and let the nannies

rear the kids, or I would give one hundred per cent to the kids for a number of years. I decided that I would give one hundred per cent to the kids for five years. There is no doubt about it, but women have this guilt feeling. While my partner travels all the time, he comes back at weekends and only feels exhausted; whereas now that I am back working again I feel guilty. I try to spend more time with the kids, but my partner does not feel one bit guilty about the kids (Human Resources Manager, Computer Company).

The managers also spoke of the difficulties they faced when allocating time between their careers and personal lives:

My husband works in London and I work in Dublin, which was quite a tough decision to make because it does affect one's marriage relationship. The fact that my husband is still in Britain is difficult, because I am a married person here and acting like a single person. But, if I had children I could not do what I have done. Where would the children live? — in Dublin or London? Many women have to choose between career and family (Managing Director, Manufacturing Company).

The engineering industry is a very difficult industry to combine work and family. There is no recognition of any kind of childcare facilities and flexible working hours, so women have to choose between career and family. In my experience most of the responsibility of child rearing falls on the women (Senior Engineer, Manufacturing Company).

I believe that women choose between career and family. In my case it was my dream to have an international assignment. Earlier in my career an international assignment came up but I could not take it because I was married; my former husband was in his second marriage and he had kids, and I played a major role with his kids, so at the time I had to choose between the family and work. At the time I let the work opportunities go because of the family, and then I separated two years ago. Fortunately this international assignment came up and I was free to take this because I do not have any family commitments now (Human Resources Manager, Financial Services Company).

Hochschild's (1989, preface) study established that 'careers were originally designed to suit traditional men whose wives raised their children'. Similarly, Fierman (1990, p. 40) suggested that 'the 1980s effectively destroyed the notion that women could have it all, that is, a successful managerial career, a fulfilling marriage, *and* children'. Fierman concluded that the career ladder in the United States is typically predicated on the life cycle of a man. This research supports Fierman's observations regarding the difficulties for managerial women to 'have it all'. The married interviewees with children spoke of the difficulties they experienced when they took time out to have children, for example, the assumptions made by some male managers that they would now be more interested in their families than their careers. One of the interviewees believed, even though she was as experienced and as well qualified as her male counterparts, that she did not get a particular position because she was a woman and was pregnant:

> In our generation the obstacles are not very overt. I think they are quite covert. There was one job that I did not get and I think it was because I was a woman and I was pregnant. That was in the United States. I believe there was covert discrimination there. I think every woman encounters both covert and overt discrimination, and I have experienced it both in my academic life and in my medical life (Medical Consultant).

The managers also spoke of the additional stress they experienced in attempting to balance a senior career and family life, often with very little support from their partners. One of the eight divorced interviewees stated that her career used to be a major threat to her former partner and that he could not cope with her success. The respondents believed that, because of the extra strains and guilt feelings which women experience in balancing an international career with child-rearing responsibilities, the majority of female managers choose between a career and family. The research revealed that female international managers may have to make this decision because (i) of what they perceived to be the relative inflexibility of organisations, (ii) of the assumptions by home-country senior management and societal assumptions that a woman's primary role is that of a mother and not an international manager, and (iii) career success is still based on a male career model which ignores the influence of marriage, pregnancy and children, and household duties. The views of the participants also concur with Astin's (1985) findings, which noted that childhood socialisation and early childhood experiences are important influencing factors in shaping occupational interests. Astin believed that basic work motivation is the same for men and women, but they make different occupational choices due to early socialisation and because opportunities are different for men and women.

The results of research in the United States, by Kleiman (1992, p. 6), indicated that women in lower management levels are likely to encounter the glass ceiling, thus preventing their advancement into middle management. Kleiman concluded that 'the height of the glass ceiling has been found to be much lower than first thought'. The research confirms Kleiman's study, as the participants suggested that one of the main barriers for women in international management is getting to senior management positions first in their home organisations, as one participant suggested: the ceiling moved up as she moved up. O'Leary and Johnson (1991) found that women managers in the United States who reached senior management positions in previously male-dominated areas do so at the cost of isolation and loneliness. The findings from this research confirm that the participants employed in traditional male-dominated areas in Europe, such as medicine, accounting, law, and engineering, also experienced loneliness and isolation, just as their American counterparts did. As outlined by the interviewees, the strains of coping with loneliness and isolation, because of the lack of networks, high visibility, and tokenism, contribute to the extra burdens women have to overcome to reach senior managerial positions. The managers also expressed their views on isolation and loneliness, factors which they believe contribute to the glass ceiling:

> I feel isolated sometimes. My sister who is a doctor and my friends who are teachers and nurses all seem to have loads of women friends, but I don't. Because of where I work I don't meet many women. Women don't tend to have the type of networking back-ups that men have, and that is a lack (Senior Engineer, Software Company).

> It is isolating for women in senior management. In a team, for example, when you are the only woman it is not quite as natural for a woman to go and do the typical things the guys might do after work, like having three or four beers together. The guys can sit there knocking back the beers giggling, and talking about sports. It is slightly lonely (Account Executive, Technology Company).

> I am constantly aware that I am a woman in a man's world, and that there are barriers that need to be overcome. I find that I have to prove myself and I believe that a man would not have to do this (Vice-president, Pharmaceutical Company).

From the comments of the respondents, it is clear that the glass ceiling is still in place for women managers in Europe. The above discussion highlights that many female managers encounter more barriers in their career progression than their male counterparts do. An analysis of the interview data confirms that both glass ceilings and glass borders are still perceived to exist for female managers. The research suggests that these barriers are not confined to European countries, but exist in all countries in which the participants have worked. As suggested in the interview data, these barriers are both covert and overt and are experienced by female managers in their home countries and host countries. It is evident that additional barriers exist for women in international management, as studies have shown that the number of female managers pursuing international careers still remains much lower than the number of their male counterparts, and also lower than females in domestic management. The interviewees believe that because of these additional barriers many female managers may choose not to partake in international assignments. In this regard the fifty interviewees considered themselves to be 'unusual' in pursuing senior international managerial careers.

The fifty managers, all of whom have reached senior management positions, believe that they need to be as well qualified, or in some cases more qualified, more ambitious, and more mobile than male managers. The respondents suggested, in addition to these traits, that they broke through the glass ceiling in their own careers because (i) they persistently asked for their next career move, rather than waiting to be offered the next move, and (ii) they were better than their male counterparts at balancing a number of functions at the same time. The respondents believe that:

> Women have to be much more outspoken about what they want. When men come to promote people, they look to people like themselves. The women might be achieving the results, but they are not shouting about it, so they don't get promoted. And that is why women need to be much more self-confident, and to say what they want, and say things like 'if that job ever comes up, I want to be considered for it'. If women don't do that, they are going to continue to be left behind. I don't think enough women do this. But, for myself, I am very career minded and I go forward and say 'this is what I want'. I ask where is my next career move? And I keep on asking and badgering people until I get answers and I think that is very important, and I don't think enough women do that. They sit back and they wait. You must let your intentions be known. I constantly keep saying what I want. After my first appraisal in the company I said to my manager, who was the financial controller, 'I want to be running my own division'. I thought he would collapse off the chair. I added, 'I don't know how long it is going to take me to get there, but, that is my ultimate aim'. Another thing is that, on

the personal front, you have to get yourself known and that is part of pushing yourself. Overall, flexibility, getting known and letting people know your career aspirations are important to break through the glass ceiling (Managing Director, Manufacturing Company).

I always went ahead and looked for the next promotion. That was important. In my previous employment, when I did a job at a certain level for one or two years I would get bored and I would go and ask for the next promotion. I would always ask for a chance. And then when I made progress I realised that I was very lucky to be given a chance and I took advantage of that. A lot of women do not do this (Partner, Management Consultancy Firm).

As stated above, the managers believe that in order for them to break through the glass ceiling they need to be better than male managers at balancing a number of functions simultaneously. The respondents suggested that they developed this ability from their childhood experiences and their socialisation as children. The respondents recalled from their childhood socialisation their fathers being singularly focused on work outside the home, whereas their mothers needed to develop the ability to balance a number of different responsibilities:

The glass ceiling is all about hidden, unspoken and indirect things. The invisible barriers are discomfort, lack of trust, and generally having to convince men in the organisation that you are powerful enough to run the organisation and to achieve results. Men concentrate on achieving results, and they don't want anything to get in their way. Their whole life is like that, therefore, they want only people on the team who can achieve results. Any female entering the organisation for the first time or coming to a new country is going to be rigorously tested. Women, blacks, Jews, and all minorities are tested. Men concentrate on results, whereas women are much better at balancing a number of things and that is very discomforting for men. All of this goes back to our socialisation, and all of it has to do with our mothers who could and had to manage fifty things all together, and that was the only thing we ever saw. At the same time, we were very aware that our fathers had only one thing to do: he went out to work and came back again. It all goes back to our childhood, thus, women are much better at keeping a number of different balls in the air (Chief Executive, Insurance Company).

There is no question about it, for women to break through the glass ceiling they have got to be better at balancing more things. I think there are more obstacles, particularly in the initial stages of an international career move. There are difficulties in trying to be accepted, trying to understand the culture, getting your arms around the business, and understanding different ways of doing things. I have to balance all of that with two little children, one who is fifteen months and the other who is three and a half. I don't think the main obstacle is childcare, however, but I think the biggest challenge for us is balancing all of that with my husband's circumstances. One of the biggest problems for women managers are their spouses who are not working and whose expectations and careers are put on hold when they move with their wives (Managing Director, Manufacturing Company).

The research illustrates that many of the barriers which prevent female managers from reaching senior managerial positions in their home organisations are similar to those experienced by female international managers. The research further reveals that it is necessary for the participants to have senior managerial experience in their home organisations before being considered for international managerial positions:

We have 7,000 employees, and at my level there are not very many female managers. I certainly had many barriers getting to my position in my home organisation because of my gender. The company is not particularly women-friendly. A woman is supposed to have the necessary senior experience before she is given the chance of an international position, whereas a man who is working in area A is often given the chance of an international promotion to area B or C, where he may have no experience at all — whereas, a woman would be told that she does not have the qualifications. That sort of thing has gone on (Managing Director, Telephone Company).

I had a senior position in the Swedish administration system before I came here. I do not think that I would have been given the opportunity for an international position if I did not have this position first, in Sweden, because men tend to recruit men. It has nothing to do with intellectual ability (Director, European Commission).

We have 250 employees here right now, with only three women in senior management positions. The company is Swiss, so it has many male managers. It is unusual for the company to have a woman in senior management. I remember once when I went to a meeting and they didn't know what to do with me as I was the only woman. I am an American and

I worked in England for five years and before that I gained senior managerial experience in the States. I believe that if I did not have this experience I would not be here today. There is a selection programme in the company for people with high potential to go to a lot of companies all over the world, but it is mostly men who are chosen. Maybe this will change, but I think it will be a long time before things change regarding societal attitudes to women having careers (Financial Controller, Pharmaceutical Company).

In summary, the research illustrates that the barriers which prevent female managers from progressing to senior managerial positions in domestic and international management include (i) the obligation to balance home life and career, (ii) isolation and loneliness, (iii) constant awareness of being a woman in a man's world, (iv) having to prove oneself to others, and (v) having to work harder and to be better than male counterparts. The respondents shared the view that the glass ceiling in home countries is a contributory factor to the low participation rate of women in international management.

3.2 Mentors

Another of the thematic areas arising from the interviews is that of mentoring. The data regarding the role of mentors, in the senior female international career move, are presented and discussed in relation to other studies on mentoring. In addition to the important role of mentoring relationships in the career success of female international managers, the research suggests that mentors may have a special role in improving the quality of organisational life for female managers. The interview data provide answers to one of the questions raised in the first chapter, regarding the role which mentors have on the career of the senior female international manager.

From the results of the current investigation and the results of other research studies, evidence is accumulating that female managers have to overcome more barriers in their progression to senior management positions both inside and outside the work environment. As a result of these additional barriers, studies have established that women need more psychosocial support than men do (Davidson and Cooper, 1992; McDonald and Korabik, 1991). The current findings confirm the work of these authors.   Organisational sources of support for managers include mentors, role models, and networks.   Previous studies have identified the lack of mentoring and networking relationships as the most significant barrier facing women managers in their transition from middle to senior management in *domestic* organisations (Dreher and Ash, 1990; Noe, 1988; Levinson et al., 1978).

Forty of the fifty interviewees had the experience of either formal or informal mentoring relationships.   Twenty-eight of the managers had been mentored by males only, six had been mentored by females only, and six had been mentored by both males and females.   All ten interviewees who did not have mentors believed that they would have benefited from such a relationship, especially in the early stages of their careers.   The sentiments of ten managers who did not have mentors can be summarised as follows:

> I wish I had a mentor in my career.   It is important to have one. I could possibly go with either a male or female mentor.   In the early years in particular it was something that I could have done with.   With a mentor you would be able to put the local issues on the table, for example, how would I handle this or that, and it is something that I lacked.   If I had a mentor it would have been more beneficial to my career (Account Executive, Technology Company).

> I haven't had a formal mentor in my career.   I have had people that I can sound off my ideas with and I still do that.   I believe that mentoring is a very good idea and I also believe that there should be a formal mentoring system in organisations.   But, people should not be forced to be mentors, because that would not work.   I would be very happy to be a mentor for younger people.   I don't think it should matter if the mentor is male or female (Managing Director, Manufacturing Company).

> I never had a mentor in my career.   But, I think if I had one, I would have benefited from it (Vice-president, Computer Company).

Seven of the interviewees suggested that their mentoring relationships were informal, and mentors were usually senior managers or bosses who gave guidance to them.   These interviewees spoke of their bosses, all male, who facilitated informal mentoring support.   These interviewees believed that a 'good boss' acted as a supporter and adviser for them, helped to develop their reputations, helped to get their names known to senior management, set high standards for them, and stimulated their personal motivation:

> Long before the word mentor was invented, I was fortunate to have a couple of bosses who were helpful in that way. It was very informal. What you need is someone to discuss issues with and whom you can trust and who sometimes helps you to find a way out and to help you solve problems. I have two sons, and when they were very young it was not acceptable for me to go home and pick up the children from school, so sometimes there were very difficult situations. But, I was very fortunate that I had a boss who arranged meetings so that I could leave when I needed to, and accepted that I took papers home and did work at home, without talking to anybody else about it. So it worked thanks to a very good attitude from his side (Director, European Commission).

> I had a male mentor, but it was not that formalised. We had a process at one point in the company where there was this idea of 'godfathering', whereby we would be allocated a senior manager whom we would be able to go to in our sector and bounce ideas off. Mine has always been very informal, with a boss that I worked with a number of years ago, before I moved abroad, and whom I have kept very close to. I would consider him as a mentor. I don't think that this is as important for one's career as much as for one's level of sanity. I have had two mentoring relationships, and they have both been with men. I have found these relationships particularly useful in situations which I have found difficult or if I have been going through a rough patch in my career. These men have tended to be a bit longer in the tooth and a bit older in career terms, but, I have found that invaluable (Manager, Oil company).

The twenty-eight interviewees who had been mentored by males talked about the absence of female mentors, which reflected the relative scarcity of women in senior management, who might otherwise have been a source of mentors. Davidson and Cooper (1992) also found that successful female managers often report that at least one of their superiors (usually male) has been instrumental in helping their careers. The research results indicate that, there are not enough women in senior international managerial positions yet to act as mentors for other women. As a result, female managers are more likely to be mentored by males. The findings establish that the mentor's gender does not influence the effectiveness of the mentoring relationship. None of the thirty-four interviewees that had been mentored by males had experienced any difficulties with cross-gender mentoring. All thirty-four believed that their mentors did not view them just as females, but saw their mentoring roles as aiding the career advancement of their managerial protégées. This finding is consistent with research conducted on the effects of gender and mentoring by Monks (1998) and Noe (1988). This challenges prior research by Arnold and Davidson (1990) and Fitt and Newton (1981) who suggested that sexual tension was an issue in cross-gender mentoring. Thirty-eight of the interviewees added that females are more likely to be mentored by males, because of the lack of women in senior management positions:

> In a previous job I had a mentor, who didn't see me as a female, but as a professional. He gave me things to do and I initially thought that I couldn't do that, as he put me in situations where I was going to be really stretched, but I thrived on it, and it definitely helped my career. He gave me more faith in myself. I realised that I could do more than I originally thought I could and I became personnel manager and vice-president because of him. He also gave me a lot of international opportunities. I have to say that I never worked for a woman boss, because they are generally not there. I normally work on the board and again because the board is mainly composed of males I have never really worked with females   (Director, Manufacturing Company).

> I have always had mentors and they have always been male. I have never had a female mentor. They are not there at senior levels. I have never come across a female mentor. I always look for a mentor in the first couple of months in my new job and I suss people out quickly. To me it doesn't matter about their personality, but what matters to me is their business brain (Human Resources Manager, Computer Company).

> I always had mentors in my career. When I would have been making my way up in organisations, they would have been powerful males at that time. And, certainly, in the organisation in which I spent most of my young career there were some men who were very good at mentoring. It is important for everyone to have a mentor, in particular for women, because it gives them information about the organisation which they are not used to having. A lot of research which has been done in the United States showed very clearly that women who first made it to the top in big organisations tended to have received formative information from their fathers whom they were closer to, information like how organisations work. The one thing that is hard for women is that there are not enough women in senior positions for them to have female mentors. But, there are men in organisations who are suited to

this purpose, and I really don't think it matters too much whether the mentor is male or female as long as they can provide the information, and a lot of men tend to think that information is power (Chief Executive, Insurance Company).

When I was 28 years old I was working as a Marketing Manager in one of New Zealand's biggest companies. The marketing director at the time was fired, so I was appointed marketing director, but the senior management did not want to give me the same package as my predecessor. This was because of my age and probably being female and not being Australian, because the company was run by Australians at that time. I think there was a whole host of other reasons, like lack of confidence in me, for example, wondering if I was really going to be able to deliver and make such a big leap in job terms. The man who stuck his neck out and gave me the opportunity was a very good mentor to me. He really kept me in touch with what was going on, and what the important issues were, what different people's feelings were, and how to approach things so I would get the best chance within the group. I learned an awful lot, but had it not been for the kind of feedback I got from my mentor it would have been much more difficult. A year later, I was appointed marketing director and it was only then that I realised what I had been missing out on, in terms of the whole package and the benefits and so on, and the kudos from it. So, that is a very good example of having a mentor. An example of where I did not have that kind of relationship was when I was working for a company in England. I went into that company at a very senior level, working part-time. Later they asked me to work full-time, which I did. But, I was given what was an impossible job. That is really the only time when I ended up really struggling with my career. I didn't have access to anybody who was able to point me in the right direction. It was a very political organisation and it was a big disadvantage for me not to have a mentor. If I had been male it would have been different because in that organisation it was all about male bonding and male drinking and so on. I had a small child at the time, so I worked very hard to get my job done and to get home. The last thing I wanted was to go to the pub (Marketing Director, Telecommunications Company).

The research revealed that, in an international management context, a mentoring relationship is even more important than in domestic management. The participants believed that while partaking in international assignments, mentors provide the contact and support from the home organisation which in turn facilitates re-entry — in addition to improving the self-confidence of protégées, increasing their visibility in organisations and increasing their promotional prospects. The participants also believed that the opportunities for them to partake in international assignments would have been partly attributed to mentoring relationships. The interviewees suggested that, in the absence of family and friends, their mentors also provided many support benefits, and also helped in keeping them in touch with their home organisations, which in turn reduced the 'out of sight, out of mind' syndrome.

Clutterbuck (1993) asserted that everyone needs a mentor. Clutterbuck and Devine (1987) pointed out that the benefits of a mentoring relationship are not limited to the protégé. The mentor is said to achieve increased job satisfaction, increased peer recognition, and potential career advancement. The forty interviewees who had the experience of mentoring relationships acknowledged that the benefits provided by their mentors began in their home organisations, for example, in providing career direction and psychological support. These interviewees suggested that their advancement to international management may be partially based on the successful development of mentoring relationships. This finding supports the conclusions of previous studies on mentoring in domestic organisations, which reported that more women than men who advance to senior management positions had mentors (Burke and McKeen, 1994; White et al., 1992; Ragins, 1989; Clutterbuck and Devine, 1987).

Six of the interviewees who had been mentored by both males and females believed that they were fortunate to have had the experiences of mentoring relationships with both genders. These interviewees believed that they had 'the best of both worlds', but suggested that it is the capability of the mentors that matters most, and not their gender:

Having a mentor is important. I had one formal mentor and a number of different informal mentors. The formal mentor acted as a career manager for me. When you are overseas, a home-based mentor is someone who provides that link when you are going to return. Having a home-based mentor, while I was overseas, kept me in touch with what was happening back home in the company, and that is incredibly important. Sometimes, if you want to find solutions or if you want to sound things off and you have a close relationship with your mentor, you can use that person in a confidential situation to sound things off. This is very important. Three of the mentors I had were men and two were women, and it was their different personalities and their different contributions that mattered, rather than their gender. Of the two women mentors that I had, one has children and it has been really refreshing for me to see that she is very senior, that she has kept a balance in her life, and she hasn't become macho. She is not working towards all these macho things like the different images of the long hours and all the rest of it, so it is quite good to see. So, it is refreshing to see that you can get there and not sacrifice yourself in getting more like men (Human Resources Manager, Telecommunications Company).

Cooper and Hingley (1983) suggested that women need female mentors who can act as role models. They believed that women may miss opportunities for career advancement if they lack female role models. This lack probably gives rise to responses which mirror the behaviour of successful male executives, which may further isolate women as their lifestyles do not easily adapt to the male managerial model. Other research has also shown that where a female mentor is available to act as a role model, it is likely that the aspiration levels of managerial women will be raised, even for work traditionally done by males (Barclay, 1982; Hackett and Betz, 1981).

Forty-nine of the interviewees asserted that many benefits can result from a mentoring relationship. These forty-nine managers believed that a mentor who guides one's career through the early stages is almost essential to success. Only one interviewee expressed any caution about a mentoring relationship, while admitting to its support role:

> I think people can become over dependent on a mentor. I believe that the best thing to do is to take the very best from everybody. Taking somebody under your wing to get them started is a help; but I wonder about long-term relationships (Director, Computer Company).

The forty interviewees who had mentors believed that the benefits provided by mentors, regardless of gender, has undoubtedly facilitated their career advancement. Ten of the managers are now providing a mentoring role for junior staff members, mostly for younger females:

> I love to mentor people. Most of them are women, but not all. It is a different interaction if one is mentoring a male or a female. I believe that I have a lot more in common with women, because we face some of the same challenges in terms of how we communicate, how we react to things, our family situations, children and the balancing of chores (Partner, Management Consultancy Company).

I have many females working for me, which is just a coincidence because they were in the department when I took it over, and I try to spend some time mentoring them (Human Resources Manager, Computer Company).

I was officially a mentor for men, while unofficially I was a mentor for women who asked me to mentor them. I would spend some hours discussing their situations and problems. I believe the women have chosen me because there are not very many senior women managers (Director, European Commission).

The managers also suggested that mentoring in organisations outside the United States is a relatively recent development and, therefore, denied to many female managers who worked in an exclusively European context. A critical question is whether organisations can create conditions that encourage females to take on the role of mentors, as it is clear from the research that there is a scarcity of senior female mentors. The research reveals that managers who do not experience the benefits provided by a mentor, as discussed above, could in turn be a contributory factor in explaining the scarcity of female managers in international management.

3.3   Tokenism and Lack of Female Role Models

As highlighted above, there is a scarcity of senior female managers to provide mentoring support to junior managers. The data presented in this section deal with (i) the additional difficulties experienced when female international managers are in the minority group, and (ii) the lack of female role models for senior international managers. The research helps to provide an understanding of two of the questions raised in the first chapter concerning (i) whether there are additional difficulties for the female international manager as part of a minority group, and, (ii) the lack of female role models for female international managers.

Being a 'token' senior female manager in an organisation can create extra burdens and stresses for that manager. Davidson and Cooper's research (1992) revealed that increased visibility can lead to loss of privacy, and further add to the stresses and strains experienced by senior female managers. The female managers who were interviewed by Davidson and Cooper and who worked in male-dominated organisations, complained of the disadvantages associated with their high visibility. These disadvantages included the highlighting of their mistakes and associating these with gender, as well as receiving personal attention for their sex characteristics rather than for skills, which meant that they had to put extra effort into getting themselves taken seriously. Similar findings, which were expressed by the participants in this study concur with Davidson and Cooper's findings with forty-six interviewees believing that, because of being in a foreign country, their feelings of isolation and tokenism were far more pronounced than in domestic management settings. Their additional feelings of isolation were compounded by language, culture and gender barriers. The interviewees remarked that home-country senior management should recognise that without the social support of other female colleagues the token woman's progress is likely to be hampered. Forty-six managers suggested that tokenism, isolation, the lack of role models, and being test cases for future international female managers were significant contributory factors in explaining the scarcity of women in international management:

> When I worked for a very large firm in New Zealand I felt quite isolated because the group's Managing Director there said to me that he happened to have a point of view that women in senior management were actually a bad thing. He was happy to agree with me, however, that there are exceptions to that rule, but as a general principle he does not think it works. I think that he was a chauvinistic male. He was in his fifties, so a man of a different generation. He liked the status quo and he did not see any reason why it should change. He also said that if I quoted him, he would deny it. And that was quite isolating. I also remember attending a conference of the top fifty companies in New Zealand and I was the only woman executive there among forty-nine men (Marketing Director, Telecommunications Company).

> I am constantly aware that I am a woman in a man's world, and that there are barriers that need to be overcome. I find that I have to prove myself more than a man would have to. This is because I am very visible and also because of the impression that I am very young. I get the impression that the company believes that it took a risk in taking me, because of my gender and age. My predecessor was a male and he looked older than I do. The way you look is the way people perceive you. I am constantly fighting this thing that I look relatively young. It has to be said that most of the men at my level are ten to fifteen years older than me, in my direct peer group, therefore, I am very young for my position. Sometimes the male managers are patronising to me. They have been known to say things like 'you are

very good, but', and there is always a but, and then I feel like punching them on the nose (Vice-president and Controller, Pharmaceutical Company).

When I joined this firm I believed that I was being treated differently because I was a woman. One time it had to do with promotion and salary. When I was to be made a partner — in fact the first woman consulting partner in Chicago — I was held back a year, because senior management was concerned that I would fail. So, they decided not to take the risk and left me as a senior manager for one more year, and then promoted me the next year. I was very disappointed and frustrated when I was kept back a year. The only reason that I was held back was because of my gender (Partner, Management Consultancy Company).

Ten of the interviewees who relocated to Belgium believed that, because of gender, they were further isolated and treated as test cases for future women. These interviewees perceived, from their collective experience, that Belgian organisations are still dominated by a male hierarchical system, which highlighted their token positions. The interviewees also believed that female managers are expected to work harder than their male counterparts, and are always aware of being in 'a man's world'. One of the interviewees stated that Belgian society is very male dominated, and also expressed that an old-fashioned attitude prevails which implies that women should stay at home with the children. She also stated that because she was a woman and was coming in to take over the number one position in a male-dominated organisation in Belgium, she was seen as a threat to her male colleagues:

I feel a sense of isolation as a woman manager and also because of the culture-based hierarchical system here in Belgium whereby you are not friends with your boss. Judging from my culture in Sweden, hierarchy should not be a barrier to relationships. Sometimes I feel the staff here do not understand my behaviour when I walk around the corridor and get friendly with them. I don't even know the difference of who is an A, B, or C grade, and I don't see that as important. What I lack here is discussion with other women in senior positions. There are a few other Swedish women here in the Commission and sometimes we meet and complain, especially when we are tired. Last week, I felt tired and I thought I would quit, as I didn't want to take any more. Then I met with some of the other women who are doing my kind of work and we discussed things, and I felt support through these women and then I felt strong again (Director, European Commission).

The three interviewees employed in Germany reported similar feelings of isolation and tokenism. Two of these three interviewees held senior positions in banking institutions and had no other female colleagues at their level. These interviewees also perceived German organisations to be very inflexible, and believed that German societal norms still value women as mothers rather than as managers. The American interviewees who relocated to Ireland believed that it was easier for them to be accepted as senior managers in Ireland than in the United States. One of these interviewees believed that attitudes towards female managers were regressing in the United States, and that there was more tolerance of female managers there during the 1980s than during the 1990s. Similarly, two Irish interviewees who had worked in the United States reported that they experienced more discrimination and bias against them in the United States than in any of the European countries they worked in.

Thirty of the interviewees reported that they were the first females to represent their companies in international assignments. These interviewees spoke of additional problems they experienced, which were associated with tokenism, isolation and exclusion, and which they believed their male counterparts would not have to endure. Only four of the interviewees expressed that they did not experience a sense of isolation:

> I believe that I am in an artificial environment in human resources because there is a large proportion of women there. My colleagues are female, so it is difficult for me to comment on how it would feel as a senior female in the engineering part of the company. I imagine that at times it can be a bit isolating, but, I haven't come across that (Human Resources Manager, Telecommunications Company).

According to Kirkham (1985), one of the key differences between being a member of a majority group and being a member of a minority group is that majority group members do not think about what it means to be a member of that majority group, whereas minority group members give much more thought to the meaning and effect of being in that minority and to the dynamics of the majority group. Tanton (1994) suggested that being members of a minority group can lead to loneliness at work and can also give rise to a number of other uncomfortable roles or issues for female managers, such as being the outsider, having to strive to avoid letting women colleagues down, little recognition for achievements, and being taken for granted. The research confirms Tanton's work, as interviewees reported loneliness, exclusion, and isolation, particularly at the early stages of their careers in their home organisations. One of the interviewees spoke about two types of uncomfortable situations which she experienced in her home organisation. The first situation was when her male counterparts 'chatted her up, and propositioned her', and the second situation was when older, traditionalist men patronised her. She believed that these situations act as barriers to women's career advancement.

As suggested earlier, another difficulty facing female managers, especially international managers, is not having female role models to follow. The research confirms previous research by Freeman (1990) and Davidson (1987) which suggested that female role models in higher managerial positions positively influence the careers of other women. Research studies have established that being a token woman manager not only means having no female peer support, but is likely also to mean working in an environment without female role models in senior management positions:

> In Ireland there are certainly not enough women in senior management to act as role models for younger women. There are a few, of course, but one could count them on one hand, the most obvious one being the President of Ireland. But, in business, there are few women who are role models and who have done exceptionally well. There is no reason why there should not be at least as many women at the senior level as there are men (Manager, Tourism Promotion Agency).

As discussed above, women in international management, typically, do not have female role models to follow. Adler's research in North America (1994), revealed that the majority of female expatriates did not have female role models to follow. Similarly, in this research, thirty of the fifty interviewees were the first female managers to partake in international assignments for their organisations, and they also believed that they were test cases for future female international managers. Forty interviewees believed that having a female role model would have been advantageous to their international careers. These sentiments concur with the findings of Davidson and Cooper's (1992) research on female managers in their home countries, who found that performance pressure is intensified when women are appointed to particular positions in order to act as test cases for the future employment of other women at similar levels. The interviews indicate that it is more difficult for a younger female manager to be taken seriously when she is the first female to represent her organisation internationally. One interviewee who worked in Japan stated that, because she was young (late twenties), she had to be very careful not to disclose anything that might reveal how young she was. She believed that being relatively young was a bigger barrier than gender. Similarly, another interviewee who worked in Belgium believed that, even though she was in her thirties, she looked very young, and found male managers patronising towards her.

Of the fifty managers, forty considered themselves as role models in their organisations, seven did not consider themselves as role models, and three said that they did not know or had not thought about it previously. Five of the seven interviewees who did not consider themselves as role models stated that they were quite proud of what they were doing, but thought of themselves as managers rather than as females. The other two interviewees who did not consider themselves as role models believed that they grew up in households 'where there was nothing less expected of girls', so they believed that if males and females were equally encouraged from a young age, they should be able to achieve without being aware of being female. All forty interviewees who considered themselves as role models stressed that they did not want to sound 'over important' when regarding themselves as role models, but as there was a scarcity of senior female international managers, they considered it necessary for them to fill this vacancy in order to help other female managers:

> To an extent I would consider myself a role model for other women in the organisation. For women who work here in the organisation I would make a special effort to coach them. I don't know if they regard me as a role model, but I would like to think that they do. I would talk to them, and if I felt they were doing something that was not helping their career I would take them aside and say to them that this leads to this and so on, which I think is helpful (Plant Manager, Pharmaceutical Company).

> I would never have considered myself as a role model until I came back from my international assignment. Now people are approaching me on a daily basis asking me about my experiences. When I came back from my international assignment I was given a high step promotion ahead of a lot of people. So I would say yes, I would be a role model. (International Assignment And Repatriation Manager, Telecommunications Company).

> I am a role model, whether I admit it or not. I never really realised what impact one has as a manager, because one doesn't really think that of

oneself doing anything so brilliant, because of growing into the role, and because of feeling comfortable in it. I never realised what effect my responses would have on certain people. I never realised before that people know exactly what you are doing and what you are saying and what you are wearing. There is no formal dress code within our organisation, and Friday is jeans day. I don't abide by those rules, I always try to look smart, because that is something that comes to me naturally (Customer Services Manager, Computer Company).

Very definitely I see myself as a role model, but I didn't come to the organisation with that in mind. Women have come to me and asked if they could talk to me. As a woman they ask me if I can help them because as women there is a bond between us (Technical Support Manager, Computer Company).

I would like to think of myself as a role model. I would like for the girls in particular and even the guys to walk away from the department and say that they learned from me. Not only learned from me while sitting down with them going through the day-to-day stuff, but that they learned by watching my performance at meetings and from my performance with suppliers. I would like to believe that the girls would think that if I can do it, so can they (Purchasing Manager, Manufacturing Company).

I suppose to a certain extent I would see myself as a role model for other women in the organisation. I would like them to think if she can do it, it must be dead easy! (Human Resources Manager, Computer Company).

The forty respondents, who considered themselves as role models, hoped that when younger female managers saw that other females had previously partaken in international management, particularly those with children, that it was possible for themselves to aim for and achieve international assignments. These forty managers believed that the actual partaking in international management assignments helped them to become role models. These interviewees also believed that as role models they could help to change the attitudes of both males and females in organisations. They believed that they could inspire and encourage younger females to partake in international assignments, and that they could help male managers to take a more positive attitude towards women in international management. The interviewees further suggested that as more senior female managers were prepared to act as role models, then, perhaps, the number of women partaking in international management assignments should increase.

3.4 Networking

As discussed earlier, female managers in token positions, in comparison to their male colleagues, suffer more career disadvantages. The data presented in this section assert that female international managers who are not part of a support network experience even further career disadvantages. In particular, the benefits derived from being part of a network group are more significant for those managers who have not had the experience of mentoring relationships. The research question addressed in this section, as outlined in the first chapter, relates to the role which networking has on the career of the senior female international manager.

Smith and Hutchinson (1995) noted that there is not much empirical research literature available on interpersonal networks. Previous research studies of networking in domestic organisations, however, have indicated that in many organisations the concept of networks is understood to mean a male club or an 'old boy network' model (Davidson and Cooper, 1992; Ibarra, 1992). The findings indicate that, throughout Europe, the old boy network is still strong in most organisations, and particularly in established industries, such as medicine, accountancy and law. The participants believe that, given the absence of family and friends while abroad, the benefits provided by formal and informal networking in international management are of even greater value than the benefits provided by networking in domestic management. Despite these benefits, however, the participants believe that women are further disadvantaged from networking as gaining access to or male-dominated networks is still the most significant barrier. Forty-three of the participants believe that there is a lack of networking for females in senior management. The managers perceive that quite an amount of business is discussed and that useful contacts are made when male managers network informally, but that as females they are excluded access to these informal situations:

> There is as lack of networking for female managers and maybe it is worse in Ireland. I got quite a shock when I found out that there were all-men golf clubs, and with special days for ladies. Even if you have a handicap of eight, you have to beg and plead to be allowed to play on a Saturday or a Sunday, and the only discussion point I had was 'you pay only half price', and I said 'well I am willing to pay full price', and then they even had to think about that. It would be beneficial for women if they had more informal contacts. From the conferences I have been to, I see that there are

quite a few women out there in managerial positions, but we are new, and we are up-coming and we have not shown what we are made of, and what we can do in an almost all-male environment. I still think women have to work harder than men in the managerial environment (Customer Services Manager, Computer Company).

In Ireland I have found that there is a lot of networking for men, and it seems peculiar to me that a lot of business is done informally. I came here after working in the United States for eleven years, so I am not shy, but, there is the old boy network that women are excluded from (Senior Research and Development Engineer, Computer Company).

Many of the male network systems are not officially through network associations, but are through rugby clubs, football clubs, golf clubs and so on. It is like a natural ready-made contact system that exists, but which women do not have as much ready access to. So, women have to try harder and they have to take individual responsibilities for their own careers. In general, the networking opportunities for women are not as extensive as for men (Manager, Tourism Promotion Agency).

This research confirms the work of Burke and McKeen (1994) who suggested that managerial women are still less integrated with important organisational networks. The research indicates that negative attitudes towards female managers were found to vary by industry, with a more hostile corporate climate prevailing in established industries. The participants believe that because they are in a minority group, they feel isolated by male colleagues. The participants also suggest that the exclusion of females from male managerial groups perpetuates the more exclusively male customs, traditions and negative attitudes towards female managers. The negative effects of these covert barriers include: blocked promotion and blocked career development, discrimination, occupational stress, and lower salaries. The respondents also believe that they are further disadvantaged from networking because of their additional family and home commitments and, generally, have far less time to network than their male colleagues:

There is a lack of networking for women in senior management, but maybe we are not like men in looking for things like the old boy network. I would not be interested in that and I would not have the time for it. I just want to go home and do what I have to do. For example, last night I wasn't home until 8.00 p.m. and the home was unhappy because mammy was home late. I have three children, one ten, one eight, and I have a small baby who is two, and when I come home the two-year-old's face just lights·up. He does this for his daddy too, but obviously his world is not complete until his mammy comes home. So I wouldn't have a lot of time for networking (Chief Accountant, Computer Company).

To be quite honest, I think women have less time than men for networking. Networking has to take place to a great extent after work and on top of your job. If you are a woman with a family, you have less time. Men have more time for networking. Working women are very busy (Human Resources Manager, Computer Company).

There is a lack of networking for women in senior management. I work quite long hours and I have a son and a partner, so I really do not have time to network. But, I think one should really make the time to network (Plant Manager, Pharmaceutical Company).

Despite the shortage of time available to female managers for networking, however, forty-three respondents suggested that if there was a professional networking organisation available for female managers they would ensure that their schedules permitted joining such an organisation:

There is not a well developed professional women's network here in Ireland as yet. I have not found the right organisation yet. I have investigated four organisations and none of the four seems to have the type of people that would have things in common with myself. There is a lack of this type of organisation for senior business managers. There is an organisation called Network which tends to be for entrepreneurs, women who are managing their own business, but that is not what I do. I certainly do not have time for a lot of networking because of three young children, but if it were part of a professional organisation with time well spent I would make time for it. There is an opening for a professional networking for business women (Human Resources Manager, Computer Company).

According to Davidson and Cooper (1992), the task for female managers of breaking into the male-dominated 'club' of managers can prove difficult, and this difficulty thereby denies them social support, contacts, opportunities and policy information. Similar findings resulted from this work, with all of the interviewees expressing awareness of old boy networks, and the difficulties associated with breaking into these. The interviewees spoke of 'male bonding' which takes place after work hours, during sporting events, and in clubs and bars which they felt excluded from. The respondents also noted that male managers in their organisations spent more time networking after work hours than female managers. As gaining access to this 'male club' has proved difficult for the participants, some of the interviewees have established their own informal female or mixed-gender networks. The views of the interviewees reflected previous research by Davidson and Cooper (1992) which indicated that, although it is beneficial for female managers to network in these newer groups, there are still more benefits to be gained from networking in established male-dominated groups, as power in organisations is still predominantly held by men. Five of the interviewees were members of networking groups for female managers within their own companies. Four of these interviewees were members of networking groups which were already in existence in their organisations and one interviewee was responsible for setting up a female networking group in her organisation:

> We developed a women's networking programme in the corporation I previously worked for. The corporation took a great deal of interest in that from a corporate and legal point of view. They wanted to become involved, which they did. They were concerned about the purpose and the scope of the organisation, and they were very concerned about our reason for forming. We responded by inviting them to participate. We are a female organisation and our purpose is to share our experiences with other females to help them overcome obstacles. It has nothing to do with male bashing, it is not a coffee morning, it is not a bunch of hens. These are the types of things you hear: 'Ah, it's hen time'. I am not even offended by that type of comment any more, because I know there is a level of fear and it is that negative type of male attitude which produces those type of comments. We used to meet monthly and during this forum we had an agenda, hosted guest speakers, and kept very detailed minutes. Our invited guests included women executives who talked to us about their backgrounds and about what they were doing, but it was primarily for networking. The network is not about reacting; it is about becoming proactive; it is about strength in numbers; it is about sharing — and we need to share this so that we can overcome obstacles, because there are obstacles out there, whether they are overt or implied, they do exist (European Technical Support Manager, Computer Company).

One interviewee who works in the medical profession believed that the professions of medicine and law are still very male dominated, and she is currently involved in setting up a networking group for senior female medical professionals:

My colleagues and I have discussed setting up a women's networking group and giving it official recognition and not to let it be seen like the old boy network. I have some ideas of how it might work, but I don't want it to be seen as a busy bees' club. I would like to see it set up so that it has a positive role and not set up so that it looks threatening. Men find women together very, very threatening. It is also interesting that men equate women working together with trouble. I don't know why this is so, because women in positions of authority can have a very calming influence. With a lot of men in authority the decisions can be based on male egos, but when you bring a woman into a position of authority it often dampens down any aggression. I think the old boy network is still alive and well, and of course there are the conversations in men's loos, and general male bonding (Medical Consultant).

Four of the interviewees were critical of networks which catered exclusively for females:

The difficulty in Belgium is that women are not accepted in clubs like the Rotary Club and the Lions Club. Then you have clubs where only women are present, and that is something that I do not agree with because it does not reflect the reality of society (Bank Manager).

I am very wary about setting up women's groups because straight away we are isolating ourselves. We are always saying that we want to be treated equally and we want to work equally with males and females. So, I am very, very wary of women-only groups (Human Resources Manager, Computer Company).

These four managers believed that it is not necessary to restrict membership of these networks to females only, and that female managers should actively encourage male managers to join. Five interviewees believed that female networking groups were established in their companies because of the dominant old boy network, and the benefits that were seen to be derived from networking:

Our organisation is very good and organises a structure for women to network and it provides a lot of money for this and the network functions well. You get out of it what you put into it. I have worked for the company for twelve years and I have a huge network of people, not just women, but men as well. The only way you achieve and get on is to have that network. I would not say that it should necessarily be restricted to women only. We have the old boy network, and that is most certainly here and I think it will always be here. The key is to try to nudge into networking and get a piece of the action. Networking can be exclusive, but I am beginning to have discussions with my female colleagues when making internal professional decisions. I almost feel myself being sucked into an old girl network, which I guess feels comfortable. It feels that there is a source of information in the network about the whole working environment that otherwise you would not have (International Assignment And Repatriation Manager, Telecommunications Company).

Research by Adler (1987) and Harris (1995a) suggested that female managers can miss out on international appointments because they lack mentors, role models, sponsorship, or access to appropriate networks — all of which are commonly available to their male counterparts. The experiences of the interviewees in this research confirm work by Adler and Harris. The findings indicate that the exclusion of female managers from business and social networks compounds their isolation, which in turn prevents female managers from building up useful networking relationships which should be advantageous to their international careers. The interviewees noted that peer relationships and interpersonal networks provide additional sources of organisational support for managers. Kram and Isabella (1985) examined the role of peer relationships and similarly found that they provided a range of developmental supports for personal and professional growth at all career stages. Burke and McKeen (1994, p. 74) suggested that peer relationships provide several career and psychological functions. Peer relationships, 'unlike mentoring relationships, were characterised by mutuality, with both individuals experienced at being the giver as well as the receiver of various functions'.

The interviewees further suggested that men, as the dominant group, may want to maintain their dominance by excluding women from informal interactions. The interviewees also suggested that exclusively male networks may be responsible for developing and nurturing negative attitudes and prejudices towards female managers. Since males still hold the power in the majority of organisations, the participants believed that if they could gain access to these networks, which would previously have been exclusive to men, that many benefits should result, in particular visibility and access to informal discussions with senior management. Forty-six of the managers perceived that there are more benefits to be gained for career progression if they can penetrate male networking groups. Given the difficulties outlined in gaining access to the old boy network, these participants believed that benefits, such as psychological support, camaraderie, and general sociability, could result from networking with females or in a mixed-gender group. The interviewees believed that if females had more access to networking groups they could be socialised in both the formal and informal norms of the organisation and gain advantages from these. As discussed, the research suggests that two significant obstacles for female managers regarding networking are (i) access to male networks, and (ii) having less time available for networking due to domestic commitments. The research suggests that if female networks become stronger and begin to have more power, then perhaps more females will reach senior management positions and in turn partake in international management.

3.5 Male/Female/Individual Style of Management

It is clear that management, and particularly senior management, remains dominated by men. As senior management is male dominated, female managers sometimes wonder if they should attempt to manage like their male counterparts in order to break through the glass ceiling. The findings presented in this section reveal the managerial styles adopted by the fifty participants and provide answers in relation to their chosen managerial styles.

This research confirms that, in all the countries that the interviewees have worked in, the stereotype of the white male manager still persists. One of the interviewees, who worked in Germany, Switzerland, Ireland, Spain, Mexico, Brazil and the United States, said that in her experience male managerial stereotyping is more prevalent in the United States than in other countries. Similarly, another interviewee noted that, from her twenty years experience in the United States, different generations of male managers exhibit different behaviours towards female managers. She noted that, first, there is an older generation of male managers who are very definitely opposed to females as managers. Second, she classified the next generation as more neutral. Third, she believed that the younger generation is now going back to the old way and is being mentored by males of the first generation. Three of the interviewees also reported being repeatedly mistaken for secretaries at meetings during their international assignments in the United States.

Of the fifty interviewees, thirty-nine managers suggested that they have developed individualistic management styles. Seven perceived themselves to have adopted a female management style, and two believed that they adopted a male management style. Another two answered that they did not know what managerial style they practised, but added that they believe that they incorporated the best traits from both genders. The two managers who deliberately adopted a male managerial style stressed that they did not want to be seen as 'masculine type women'. They believed that as they worked in predominantly male environments it was necessary to adopt this role:

I adopt a male style of management, but I try to modify this as it bothers me a lot (Medical Consultant).

You should ask some of my staff what type of management style I adopt. I hope they would say masculine. I am very matter of fact. I have always worked primarily with men. I have no idea of how I would feel working with a lot of women. I have always been in male dominated environments. I don't think that I would be perceived as being overly feminine, but I surely hope that I would not be perceived as being masculine. I would hope not to be seen as a masculine type woman (Managing Director, Manufacturing Company).

The thirty-nine interviewees who perceived themselves as having developed and adopted individualistic management styles believed that managerial sex typing is a major barrier to women's opportunities. This finding confirms previous research studies by Schein et al. (1994) which established that male sex typing of the managerial job is strong, consistent, and pervasive and appears to be a global phenomenon among males. According to Marshall (1984), sex role stereotypes relating to management seem to have evolved in a way that males are typed as being more task-oriented, objective, independent, aggressive, and generally more capable than females in handling managerial responsibilities. The managers in this research believed that these attributes are still used to categorise the successful male manager. Two of the interviewees, however, suggested that when their managerial styles occasionally appeared to be assertive, their behaviour was perceived as aggressive, and was not accepted as assertive by their male colleagues. Female managers are generally stereotyped as being more passive, gentle, consideration-oriented, more sensitive and less suited than males for positions of senior responsibility in organisations (Marshall, 1984). The interviewees in this research who did not adopt a typically 'female' managerial style stated that they did not want to be associated with the 'mother' role in their organisations. Research by Schein et al. (1994), on male management students in five different countries and on male corporate managers in the United States, established that international managerial stereotyping illustrates the unfavourable way in which female managers are stereotyped. The participants in Schein's (1994) research viewed female managers as much less likely to have leadership or analytical ability, and less likely to be competitive, ambitious, skilled in business matters, or to desire responsibility. The research also indicates that the managers believed that they are unfavourably stereotyped, while all managers believed that they were generally more qualified than their male counterparts, and were equally as ambitious and competitive.

The thirty-nine respondents who stated they adopted an individualistic style of management, added that they did not want to be stereotyped as typically male or female. Thirty-seven of these thirty-nine respondents worked in male dominated organisations. They believed that they were socialised in the male managerial style, and consequently their original management style would have been male. The thirty-nine respondents believed that they developed 'individualistic' management styles, because a stereotyped male or female style denies, to both men and women, the ability to exercise broader characteristics. These interviewees noted that their individual styles of management evolved as their careers progressed and as their confidence in themselves increased to allow them to behave as individuals. They believed that they could be as 'macho' as any of their male colleagues when some situations arose, but they also believed that when necessary they could be as feminine as any of their female colleagues. In their career progression to senior management positions, the interviewees believed that whatever managerial style they adopted it caused difficulties for them. If they decided to adopt a male style of management, the females in their organisations often isolated them and viewed them suspiciously, while their male colleagues viewed them as unconforming and unpredictable.

One research and design engineer said that she heard her male colleagues say that their subordinates would not be interested in hearing the newest developments, but she believed that this was an excuse to maintain power in 'the male club'. She also stated that, in her experience, subordinates were always interested in discussing the latest developments in the field. The interviewees suggested that partaking in international assignments helped them to change their former management styles, as they developed their own style of management which they felt more comfortable with. The following typifies these sentiments:

> I developed my own managerial style over time. First of all, when I started out in management, I tried to be more male. Looking back on myself in the earlier days, I had to swear as good or as loud as the next guy. I had to be as aggressive as the next guy, and I got on that way. It was when I went to Singapore and I became part of a totally different environment, where to swear would be so rude and so insulting and they would be so horrified by it. I looked inwards on myself and it was actually good for me from a self-assessment point of view. I said 'Hold on a second, how did I get to this stage?' I know I'm doing a good job, but why did I have to take on all of these qualities to let myself be noticed as a person in charge. So, I actually changed my management style. First of all I dropped the habitual cursing; there is no benefit in women cursing and swearing. I became more structured. If I wanted to be definite about something I became more assertive in my style and the shouting and roaring stopped. This came from confidence within myself. My style of management has really changed from being a masculine style, to my own individual style. I feel strongly about the way I dress; if I am away on business, I don't like the briefcase image. I really don't want to be like a man in a business suit; even now my bag is a doctor's bag. I feel women can do it, and I think we can complement each other's gender (Director, Manufacturing Company).

> I think that I adopt an individualistic style of management, in contrast to reacting in a very typical female way. There are situations in which it is extremely good to react in a female way, but there are also situations where that is not the way to react. I am very conscious of that and I like to react in the way which I think is the best way. I don't think I am very typically male in some situations and I don't think I am very typically female in other situations. I try to be fair and open and I like to avoid the emotional reactions — even though sometimes I would like to pull my hair out and cry and ask why is somebody behaving in that way, and why is somebody being so nasty to me, or why are they ganging up on me? I try to avoid that sort of situation, but it is difficult sometimes (Plant Manager, Pharmaceutical Company).

> There are very good managers who happen to be male, and there are very good managers who happen to be female. There are also poor male managers and poor female managers. There are principles of good management practice which should be adopted regardless of gender. I would seek in my own management style the best principles of

management practice, which is about communication: being firm, being fair and being friendly — the three Fs — and developing my own individual style. Good management is ultimately about fair communication and having a policy of good upward and downward communication. Communication is essentially the key to good leadership and good management. If managers practise skilled communication, whether they are male or female, they should be able to obtain the best result. Females and males need to adopt best principles and try to enact those rather than adhere to what are supposedly expected male or female manager characteristics (Manager, Tourism Promotion Agency).

I am a strong believer in the hybrid style of management because it is very complementary. When you think of the typical male characteristics and the typical female characteristics, you never have a purely male or purely female personality. So, I always try to complement my management style (Human Resources Manager, Financial Services Company).

I believe I have always been myself. I think I am softer than my male colleagues, but I have been told that I am quite hard and firm to work for. I am very demanding. We have some really good women here and I do think that we need to be better than men to get on. I changed after I came back from working in America. I felt that I had grown while I was there and that I had another facet now to my character. America also showed me that there is more to life than work (Manager, Retailing Company).

Forty-two of the interviewees suggested, because of the scarcity of senior female international managers, that their managerial style was very visible, and colleagues often questioned their behaviour and reactions far more than that of their male colleagues. The findings suggest that female managers are in a 'no win' situation, whether they adopt a male or female managerial style, because of the difficulties associated with each style. The participants further suggested that male home-country senior management may perceive that the managerial style female managers choose to adopt in the home country may be inappropriate in certain international assignments.

All of the seven interviewees who said they practised a female managerial style believed that this style came naturally to them and said it would have been more stressful for them if they were expected to behave like men. The findings from this research differ from Davidson and Cooper's (1992) research, which suggested that the 'mother' role was by far the most common role reported by female managers. These interviewees were very conscious of not adopting the 'mother-earth' role. They believed that the female managerial style had advantages for them but, most importantly, they felt comfortable with this style:

> I adopt a female style of management. I don't try to be like men at all. I am the more nurturing, caring type. I feel this has advantages because people will be honest with me and they know that I do have their best interests at heart. I think if people feel that you are being genuine about something they will know it and they will trust you, and that is the kind of feedback I get (Chief Accountant, Computer Company).

> I adopt a female management style, so I think that I am more caring for my colleagues. For example, if I learn something that my employees may benefit from, I inform them of this. I share the information as soon as possible. Whereas, my male colleagues say the employees would not be interested in knowing. They make an assumption that the employees don't care, but they do care and I know that. Knowledge is power and the men like to have the power (Senior Research and Design Engineer, Computer Company).

> It has been quoted to me that I am unusual in that I still have a female style of management even though I am surrounded by males at the top. I have seen female managers who have adopted a male style, and they have become very aggressive. A lot of female managers change their own characters and they change their own style in order to be accepted at work. I don't know if female managers have to do this to be accepted, but I think that probably in some circumstances they do have to change to be accepted. It has been easier for me not to have to change because of my human resources function (Vice-president, Computer Company).

It is clear, therefore, from the research that managerial stereotyping prevails in organisations and society. The findings suggest that this stereotyping is negative and unhealthy and is a major contributor to the glass ceiling. In an effort to overcome these obstacles, the majority of managers (thirty-nine out of fifty) decided to adopt individualistic managerial styles, drawing on what they perceived to be the best managerial traits from both genders. The managers, however, stated that their individualistic styles developed as they progressed along the career ladder. The thirty-nine managers who have adopted individual styles of management suggested that having individual managerial styles helped them break through the glass ceiling, and they now encourage and recommend junior female managers in their organisations to develop their own styles of management. The sentiments of the participants again reflected Schein's (1989) above-mentioned finding that 'to think manager was to think male'. The interviews also confirmed that in male-dominated organisations, where promotions have largely been reserved for men, women are encouraged to enact gender roles that suit men's preferences, thereby reinforcing men's power and dominance.

3.6   Career Planning

In this section research results relating to two questions raised in the first chapter are presented. First, the managers were asked if they planned their careers. Second, the research investigated whether there is a model of career development which fits the experiences of female managers.

The findings from this research concur with the findings of Henning and Jardim (1977) and White et al. (1992), with forty of the interviewees attributing their career planning to their mentors. The interviewees spoke of planning their careers in the short-term and gaining experience in various departments which gave them the opportunity to apply for senior managerial positions in their home and host organisations. White et al. similarly found that some of the women in their study believed that lack of planning had allowed them to do jobs which, although not directly relevant to their current occupations, had given them the opportunity to develop a diverse range of skills which enhanced their current performance. Only two of the fifty interviewees planned for an international career:

> I had no doubt that I would be in a successful career and in an international career. Americans do not generally speak foreign languages, and I speak fluent German, fluent Greek, decent French and I speak some Spanish and Japanese. Not too many Americans could do that. And I believe there is another difference also. Most people who get expatriate assignments, at least from American companies, do not get them just because they are qualified to be an expatriate. They get them because they are qualified to be an engineer, or whatever the requirement is. In my case, not only am I qualified to do my particular role, but I also have educated myself for an international assignment by studying languages and by the work that I did as an undergraduate in university. So, to that extent, I would definitely have planned my career. I wanted an international career, I wanted to live abroad (Managing Director, Telephone Company).

The research revealed that if women want to be considered for international assignments, they usually need senior managerial career experience in their home countries, but as discussed earlier gaining this experience has proved problematic:

> The first requirement is for women to make it to senior management in their home countries, as all the pitfalls are on the way to that, because there are still a lot of people who would have a mental block to promoting women (Plant Manager, Pharmaceutical Company).

> It is a very hard job to convince the males in the automotive world, because that is a very male world in which to promote a woman, and firstly in the home country. One has to create a very positive picture for men, one has to combine very positive skills and competencies and convince them that you are the one they want to promote   (Head of International Personnel Management, Manufacturing Company).

> I believe that female managers need to be flexible and assertive to convince home-country management to promote them. A woman has to be assertive but not aggressive to get the job she wants. Aggressiveness is accepted from males, but if a woman is aggressive she can lose everything. A man can be yelling and everybody will say that he is like that, and they will wait until he cools down and then go back to him again. But, they will not accept aggressiveness from a woman   (Senior Research and Design Engineer, Computer Company).

Thirty-nine of the fifty respondents felt that many working women are blocked in their attempts to gain access to higher occupational positions in their home countries, because of organisational and personal factors. This research finding supports previous evidence by White et al. (1992), which suggests that women have not made a significant impact on top jobs in either the private or the public sector. White et al. indicated that evidence concerning the number of women at the top is sparse, but that in any given occupation, the higher the rank the lower the proportion of women. The findings from this research revealed that, as managers progressed along the domestic managerial ladder, they planned their careers in the short term by always asking for their next career move, rather than waiting to be asked by senior management. Despite their lack of career planning, the female managers strongly emphasised their need for achievement:

Even though I did not plan my career, I always had the desire to succeed. I was always quite aggressive about what I wanted in my career and what I could contribute, so I never sat back quietly and waited for things to happen. I really think that you need to have the initiative to go ahead and make change without having to seek permission and control every time (Managing Director, Freight Carrier Company).

I don't think I planned my career, it just seemed to fall before me. I always asked for my next career move and I think this is important. I don't think a lot of men and women do this. I have always made it known that I wanted to work in the United States and I kept asking for this and I got it. If you don't ask for the next move you won't get what you want. You have got to help yourself along (Manager, Retailing Company).

I did not plan my career, but I would say that I am very determined and I also work very hard. I always set high standards for myself, but I didn't always have confidence in myself. It actually took international experience to give me confidence. In the early days of my career, there is no doubt about it, but my gender affected my career. I was a woman and it was seen that I 'should' have stayed at home. There is still a lot of that type of attitude around, and I think the older businessmen typically hold this attitude. Younger women and men are changing no doubt, but there is still a lot to be done regarding changing attitudes (Human Resources Manager, Computer Company).

Forty of the interviewees suggested that, perhaps, females engage less in career planning than their male counterparts because they are often discriminated against by organisational career policies. These interviewees perceived that male managers still select, recruit and promote people that mostly resemble themselves. The thirty-one married interviewees also suggested that it was also more difficult for them to plan their careers, than it was for their husbands, as it is still not the norm for the female's career to take precedence. Additionally, they spoke of putting their careers on hold because of the responsibilities of child minding and rearing which still rest with them. The twenty-six interviewees who have children spoke of taking extended maternity leave and career breaks to relieve the stress of balancing home and work when their children were very young. These interviewees believed that if they included such time in a career plan it would not be looked upon favourably by senior management. The interviewees also believed that it is undoubtedly more difficult for them to plan their careers based on a traditional linear male model, which does not allow time out for childbearing and child rearing or for part-time working.

The research further revealed that, because of the barriers experienced at all levels of the participants' careers, career planning is undoubtedly more difficult for female managers. Two of the interviewees said that they were forced to change their career plans and move to different organisations because of severe sexual harassment. Twelve of the interviewees admitted that they experienced some form of sexual harassment, ranging from mild to severe, during their careers:

> I had to leave one organisation because I would not sleep with my boss. He was double my age at least, so he would have been like a father image. When I returned to work, after I refused to sleep with him, he continually gave me a really, really hard time. It was terrible. The most awful thing was that I couldn't talk to anybody about it. It ended up by me feeling that I had done something wrong, and that was very, very traumatic. So, I left my job because of him. I had to leave it because of that and by the time I left I was quite devastated because he treated me so badly all the time (Human Resources Manager, Computer Company).

> I experienced a lot of sexual harassment. In Germany, where I had my first job, I left the country a month after starting, as I had two really terrible experiences with my colleagues. One was where one of my colleagues offered to drive me home from work as I didn't have a car then. He then started making advances to me. I was young and naive, and it was terrible. I was shocked. And then my boss, whom I reported to directly, made advances to me in the lift and again started touching me. It was disgusting. These were the two experiences where there was physical contact. I had lots of propositions also and that is another difficulty for women because you are viewed in this way (Manager, Standardisation Organisation).

The research revealed that, besides sexual harassment, there were other reasons for female managers to change their career plans, such as family commitments, blocked promotion, and difficulties they encountered because of their gender. One of the managers with a young child stated that her career is very important to her, but if she were asked for her very top priority in her life, she would have to say that it is her daughter. She believed that to admit to that is not a bad thing, but also believed that this is not what companies would want to hear. Another one of the respondents with three young children believed that having children 'softened her' and brought out another side of her, that might not otherwise have been brought out, which she believed was also beneficial to her career. Further analysis of the data indicated that career planning has traditionally been associated with the careers of males, and that females who departed from this male model, for reasons such as child rearing, were seen in some cases to display a lack of commitment to the organisation:

> Once you become a mother it becomes more difficult. For me the difference was when I had children, and suddenly I had an extra set of priorities and I was not able to drop everything to the same extent and go off to the other end of the earth. Management views one differently once one becomes a mother. I believe that management may think that I have not got the same interest in my job as I had previously (Marketing Director, Telecommunications Company).

> Once, when both my children had whooping cough I decided that I was not going overseas on a business trip. That was the only time ever that I actually had to decide not to go. I was booked to go on a trip to the United States, but I thought that whooping cough was not an ordinary child sickness as it could be life-threatening. I actually had to negotiate so that I would not go. I was even told at one stage that my decision was going to affect my career. But, I did not want to be 7,000 miles away when my children were seriously ill (Human Resources Manager, Manufacturing Company).

It is clear from the above discussion that female managers are concerned with advancement, challenge, and development of their careers, and the twenty-six managers who have children are also concerned with taking time out to rear children. These managers, however, believe that they are further disadvantaged, as 'time out' is not built into the male model of career development. The research results indicate that female managers are becoming discouraged by the barriers found in corporate cultures and in environments that continue to block their advancement. The interviewees suggested that, if senior management continues to ignore the fact that career paths of female managers differ from those of their male counterparts, then organisations will experience unacceptable rates of female turnover. These findings concur with the work of Gutek and Larwood (1989), which noted that a career-development process for female managers has not yet emerged. For change to occur, it is apparent that senior male managers will need to implement initiatives to eliminate organisational, cultural, and attitudinal biases in order to develop a career path to retain and promote female managers. The findings from the current research also indicate that organisations of the future will have to review the emphasis on full-time work as the norm. The participants also suggested that when a model of career development for females emerges, it is likely that more female managers will engage in career planning. The interviewees believed that if future female managers would be given the opportunity to develop their careers, based on a female model of career development, then perhaps more females would reach senior managerial levels.

4 Challenges for Female International Managers: Further Evidence

As highlighted in the first chapter, a number of questions remain unanswered in relation to the senior female international career move. Previous studies have called for additional empirical work, particularly across occupations, organisations, and national cultures, in order to increase our knowledge of women in international management. International human resource management literature has been criticised, by Kochan et al. (1992), for focusing too narrowly on functional activities and, overall, for defining the field too narrowly. These researchers argued that a new field of international human resources studies should be built around a broader set of questions. On the basis of the criticisms of previous research, Brewster and Scullion (1997) suggested that there is a need for a new research agenda in the study of expatriation and on expatriates themselves. This study of senior females in international management makes a theoretical contribution, not only to the analysis of gender in international human resource management, but also to wider debates within the contemporary literatures on career theory and on women in management. The quotations and discussion presented, in the six thematic areas which this chapter focuses on, relate specifically to female international managers.

4.1 The Trailing Spouse

As an international assignment usually requires a trailing spouse to forfeit the accustomed structure and continuity of his life, this can make dual career issues highly problematic for the expatriate couple. This research regards the 'trailing spouse' as the partner in the secondary professional role. Each dual-career couple faces different difficulties, for example, based on the couple's marital status, host-country work or visa regulations, and the trailing spouse's occupation. This section presents data from the interviews to help answer one of the questions raised in the first chapter, concerning the additional difficulties for female international managers when the male partner is the trailing spouse:

> Women may turn down international career moves because of the trailing spouse issue. If you are a two-career couple, then having a trailing spouse is a very significant concern (Human Resources Manager, Automotive Energy and Component Company).

> Obviously, it is more difficult for women to move if they are part of a dual-career couple.   There would be difficulties in working out an agreement between the couple, and that is a major factor preventing women from taking international assignments.   No company is going to accept responsibility for two people and it is a very rare occasion when the second person can find a job.   There might be problems with work visas for the second person also (Chief Executive, Insurance Company).

> I believe that it is extra difficult having a male trailing spouse because it is more unusual, and the pressure is really on him, to a large extent.   That is all the more reason why I am eternally grateful to my trailing spouse. I don't think that a lot of men would be prepared to do this. It takes very special men, and men that can put up with the sort of comments that people make about the situation.   He has come across a lot of comments from people.   People say to him openly that they cannot believe that he is a trailing spouse. People say all these 'wonderful' things to him like that he must have the patience of a saint, and that must make it worse for him (Counsellor, Government Department).

Studies of domestic managerial transfers have, generally, found that companies need to take a proactive approach to dual-career couples if they are to attract and retain the best employees. The findings from this research suggest that a proactive approach to dual-career couples is more important in the case of international transfers, as additional difficulties with visas and work permits have to be overcome. According to Handler and Lane (1997), there is a dearth of literature informing the human resources practitioner of what multinational companies are doing to confront dual-career issues. Career prospects for the trailing spouse, especially in the geographical vicinity of their partner's assignment base, become an important consideration. Twenty-eight dual-career couples relocated to facilitate the careers of the female partners, but none of these couples received any assistance from their home organisations. The research indicates that every couple had to devise their own particular solutions to cope with additional difficulties associated with the male trailing spouse. Forty-nine of the respondents believed that most dual-career problems are left to the couple to resolve, with no help from their organisations. Of the fifty managers interviewed, only one knew of a trailing spouse being facilitated:

> Our company is quite good because it has started putting various policies in place, such as, looking at what assistance we can give the spouse. I know of two occasions here where the trailing spouse has been the husband. One case worked out very well, but the other case ended up in divorce. Our company will now pay for the education fees of the trailing spouse at university and that is a good package as some of the education fees can be quite expensive. It is a good idea also because if there is a problem with working visas what are the spouses supposed to do? (Human Resources Manager, Automotive Energy And Component Company).

The research confirms findings by Brett et al. (1992) and Davidson and Cooper (1983), who highlighted that female managers in dual-career relationships are more likely than their male counterparts to have partners with professional careers. All thirty-one married interviewees are married to professional partners. This created further personal difficulties as the research established that throughout Europe it is not the norm for an organisation to arrange an international relocation for any personnel in order to facilitate the career of a partner. Carmody (1989) and Shellenbarger (1992) noted that, despite profound changes in workforce composition, organisational policies and practices are still largely predicated on the outmoded assumption that employees are predominantly males from traditional families — the traditional family being one in which the husband is the sole breadwinner and the wife the home maker and child rearer. The findings confirm the work of Carmody and Shellenbarger, as the German interviewees stated that it is still unusual for a woman to have the primary career. These interviewees believed that German societal and organisational norms remain very traditional, and that in their organisations they would be considered to be quite unusual because they, as women, are in senior managerial positions. The managers also suggested that it is considerably more difficult when it is the male partner's career that is 'put on hold':

In Germany it is very, very unusual if the husband's career takes second place. One of my colleagues here in the bank is married and she has one child and she works here full-time. Her husband works half days and a lot of people have been surprised with this. It is not the normal way (Bank Manager).

Of the thirty-one *married* respondents, sixteen respondents believed that the progression to the top of their managerial careers was facilitated by the careers of their spouses becoming the secondary careers. These interviewees stressed that they were both lucky and unusual in that their careers took *priority* over those of their partners, and they believed that this undoubtedly contributed to their career success:

I have a husband and that is another challenge. It has been extremely difficult for us. I guess it was a surprise that the actual move would be difficult because we considered ourselves pretty worldly and flexible, but we found the move much more difficult than we thought it would be. My husband originally had a job lined up here in Brussels, but that fell through. We are now here three years and since we have been here he hasn't had a full-time job. I come home at night and usually find him extremely frustrated and unhappy and he would say things like 'I hate this place'. That is very much an extra strain on me because it isn't something that I could offer any support on. He would say to me 'you just don't know what it is like, you have someone to talk to all day and I have no-one'. So from his standpoint the international move has not been a positive experience. Also, since there are so many men, rather than women, that lead the move, there are a lot of women groups that my husband cannot go to. He has found a group of men here who are the partners of high-flying women, but they are mostly older and retired men, and my husband is not yet forty. My husband and I made a conscious decision to allow my career to have priority and that was also a difficult position to reach, because my husband's career had to take second place. That is another reason why many women do not take international career moves, because their husbands' careers have to take second place, and especially if couples are planning on having children it puts the female in an awkward position (Manager, Freight Carrier Company).

When I moved from England to the United States my husband came with me. I would not have gone without him. My husband had to give up his job and the company did not compensate us for all that. My career has always taken precedence all through our married life, and I know that I am very lucky with this. We don't have any children, which helps, as I can do a lot more things. If we had decided to have children it would have been very difficult for us because I don't think organisations are flexible enough for women with children (Manager, Retailing Company).

Most people think that having an international career is exciting. In Canada it sounds quite exotic to say that you are going to live in Europe for a while. But, the reality is quite different, because it means that the husband has to sacrifice his career for three or four years. If you have small children it is vital that both parents share in the responsibility of bringing up those children, and you have to think of the children's education. My husband is actually working here now. He works as a consultant which means that he is quite flexible. When he took this job he said that our children would be his priority and he would have to do the school runs and that type of thing. So, my career has priority for these four years at least. One career has to have priority because of the huge amount of travel involved in an assignment like this and because of the school breaks as one does not have the support network of family. I missed this a lot when I came here first (Managing Director, Freight Carrier Company).

Two of the trailing spouses decided to retire early from their own careers to facilitate the careers of their partners. The two interviewees in this situation emphasised that having supportive partners, who took care of the cooking, shopping, and housework, undoubtedly contributed to the success of their careers. These two trailing spouses are members of the Brussels-based STUDS (Spouses Trailing Under Duress Successfully) group, and, along with approximately fifty-eight other male trailing spouses in the group, provide support for their executive partners' careers, as well as holding golf outings, fund-raising events and social evenings. The STUDS group provides a social network for the trailing spouses, which in turn helps them to settle in their new location:

My husband retired when we moved and undoubtedly that made it so much easier for me. I would say that is the single largest factor which allows me to perform to my full ability at my job. The one outside factor that has made all the difference to my job has been the support of my husband. He is fabulous. He cooks for me all the time. When we moved here to Brussels he got involved with the STUDS (Spouses Trailing Under Duress Successfully) group, and this meant that we had a whole new social element and that was really good. There are about sixty men in this group who follow their high-flying partners around the world. I believe, number one, STUDS helped us to make new friends and, number two, if you look at any of the research on expatriates you will see that the ones that don't make it are the ones where their spouses don't settle. If the spouses and families don't make it, then the employees don't make it (Managing Director, Telephone Company).

Potter (1989, p. 29) suggested that 'companies with successful family-related policies will be able to increasingly attract the cream of the crop in future workers'. This research confirms Potter's findings, as the interviewees foresaw problems for organisations which do not have positive policies on dual-career issues, and they believed that the absence of these policies should lead to difficulties in attracting the most suitable expatriates. The respondents did not expect organisations to spend substantial amounts of money to help them, but believed that much could be done at relatively little expense, such as financing educational courses for their partners. The interviewees perceived that family-related policies are not yet adequately developed in the organisations where they worked. In this regard, the interviewees spoke of the lack of organisational recognition for their partners having to put their careers on hold.

The results of Australian research by Pierce and Delahaye (1996), suggest that organisations may no longer be able to assume that the male partner's career will always take precedence, and that the female partner will always subordinate her career aspirations to those of her partner. This research confirms the earlier work of these authors, as only two of the interviewees regarded their own careers to be relatively less senior to the careers of their partners. Incidentally, these two interviewees pointed out that they chose to adopt the relatively secondary career role, because of their partners being relocated. These interviewees added that because they have young children, it suited them to temporarily adopt this role and to cut back on professional commitments, but in future they may review their roles and relative positions.

The interviewees also identified the necessity for both partners to work around the optimum financial arrangement, because of the implications of one partner having to give up work due to an international transfer would be quite significant. As the difficulties associated with male trailing spouses are quite significant, three of the married interviewees decided on commuter marriages, and their views concurred with the findings of Taylor and Lounsbury (1988), which suggested that commuter marriages are likely to increase proportionately among working couples as the labour force participation of women continues to rise. Eleven of the thirty-one married interviewees stated that their careers were *equal* to their partners, and have commuter marriages, meeting only at weekends rather than sacrificing one career:

> It is very interesting when you fly from Dublin to London on Friday night and back on Monday morning to see how many other people are also doing the same, there are quite a number in the same situation. I know one woman who commutes from France to New York every weekend. Before this she commuted from Paris to London for five years. If people want to do it they can, but it is very tough (Managing Director, Manufacturing Company).

> I am responsible for the overall site here in Ireland, but I am also director for international quality assurance, which means that I manage groups in the United States, Tokyo, Beijing and Taiwan, so, I always have too much travelling. I wake up in the middle of the night and I look in my briefcase for my ticket to see where I am! I followed my husband's career for several moves, but now I am here in Ireland and my husband and son are in the United States. In the summer all the family are together here in Dublin for a month or two. My son has an Irish nanny, he is eight going on forty, he sends me e-mail messages and fax messages every day (Director, Computer Company).

Only two of the interviewees acknowledged that their partners' careers were the main careers. This created further difficulties in planning their own careers. The results also showed that achieving a balanced lifestyle is important, but difficult for dual-career couples:

> I went to New Zealand with my husband, as he had a job to go to and I didn't have a job. I decided that I would look for a job while I was there and I got a job after three weeks, so I was very lucky as it just worked out for me. When you are in a dual-career relationship it is very difficult balancing the two careers. We have come to the conclusion that somebody has to take the lead and somebody has to take the second role, because you can't operate two executive careers at the same time. Then my husband was moved to London, so I moved with him again. I got a very good promotion in a company which I had been working for in London in October 1993, but in November 1993 my husband was moved to Dublin. So after a month we had this dilemma about what we were going to do. We decided that he would set up home in Dublin and I would stay in London. We had a young child and two countries to commute between. My husband found it very difficult when I was not with him. He felt that there was a lack of commitment from me to the relationship, and I found it very difficult because I was managing a

home, a job and I became pregnant again. It was not a planned pregnancy so it was all very difficult. That was a very tough year, so then I decided that I was not going to work at all. I decided that I was going to take time out and move to Dublin, and that was really the hardest thing of all, adjusting from working so hard to doing nothing at all. I did that for two years, and then I came back to work again. I look at the number of people who are separated or divorced in my peer group and most of the causes have been people living two separate lives. My husband has a very good job, but he is away a lot. He goes to work at 6.30 in the morning and is not home until late at night, and if you have got two of you doing that your paths just do not cross. So, that you have to make some trade-offs, like where are your priorities going to be and I decided it was going to be my family first. So, my husband's career now takes precedence, because if one stands back one has to decide which career is going to be the main career. With two small children now, that suits me at the moment, but in ten years time it might be quite different, who knows? (Marketing Director, Telecommunications Company).

The personal satisfaction of the trailing spouse is particularly important, as spousal failure to adjust is the most common reason for expatriate failure. The limited research which has been conducted on international managers who are in dual-career marriages suggests that spouse-related problems are more serious when men have to adjust to the role of secondary breadwinner. Spouses accustomed to working and having a career may be particularly frustrated if they cannot work, or if they encounter difficulties in finding work. Within this research trajectory, Punnett et al. (1992) suggested that additional emotional stress is experienced when the spouse in this position is male, and this can lead to some dual-career couples preferring to avoid international transfers, thereby sacrificing the female partners' career advancement. Five of the interviewees spoke of the additional stress they experienced when their husbands had difficulty in finding work in their new locations. Herbert and Daitchman (1986) noted where an employee refuses relocation, because of the potential impact on their partner's career, that this may amount to 'career suicide'. The respondents confirmed the work of Herbert and Daitchman regarding the difficulties they experienced when considering relocation because of their partners' careers.

The research results show, from the perceptions of the thirty-one married respondents, that an international career move is much more difficult when the male partner is the trailing spouse, confirming previous research by Harris (1995b) which suggested that sociocultural norms relating to career models make it relatively easier for women, than for men, to make these transitions. It is clear from the research that it is not yet the norm for the male partner to be the trailing spouse. Twenty-eight respondents who had male trailing spouses noted, in all cases, that the presumption in social settings was that the female was the trailing spouse. Whenever it was pointed out that the international move had taken place because of the female's career, people generally did not know how to react to this, and the couple were often considered an 'oddity'. The twenty married managers with children also mentioned that it was more difficult for them to adjust to a new neighbourhood, particularly when the other women in the neighbourhood did not work, and their neighbours considered it strange that a man should stay at home and be the trailing spouse. They also remarked that their neighbours perceived them as 'always working', and 'too busy' to be invited to neighbourhood gatherings.

Analysis of the data also indicates the importance of trailing spouse issues to expatriates, and suggests that the effective handling of trailing spouse issues should be a matter of growing concern to home-country management. Ninety-eight per cent of respondents are currently employed in organisations which do not have any policies to assist dual-career couples. Further analysis showed that ninety-two per cent of interviewees believed that the success or failure of expatriate assignments is directly related to the happiness of their spouses. This figure is consistent with the literature, indicating that spousal and family problems are the chief cause of difficulties relating to expatriate assignments (Handler and Lane, 1997; Tung, 1982).

In the absence of home-country organisational policies on dual-career couples, the thirty-one married participants have coped with this particular difficulty in a variety of ways, such as: commuter marriages, putting the male career on hold, giving priority to the female career for a number of years, or the male partner retiring from employment. As discussed above, these options are still not socially accepted as normal. Seventy-four per cent of the interviewees believed that many female managers did not partake in international assignments because of these additional difficulties. This seventy-four per cent asserted that the issue of the male trailing spouse is a major contributory factor in explaining the scarcity of female international managers. They also believed that many male partners would not be prepared to put their own careers on hold, and sixteen of the senior female managers believed that they would not have made it to the top of their careers if their partners had not sacrificed their own careers. All of the findings concur with DeCieri, Dowling and Taylor (1991) and with Adler (1986), who suggested that, by failing to assist the trailing partners of dual-career couples, a firm increases the risk of a trailing spouse's unhappiness which in turn contributes to the expatriate's poor job performance and/or premature return. Despite the additional difficulties involved when the male partner is the trailing spouse, this research has indicated that the low participation rate of females in international management, and who are in dual-career marriages, cannot be attributed solely to problems arising from dual-career marriages. The thirty-one married participants suggested that dual-career problems are not insurmountable, but that it is essential to have the priorities of one's personal life in order before embarking on an international career move. Overall, therefore, it is evident that additional difficulties exist when the male partner is the trailing spouse, but as the above evidence illustrates these difficulties are not insurmountable.

4.2   International Career Versus Relationship and Childbearing Conflicts

As detailed above, the male trailing spouse is more problematic than the female trailing spouse for international mangers who are in dual-career relationships. A closely related area concerned the conflicting demands of work and home where there are children involved in the international move. The interview data presented in this section first explore the challenges faced by unmarried female international managers and suggest that they have more difficult lifestyle choices to make than their male counterparts. Second, the research confirms that international mobility for the married female manager is further restricted when there are children to be considered. In particular, this section addresses one of the questions posed in the first chapter, regarding the level of responsibilities female managers have in relation to home and family members.

As discussed in the third chapter, work–family conflict is not only experienced by married female international managers, but being single also presents its stresses and pressures, for example, in maintaining personal relationships:

> The main difficulty for me, as a woman, is combining my career with my private life. Firstly, a lot of men can't handle this and, secondly, my job is so hard that during the weekend I don't have the energy to go out. I get up

at 5.20 a.m., I am at my office at 6.45 a.m., and I work through until 6.00 p.m. or 7.00 p.m. I then go to a sports club and after that I fall into bed. So, it is very difficult to maintain a social life. But, all of this is a challenge. It is definitely more difficult for women to try to balance everything because there is no woman who has a problem with a man having a good career, whereas, men have problems with women having 'important' careers. For me, for example, it is very difficult. My boyfriend is in London, I am here in Frankfurt, my apartment and my car are still in London, but I will keep them there for the moment, as I can go there at weekends. I am here only two weeks and so far I have been on a training course in Orlando, a conference in Berlin, and I am going to London for the weekend — so it is very difficult. Quite a few of my previous relationships have broken up because I work too hard, and I couldn't do traditional housework like sweeping the floor and being awake at night with a baby (Bank Manager).

I moved from France to England three years ago. The move was difficult, firstly, because of the language and, secondly, I was given only short notice. I was wondering what would happen and how it would all work out for me. Socially it was difficult for me. It was more difficult because I am a woman. Because I am single I don't fit socially here. I missed my relations. At the beginning I worked fourteen hours a day so that I could get on top of everything, and I did not have time to feel lonely. Then I was so tired going home I did not have time to miss people; it was survival that mattered (Legal Director, Manufacturing Company).

Ten of the participants were single, another eight were separated or divorced, and one was a widow. The single managers believed that, despite the difficulties of maintaining personal relationships, by remaining single they were limiting their conflicting roles. They also believed that it was easier for them to partake in international assignments as they had only themselves to consider in the relocation process. The following quotation typifies the views of the unmarried managers in the survey:

The more moves one makes the easier it gets. I have had a good number of moves and I travel a lot within this job, but most of my working life has been 'have bag will travel'. I have never had a problem due to gender while travelling abroad; you just look after yourself (Manager, Tourism Promotion Agency).

Seven of the ten unmarried interviewees maintained that remaining single had proved a distinct advantage for their careers, as this enabled them to make longer international career moves. The single managers also moved internationally more *frequently* than their married counterparts. Of the thirty-one married managers in this survey, eighteen had made one international career move, nine managers had made two international moves, and four managers had made three international moves, although not always with their partners. The greater frequency of international moves by single managers was reflected by one of the unmarried respondents, who had moved, for example, to Germany, the United States, Switzerland, Spain, Mexico, and Brazil. Another single manager had moved to Switzerland, Germany, Britain (on a few occasions), the United States, and the Cayman Islands. Similarly, the eleven married interviewees in this research who did not have children spoke of choosing a career in preference to children, and of devoting themselves one hundred per cent to their careers. These interviewees believed that if they had decided to have children, senior management would perceive them to be more interested in their families than in their careers.

The views expressed by the *married* females claimed that female managers experience the conflicting demands of work and home to a greater extent than that experienced by their husbands. These demands are perceived to be more stressful for female managers when international assignments are undertaken, both in the context of the trailing spouse as discussed above, and from the general conflicting demands made by work and home. An examination of the senior female international career move, indicates that work–family conflict is a major source of pressure for female managers. The interviewees believed that male international managers experience less stress from balancing work and family situations, as females still tend to take on the major responsibilities for organising family members and the home. The thirty-one married respondents confirmed that it is much more difficult to move internationally with a family. This finding supports previous findings from research with female managers in *domestic* management positions, by Davidson and Cooper (1992, p. 140), which found that 'more and more executive women who marry are having difficulty in their dual managerial roles as corporate manager and family manager'. There is a lack of empirical research on the senior female *international* career move, particularly outside the United States, a situation which makes comparisons with other research difficult. Family management difficulties were also highlighted by the respondents, as well as by the domestic managers in Davidson and Cooper's study, concerning *role* conflict between demands of career, home, and children; *time* conflict in managing a home, children, and career; the condition of not being geographically mobile; feelings of guilt about not being a good wife or good mother; the lack of emotional and domestic support from husbands; and, having to take work home with them. The twenty married respondents with children, reported that partaking in international assignments created more conflict for them, and they were always conscious of the difficulties their careers caused for family members:

It is much easier to move if you are single when you have no ties. I can see it with people around me who are single. It is a breeze for them, whereas, most of the people who are married have the trauma of organising the family. If you are single you can have fun and a great social life. There are none of those extra worries. It is because of family reasons that a lot of women do not take an international assignment. I have told my children that there is always a possibility of moving. When I told my eleven-year-old daughter recently that we are moving to New York, and that she would be near her grand-parents, hoping that it would be the easiest of all possible options, she said 'You have ruined my life'. Then, her second point was that not only would she be the only new kid in the new school in September, but in four or five years time, she would be the only new kid again in a new school in Dublin. So, really, the family is the most difficult aspect of moving for women. You can see all the dimensions of family life that are affected by the move. Your heart bleeds when your children have to leave their friends at school, and maybe having to go to school in a different language. That is a big factor that a lot of people have to deal with. In fact, a colleague of mine said that when he discussed the possibility of going abroad, his sixteen-year-old daughter put her foot down and said that if he was going she was not going. So, what do you do? (Counsellor, Government Department).

One has to organise oneself very well and the professional side and the home side of one's life has to be considered, and balancing the two is not always easy. That is one of the main difficulties, and my friends would also confirm that. A lot of women end up giving up their careers because they find so much pressure on them trying to balance everything, and definitely it is a lot harder for them than for men. Men do not have to think about all the home responsibilities when they go away. Men just don't think the same way. It is a lot, lot easier for them professionally. If I compare myself to any of my colleagues, I wish I had a wife at home. I find that when I am travelling I still have to rush home to get a travelling case ready, whereas for men their wives will sort out their case of clothes, and the men do not have to sort out the food for the children, or babysitting, so it is totally different.

When you live abroad it is an extra difficulty because you do not have the support systems of home (Vice President, Computer Company).

Women have a lot more things to think about if they have a family. They have to think about the dual-career situation. They have to think about schools. Children are not always mobile. They are mobile up to the age of ten or eleven, and after that you have to think about how they are going to get their qualifications for life, and life should not be too disruptive for them. But, most of the housework falls to the women. We have someone who comes in once a week to clean, but I do most of the work around the house in comparison to my husband. My husband is very good, he picks our daughter up from the crèche more days than I do, but I spend more time with her. My life is an absolute helter-skelter. It really is. It is a complete helter-skelter, and I would love to get off. But, I'm not sure how long I would be happy if I got off. I think I would love to stop, I really do. But, I am not sure about what I would do. I have a mother who is 83, who lives on her own in Northern Ireland, and I go up every fortnight to her and spend the weekend with her. Women also bear more responsibilities towards their own parents than men do for their parents. My mother is staying with me now for a fortnight and that is more work; for example, I got up this morning and prepared lunch for her before heading to work (Human Resources Manager, Computer Company).

I have a little three-year-old girl, so, with the move, my personal life was harder than my work life. Actually, when I looked at this job I was working in the United States and I told the managing director who interviewed me that unless I could find good childcare I wouldn't move. I told the managing director that I had to be happy about the childminder or I wouldn't travel otherwise. First of all I came here to look at the work situation and I also looked at childminders before I finally accepted the job. If I were a man, that would not have arisen (Financial Controller, Pharmaceutical Company).

It is always, always women that will take care of the family and the children, even in families where there is supposed to be an equal relationship. This is why I believe that women do not accept international career moves — of course it is! The woman is always to blame if the children are unhappy. There is also a guilt feeling that women experience. I don't know if this is a biological thing or not (Director, European Commission).

Hall (1990) noted that fathers have a choice about whether to make their new family status and family needs visible, and when they do choose to modify their work schedules they frequently do so in a covert way. For women, on the other hand, Lewis (1994) noted that there is no question about the visibility of motherhood. Insofar as they have a choice, it is between making their family needs invisible by conforming to traditional patterns of work, or to modify work schedules, often at considerable cost to career advancement. The interviewees remarked that by the time a woman reaches her thirties she is often beginning to establish herself in her career, and at the same time is reaching the older years in terms of childbearing. In organisations where long hours at the workplace are considered important for career advancement, new mothers are often faced with identity dilemmas and difficult career decisions. Twenty-five respondents expressed career-related concerns about the dilemma on whether to start a family or not:

> I have seen my friends trading things off because there are always conflicts. I am not married yet, so I will make my choice about children when the time comes. I do see my female friends going through a lot of angst, a lot of conflict, and a lot of guilt about the choices they make. Because, if you make one choice, of course, you are giving something else up; you can't do something else as well. There is a lot of pressure trying to be all things possible, and to do the balancing that men still don't have to do. Women tend to take on the major share of trying to balance everything. From my experience of looking at my friends and my contemporaries, it is a massive challenge for a woman to hold down a very big job and to look after very young children, and run a house, and have a social life. It is awe-inspiring (Manager, Oil company).

Knight's (1994) interviews with senior domestic managers who became mothers perceived that their organisations did not seem inclined to believe their continued commitment to work. The women also experienced difficulties in their efforts to be taken seriously on return to work. Previous research by Forrest (1989) also suggested that the stress of integrating family and work life is more acute for working mothers as, generally, women still take more responsibility for the home. The sentiments of the interviewees with children resonate the findings of Knight's interviewees, all of whom reported that they had to convince their home-country senior managers of their availability to partake in international management. These interviewees also stated that organisations tend to be inflexible in their demands, and that some of the women managers leave the workforce for family reasons only because their work environments are not sufficiently flexible in allowing them to balance work and family demands. Two of the interviewees had left employment temporarily for childbearing and child rearing reasons, but found this lifestyle to be more stressful than balancing a career and family.   They have since returned to senior positions in organisations:

> I was at the height of my career when I became pregnant . My pregnancy was not planned, as I had never planned to have children in my life, since I had been told numerous years before that I wouldn't be able to have children. It was quite a shock to the system, but once it had sunk in, I accepted that I was going to go ahead with the pregnancy. But, I was told by my boss to take myself off the succession plan within the organisation because I was a woman and I was pregnant. Having children definitely slowed down my career, but if I had stayed in the business I feel my family would have suffered badly. I made the decision not to stay in the business and, yes, it did slow down my career, as I then had a second baby and I was nearly six years out of the business. I don't know how I stayed sane while I was at home. I drank more red wine in those years that I don't know how I have a liver left. Behind closed doors with two babies is very, very difficult. During those years I set out to achieve two things, I wanted to learn to horse ride and I wanted to do a Master's degree. I achieved the Master's, but I am still not very good at horse riding, but those two things got me back out of the house. After studying for the Master's I realised that I could not stay at home. I struggled through nearly six years at home and it was not for me. I was unhappy and I realised that if I did not get back to work my kids would suffer long-term and my relationship would suffer. I am back at work only four months now in this new organisation and I am more tired than I have ever been and I am probably stressed out, but I am alive, and it is the true me. I am totally exhausted and totally overworked and totally under-staffed, but I love it. I now have to re-establish myself here in Ireland and to prove myself again, which will take a lot of effort (Human Resources Manager, Computer Company).

The findings confirm results from previous research studies, conducted with female managers in *domestic* organisations by Hochschild (1989), Lewis and Cooper, (1987) and Pleck (1985), all of which have established that women take responsibility for household tasks and child rearing, regardless of how many hours they work outside the home. The research indicates that the female expatriate manager take responsibility for running the home and raising children in the majority of cases, despite the demands of an international assignment. Seven of the respondents suggested that the difficulties associated with male trailing spouses, in international assignments, however, are more difficult to overcome than the difficulties associated with child rearing and childminding. The fifty respondents also perceived organisations to be too inflexible towards managers having to balance work and family:

> The main obstacles for women are marriage and family. I ask myself if we had kids would we still have moved from London to the States. I got four weeks notice to move, and there is no way that we could have organised kids, schools, and everything in that length of time. If I had children it would be very much more difficult. And if I had children, would I still work the hours that I do? Probably not, because I would not want my children to be with a minder so much, so you have that dilemma also. Mothers feel torn between what they should and should not do. We have a couple of women here where the husbands look after the children, but it is very, very rare. A lot of women choose between career and family. I think that if we had decided to have children it would have been very difficult for us. We don't have any children, which helps, as I can do a lot more career work. We have chosen not to have any children. I am fond of children, but I like to give them back after a few hours. I don't think organisations are flexible enough for women with children (Manager, Retailing Company).

As mentioned above, eight of the interviewees were separated or divorced and one was a widow. Being a working widow with two children also had other challenges:

> I was in a very difficult position because I lost my husband twelve years ago, one year before I entered the bank, and I had two small children. The only sentence my boss used when he saw me was 'How are your children?', and I was very unhappy about that, he never said things like that to my male colleagues. There was no difference between me and the other male managers. In fact, I was often in earlier than them and my boss never saw that. My flexibility was never appreciated. I worked very long hours even though I had very difficult family circumstances. Then, I would notice my male colleagues when their wives had gone abroad and how they made a big fuss about being temporarily alone. At 4.00 p.m. they would announce that they have to go home, and then they would say very bluntly 'I am a widower today', and I would say 'I am a widow the whole year', and they would look at me and say nothing. It is extra difficult for women balancing a career and home. You must make your choices but you must not look for second best, and if you really want to have the best at home and the best at work you cannot make a distinction between both. I found it very difficult, but I learned to live with it (Bank Manager).

The eight separated or divorced interviewees suggested that their personal relationships suffered because of the demands of balancing career and home life, particularly when spending long intervals away from home on international travel. Organisational norms of mobility and long hours spent at the workplace created conflicts and dilemmas for these couples. These eight managers also spoke of the inability of their former spouses to accept that female careers could be equal to or more successful than their own male careers. These findings are similar to those reported by Davidson and Cooper (1992) and Lewis and Cooper (1987), which observed that traditional gender boundaries in the family are most challenged when the female partner earns more or is more successful in career terms than her partner. Three of the divorced interviewees concurred with Cooper and Lewis (1993) who suggested that some women respond, consciously or unconsciously, by holding back in their careers, in an attempt to prioritise their marriages. These interviewees suggested that their career successes caused problems for their partners, therefore, in an attempt to save their marriages they held back on their career development. Davidson and Cooper (1992), however, also found that some professional women are giving priority to their own careers in preference to relationships with male partners who fail to support their career objectives. Lewis (1994) noted that there is considerable evidence to suggest that stressful work experiences, such as overload and conflict, can affect employee well-being and general mood which can, in turn, affect the quality of marital relationships. Lewis further argued that the potential for tension is greater when both parties in a couple have stressful jobs. Only four interviewees (the two sole careerists and the two secondary careerists) believed that it is not possible for both partners to hold equally senior careers simultaneously.

The eight separated or divorced interviewees perceived that their husbands felt threatened by the career success of their wives, and these managers also spoke of the guilt that was associated with their long working hours:

My career was a big threat to my husband. I was the major money earner, and it came to a point where I did everything. I looked after the children. I did the house. It was crazy. When I look back on what I have done, no woman in her right mind should ever contemplate doing all of that. I brought up three children as well as continuing with my work, and it was very, very difficult. I was riddled with guilt, especially with the first two, not so much with the third, but I managed to get through that. I had a terrible time from my ex-husband who was thoroughly confused about the situation and who was proud of me, threatened by me, and wanted me at home — but of course all of that does not go together. I do not know how I ever did all of that, but I did. I had lists everywhere and my pledge was to the children, and they could rely on this, one hundred per cent, and whatever I did I would never let them down. So, I was the one after work that drove them to their various activities. I did everything. During my lunchtime I was rushing around buying cards and presents to allow them to go to birthday parties. I would say that my intention has been to look after my children in all of their needs, but the drive in my life is my career, for myself and for my self-development and I am very excited about this (Manager, Standardisation Organisation).

I always worked, but like most women, what was most important to me was my husband and family. But then, there came a divorce when I was forty-four years old, and I found myself in Belgium with three small children and absolutely no support from my ex-husband. It was not easy. After a divorce, especially, you have all kinds of self-pity and you feel upside-down and so on. I also had this guilt feeling about my children. My daughter was thirteen or fourteen years old and she had to take care of the younger ones when I was away, because we could not afford babysitters. I used to prepare meals on Sundays for the rest of the week, but all of this was very difficult and also the guilt feeling was always there. It was very difficult for me. One day I might be on a business trip and the next day I might be on a site, and that would mean that I would be away for two nights. I used to ring the children at night, and in the morning to call them so that they would not miss school. So, it was very, very difficult on the children and especially on my little one, as she used to say to me 'I wish you were at home making cookies', and I would feel horrible about it. But, I explained to her what I had to do and she now understands what I had to do, and that I did not have a choice. In fact for the past thirteen years I have a suitcase in my bedroom and it has everything ready in it, and all I have to add are two blouses. With young children that is very difficult. When I had three young children, I still did it. I did it because I had no other choice, I needed the money (Associate Director, Pharmaceutical Company).

Forty-seven of the interviewees believed that it is more difficult for female managers than for their male counterparts to 'have it all', that is, a successful career, a good personal relationship, and children. Thirty-seven of the managers believed that females are forced to choose between an international career and marriage because of the extra responsibilities of balancing home and work life. These interviewees believed that their male counterparts in international management do not have to make the same sacrifices, as it is still generally accepted by organisations and society that the family will move to facilitate the career of the male breadwinner. The fifty managers suggested that organisations can no longer assume that this pattern is going to continue. It is, however, not yet the norm for a family to relocate internationally to facilitate the female's career.

The twenty-eight managers, whose families relocated to facilitate their careers, noted that the organising and settling in of their families to new surroundings often proved more difficult than dealing with their new professional lives. The participants perceived that much of the guilt and conflict experienced by them as female managers derived from the way parental roles are socially defined. They also believed that the role conflicts and role constraints, which they contend with, are likely to be damaging generally to women's careers. The interviewees also perceived that the historical devaluing of women's work means that women tend to be employed in traditional women's occupations which have lower pay, power, and prestige — all of which can affect women's career progress. The interviewees further believed that gender role identity, particularly in relation to childbearing and child rearing, does impact on male or female behaviours in relation to occupational expectations. The managers believed that conflicts in personal relationships, childbearing, and child rearing have a impact on the disproportionately low number of females who pursue, or are interested in pursuing, careers in international management.

It is clear from the views expressed by the managers that have children, that work–family conflicts are a major deterrent to female participation in international management. All twenty-eight managers who relocated for their careers believed that they, as females, still took responsibility for organising home and family. These interviewees believed that, in the case of international relocation for the male career, the female would take responsibility for home and family life. It is, therefore, apparent from these data, that more females than male managers have to choose between an international career or family commitments. Conflict between work and family prevents many female managers from partaking in international management. Work–family conflicts, however, are not the only barriers to the senior international career move. Other significant obstacles which were reported by the respondents will now be discussed.

4.3 Characteristics of an International Manager

The research findings presented in this section suggest characteristics required to make an international managerial career move. In particular, the findings address the characteristics which *female* managers require to make an international career move.

International assignments have a strong bearing on a company's success and are of crucial concern for the person who is relocated. Research by Adler and Ghadar (1990) and Edström and Galbraith (1977) established three general company motives for making international transfers. The first was to fill positions where qualified host-country nationals were unavailable or difficult to train. The second motive was management development, whereby managers gained international experience and training for future important tasks in subsidiaries abroad or with the parent company. The third motive was organisational development, through managers being socialised in a variety of cultures and creating international communication networks allowing for more decentralisation.

The research indicates that international transfers generally occurred when host-country nationals were unavailable. The findings, based on a predominantly European sample in an entirely European context, revealed that many similar characteristics are required by both male and female expatriate managers. The interviewees, however, generally had to convince home-country male managers of their willingness to work internationally. All interviewees believed that it was necessary for them to have senior managerial experience in their home organisations before they would be assigned to senior positions abroad. The interviewees also noted that female expatriates require additional qualities, such as: the ability to prove that they are 'very, very good', bravery, self-sufficiency, and resilience. The attributes which forty of the respondents recognised as essential were: flexibility, the approval of a partner and family, the ability to adapt to other cultures, open-mindedness, independence, and a willingness to take risks:

> The first thing we need is people with ability. Second, the whole personal situation should be prepared. Nothing can compensate in the end for that, and it is particularly difficult for a woman moving a family, because each individual member has got his/her own problems, so it is a prerequisite to have the family in order. Then you look at social competence, ability, and general skills, and somebody that can cope with different cultures and can offer a certain degree of judgement and adjust themselves to the new

environment (Head of International Personnel Management, Manufacturing Company).

You need to be incredibly flexible. You need to be able to deal with ambiguity, and to cope with the rapid pace of change. You need to be able to see things from a number of different perspectives and not make judgements only from your own standpoint. You need to have incredibly good interpersonal skills, very good relationship skills, influencing skills, and persuasive skills. You need to be incredibly good at listening — and that is listening with your ears and your eyes, watching body language, listening to the silences, listening to what is said and being able to find ways of providing feedback in the channels that they use. It doesn't harm to be humble, but at the same time you must recognise that you do have qualifications and ability that you are bringing to the job, and they are as equal as theirs, though they are different. Another difficulty is the mobility issue and this applies more to women. This is the biggest issue. I was specifically asked to go overseas before I got too old or too tied down. I think the biggest issue for overseas assignments that we, as a company, need to address are the difficulties relating to accommodating the requirements of the partners of assignees, whether they are working or not. When I look retrospectively at the international assignees in our company, many of them have been men who were able to move overseas because their wives do not have careers, or they were at the stages of bringing up young children and they thought that would be a good time for them to go overseas because the wife is now going to be staying at home with the children. Female colleagues who are working overseas tend to have incredibly supportive spouses, who are open-minded and share responsibilities, and there is respect from both sides. If a woman has not got that support and she has children, it would be very, very difficult for her (Human Resources Manager, Telecommunications Company).

According to Borg and Harzing (1995), companies have different transfer policies; some have formal systems, while others have no specific policy on this subject. The research indicates that assignee selections for international transfers generally occurred on quite an arbitrary basis, with only two organisations having managers officially assigned for dealing with international transfers. According to Adler (1991), companies can no longer afford to send any but their best people abroad, and these individuals cannot afford to fail. None of the fifty interviewees had been recalled from her international posting. The interviewees believed that a contributory factor to their success is that they all actively wanted an international management position, and they ensured that they were fully qualified before going abroad, and also had their personal circumstances in order. The interviewees, however, believed that in the case of their male counterparts, the males were very often not as senior nor as well qualified, and did not always take the circumstances of their spouses into account.

This research revealed some necessary attributes which Tung also discovered, such as ability to cope with environmental variables, and having one's family requirements in order. The interviewees, however, cautioned that a reliance on technical competencies does not necessarily ensure a successful international assignment. The interviewees stated that it is not only essential for all international managers to be technically capable both in their home and host organisations, but that it is important for them to have the capacity for flexibility, the ability to change, and to be able to take risks. The interviewees also suggested that having the ability to live and work with people whose beliefs and customs are different from one's own can be even more difficult for female managers than for their male counterparts; the participants who worked in organisations, for example, in Japan and Switzerland were treated as unusual, where it is still extraordinary for a woman to occupy a senior position in these countries. The twenty-eight managers from dual-career couples that relocated to give priority to the career of the female partners believed that the approval of their partners is essential to ensure the success of their assignments:

> You have to be extremely flexible and receptive to different attitudes, recognising that when you do go to a different country it is going to be hard for a man or a woman because you've got to understand a very different culture. You have got to be conscious not to impose your own culture. Some companies do not send women abroad because they have previously been seen as a trailing spouse. In our worldwide company there are 37,000 employees right now and I am the only woman at my level. There are not a lot of women who would want to make an international move. It is a big deal for a man or a woman. It disrupts one's entire life. I mean if one likes stability one might as well forget it. I have made lots of moves, but never outside the United States until now, and I would say moving to Ireland has been my most difficult move. Ireland would be easier in terms of language than other countries, but culturally it is different. You don't have the support system of family either, when abroad (Managing Director, Manufacturing Company).

I believe one needs to be open to other people and to listen to them and adapt to other people and not impose one's own way. I believe one has to adapt, and this takes from between six months to a year. One is a stranger at the beginning of an international assignment, which is a very difficult period, and sometimes it is frustrating because of the language. It is easier for men rather than women to be accepted because the reality is that there are so few women in this situation (Bank Manager).

I believe that being flexible and not judging other people are important. From my point of view curiosity was my guide because I believe that it is always interesting to meet new people and see what is new. I believe that if one does not feel confident as a woman, one will always be asking if one is fit for the job. Men are always thinking that they are much closer to God. It is natural for them to be asked to apply for an international position, whereas it is not natural for women (Director, European Commission).

Research, however, has established that only technical competence and knowledge of company systems have been used as the main selection criteria for appointing international managers (Barham and Devine, 1990; Brewster, 1991; Mendenhall et al., 1987). According to Borg and Harzing (1995), the selection procedures, adopted by companies for appointing international managers, accord inadequate attention to factors such as relational skills, cultural empathy and partner/family support. Brewster (1991) noted that widespread reliance on personal recommendations for expatriate postings results in selection interviews in which negotiating the terms of the offer takes precedence over determining the suitability of the candidate. The interviewees suggested, however, that the reliance on personal recommendations for appointing international managers creates further difficulties for female managers, as senior managers tend to promote those who most likely resemble themselves, i.e., males. Thirty interviewees believed because of stereotypical attitudes and the relatively recent entry of females to international management, that female managers experience additional difficulties in convincing home-country senior management that they posses the desired characteristics for making successful international career moves. These interviewees further suggested that, given the high failure rate of male expatriate assignments, females are likely to be considered as an extra risk for their organisations, and this is a further obstacle for female managers to overcome.

The above discussion shows that the male or female international manager requires a wide range of skills. Extracting from the above quotations and from the interviews, the range of skills required for international manager assignments include aptitudes for:

- managing cultural diversity,
- communicating effectively,
- managing change,
- working with others and in teams,
- risk taking and experimenting,
- developing high mobility.

Thirty-one interviewees suggested that international mobility is more difficult for the female manager because (i) of problems associated with relocating a male partner and family, (ii) until recently female managers were confused with the traditional female trailing spouses, who were generally recognised as problematic in international assignments, and (iii) the qualities required for an international career are frequently associated with a male managerial style. The research results suggested that, because of gender, female managers had to be more aware than their male colleagues of their personal safety, and twenty-five managers said that bravery was another required characteristic. Thirty interviewees also suggested, because of the difficulties they experienced in socialising and networking, that they had to be more independent than their male counterparts and had to posses the ability to combat loneliness and to enjoy being alone.

Twenty-one of twenty-two interviewees, who went on international assignments alone, spoke of the loneliness they experienced for the first few months of their assignments, particularly at weekends, when they knew they would not speak to anybody until they returned to their companies after the weekend. These interviewees observed that this was not the case for their male colleagues as the male managers were invited much more frequently to socialise with their colleagues at weekends. Thirty of the interviewees believed that a further necessary quality was the ability to take risks, and these thirty interviewees believed they were risk takers as they were the first females to represent their companies abroad. They also realised that they were perceived as a risk for their companies, because of preconceptions based on gender:

If you believe strongly in something in your career or something that might be good for the company, you need to take a risk and convince your company of this. When I came here first, I had some strange comments about being a woman, and I have been mistaken for the note-taker at meetings, which doesn't bother me. In fact, I think that is funny, and I take pleasure in handing out my business cards. Getting to a senior position is a balancing act and it means being aggressive and having priorities within the company and letting the company know that you are going to take the risk. One must know what one wants, and if one is simply waiting for instructions one is not considered to be a leader and will never be successful (Managing Director, Freight Carrier Company).

From the above discussion it is apparent that the successful international manager requires a large number of diverse characteristics, as studies of expatriate assignments reveal that large percentages of these assignments fail. Research with United States expatriates reveals that from 16 per cent to 50 per cent of foreign assignments fail (Black, 1988; Mendenhall et al., 1987; Tung, 1981). The research suggested that the two main reasons for expatriates returning prematurely to their organisations were: (i) the inability of spouses and families to settle in the new environment, and (ii) cultural difficulties:

Women are more social and it is very hard to put one's whole self into work and to forget everything else. Women like being involved in their homes and their families. It is very hard to set up a home in a country where one has no family. When you are in a family situation you are trying to keep everybody happy. If my husband moved somewhere, I think he would concentrate on his career and expect me to get everything sorted out and keep the family happy. Even though I am the one we moved for, I have to do all of that as well. I try to make my family happy. If one is by oneself it is also difficult, especially to go out socially. I worked in New Zealand and I made an effort to socialise, but it was difficult. When I am in the States and if I want to meet new friends, I can take a class, but if you go to a new country you don't know what the things to do are, and it is not always done in the same way. It is easier for men. People automatically think I am the trailing spouse; they automatically think I am not the career person. I know sometimes my husband has a hard time because people say 'Oh, your wife is the career person', and they think of it as a negative, but it is not (Financial Controller, Pharmaceutical Company).

What I have found in the companies that I have worked for is that the spouse usually doesn't settle and that has been the main cause of expatriate failures. We have sent a lot of expatriates from and back to the States and to other parts of Europe, and it is often very difficult for the spouse moving into a new environment. It is fine for the persons working, because they have fewer problems, as they are totally tied up in their work, and in most cases they are the men. Their work is challenging, but their partners are at home and do not have social support. It is hard for them to get into a community if they are not working, and then if there is a language barrier it is more difficult again. Most people adapt to their new environment, but you get the few who are culturally handicapped, and I think the main reason is the spouse not settling (Managing Director, Computer Company).

Expatriate failures can result from cultural mismatches and from not understanding local conventions and what behaviour is rewarded in different cultures. Since your work ability does not change, it is your ability to fit into the cultural or social norms which matters most (Chief Executive, Insurance Company).

I believe that a reason for some expatriate failures could be attributed to unrealistic expectations. Sometimes it might be a cultural mismatch or people might just not gel in an organisation (Marketing Director, Telecommunications Company).

I believe that one of the main reasons for expatriate failures is that they are not part of a career plan. Too often we take people because there is a gap to be filled. I have seen that happening. But, I do not think that there are many companies who are good at planning careers, for example, I received only four weeks notice when I was due to move to the United States, but then it is amazing what one can do in four weeks. It was difficult for my husband to get himself sorted out. He was always questioned going through customs, as they would not believe that he was not working. Moreover, they would not give him a social security number because they thought he was moonlighting, so that was a bit tough (Manager, Retailing Company).

In summary, all fifty interviewees confirmed that professional ability and competence to achieve the desired objectives of the international assignment are required by all international managers. The research, however, suggested that relying solely on these skills does not guarantee a successful international appointment. As suggested above, the technical ability of an expatriate remains the same, but having one's personal life in order and the ability to adapt to a new culture are increasingly important.

4.4   The International Transfer Cycle

As discussed earlier, it is clear that male and female managers in *domestic* managerial positions are not treated similarly by senior management. Because of the relative scarcity of female international managers, comparisons between male and female transfers are more difficult. The interview data, however, highlighted that the international transfer cycle, for male and female managers can be divided into three distinct phases. The overall transfer cycle is discussed in these phases. First, the selection and preparation procedures for international assignees are examined. Second, the length of international assignments is investigated. Third the re-entry stage is analysed. The research results and discussion specifically address comparative aspects of the transfer cycle for male and female international managers.

4.4.1   *Selection and Preparation for Managerial Expatriation*

According to Brewster (1993), managerial expatriation is still an atypical experience, and only a minority of employees ever experience it. The results from this research confirm the earlier work of Brewster who recorded that expatriation does involve a major upheaval for the expatriate managers and their families; and while it often proves to be a very positive experience in the long term for all concerned, the immediate transfer is frequently problematic.   For some managers the proposition of an international assignment can come as a shock, forcing them to fundamentally review their future career prospects — and the potential for major domestic problems — if the opportunity were to be accepted, and also to consider the long-term outcomes if the opportunity were to be turned down.

The research confirms Torrington's (1994) work, which suggested that there is no profile of the ideal expatriate but that culture, economic development, geographical location, and the job are important issues that should be considered in the selection of expatriates. The findings indicate that for female international managers cultural differences are often more significant than for male managers. One of the respondents, for example, spoke of the difficulties she has in assigning women to Alaska. The organisation she works for has fish caves in Alaska that are run by men who live in bunkers for a few months, and it is not yet socially or culturally acceptable for women to be employed in such work in Alaska. Many of the fifty interviewees spoke about personal security and petty crime. One interviewee who worked in France spoke of being attacked outside her apartment as she returned from work one night, despite having leased an apartment in the centre of a major city.

The importance of expatriate training for spouses and families was pointed out by the interviewees, particularly as the difficulties for male trailing spouses are more significant. The interviewees believed that if male and female expatriate managers and their families were given opportunities to participate in expatriate training and development courses, then perhaps the number of female international managers would increase. Torrington (1994) suggested that, the size of the expatriate community is also an important consideration. The interviewees believed that the expatriate community is even more important when the male partner is the trailing spouse. The success of the expatriate Brussels-based STUDS group was referred to earlier. The managers with children also stated that the availability of international schools would be an important consideration for them. These managers also stated that as children got older mobility would be more difficult, as they did not want to disrupt their education. These interviewees also believed that additional training should be provided for female expatriate managers to help them cope with the additional stressors associated with balancing work and home life in their new surroundings. The research reported that only five interviewees received any training. The interviewees believed that pre-departure training would have been very beneficial to them, particularly since they had no female role models to follow. One interviewee said that after she applied for an international transfer, she was given two weeks notice to move from England to the United States. She found this extremely difficult as her partner was also accompanying her and they had to arrange visas and make arrangements for renting their house within this time.

The interviewees believed that currently it is much more difficult for female managers to be selected for an international assignment than it is for their male counterparts. The managers believed that, because of the additional risks involved in expatriate assignments, female managers are further disadvantaged in the selection process. The thirty-one married participants also noted that home-country senior management presumed that they would not be interested in being selected for an international assignment because of their domestic responsibilities. These participants believed that if they had not asked to be included in the selection process, they would not have been considered by home-country senior management:

> For women especially, assumptions and generalisations are made, so women will have to do more about that by making their intentions known. I constantly keep saying what I want. I don't think enough women do that. Without a doubt, that is how I got to my position now. When an overseas opportunity came up in our organisation, senior management said to me 'We don't know if you would be interested because of your personal circumstances — because you are married'. I asked what that had got to do with it? I don't think that would have been said to a man, but then I made it very clear that was never an issue. I would want to consider the job first and then I would sort out my personal life (Managing Director, Manufacturing Company).

> I have just been assigned as manager of European logistics and it is a tough project, the first one to be taken on in Europe by our company. My experience, background, and knowledge were looked at in the selection process. There is a tremendous amount of travel involved and because I am a mother they asked me if this would be a problem. I don't think I would have been asked that if I were a man, because a husband knows that most of the time he has a wife at home who can take care of all the household and family things. When he is asked to take on a role all he has got to think about is managing that role. When a woman with children takes on a managerial role she still has to take into consideration the amount of time she will and will not be with her children, no matter how good her husband is. There is no backup; at best it can be a fifty-fifty deal between husband and wife, but usually it is a third party that has to come in and do the back-up, because it is never fifty-fifty (Director, Manufacturing Company).

> For four years I was in charge of financial analysis for subsidiaries based here in Brussels. Then a very interesting project came up in Asia, and I asked to be moved there. My son was four years old at the time. In the meantime, my husband had set up his own company, so the assumption was that I would not be interested in moving. But, I moved over there with our son, and my husband did not go, he stayed over here because of his new company. I think it was easier for me being there without my husband, because when I looked at other expatriates they had lots of problems with their spouses. We travelled a lot back and forth from Asia, so my son saw his father a lot (Head of Corporate Communications, Pharmaceutical Company).

I moved to Paris for four years. I wanted to move because the job was good and there was an element of career development. But, I had to fight very hard with management here in Britain to get the job (Account Executive, Technology Company).

Despite the recognition of various problems encountered with international assignments, on average, only twenty-five per cent of aspirant expatriates receive preparatory training prior to departure. For those expatriates who receive training, most training is, however, of very short duration, generally lasting only a few days. Interestingly, with the additional difficulties which have been highlighted for female international managers, only ten per cent of managers received any form of training. Baumgarten (1995) noted that in eighty per cent of the cases where training is provided, the partners are not included in the training programme. Of the five interviewees who received any form of training, no partner was included. The training ranged from short induction courses of a few days, to general training over a few weeks, and up to a maximum of three months. The remaining forty-five respondents received no formal training and were, as one interviewee described it, 'being thrown in at the deep end'. They believed that initial difficulties could have been lessened, or in some cases avoided, if an adequate training programme had been in place:

The company certainly did not do a blessed thing for me. The difficulties were more around the move rather than around people. Trying to find housing was very difficult. Eventually, the company did hire a relocation person to help us find a house, and she was helpful and gave us a couple of books and other support. Another sample difficulty for us concerned my husband who, after driving for twenty-five years in the States, couldn't find an insurance company here in Ireland to insure him because he had never driven on the left-hand side of the road — and yet they would give insurance to an eighteen-year-old. Another instance was when I went to the bank to open an account and I had a bank draft for £10,000 and yet they would not let me open an account. They eventually allowed me to open an account, but they said they would hold the money for weeks, which meant that I could not write cheques. I was treated like an international drug baron. Those are just some of the start-up problems that could have been sorted out if there was a training programme for expatriates in the company (Director, Computer Company).

The research indicates that the short time span between selection and departure was the main reason for managers not receiving training. The managers asserted that training is not only important for the expatriate manager, but since the stress associated with an international assignment falls on all family members, the issue of training programmes for spouses and families should be addressed. This finding confirms previous work by Harris and Moran (1987) and Harvey (1985) who also highlighted the importance of including all family members in training programmes.

Forty-five interviewees perceived that the selection process for expatriates in their organisations was conducted on quite a haphazard basis, with far too little time given for the preparation and training for international assignments. The interviewees also believed that their gender is still the main barrier to selection and preparation for international managerial assignments, because the stereotypical image that an expatriate manager is male still exists in organisations and society. This finding concurs with North American research findings conducted by Adler (1993), who suggested that institutional discrimination exists by which assumptions on the suitability of managerial candidates are based on societal assumptions about men and women.

4.4.2   The Assignment Period Abroad

Research studies have established that an international managerial assignment for male managers normally extends for a period of three or four years (Borg and Harzing 1995; Izraeli et al., 1980). The findings indicate that the majority of interviewees (thirty-three out of fifty) spent similar lengths of time on international assignments. Thirty-three of the managers had each experience of between two and four years internationally. The managers believed that one- or two-year assignments are too short, and thirty-one of the managers considered that a three years assignment seemed an appropriate length:

> Three years is a nice time to be away for. Three years should be the minimum because you are really only getting into the swing of things then. You really have to spend three years to make a change (Plant Manager, Pharmaceutical Company).

Five years expatriation was considered to be too long, as the managers believed that repatriation would be extra difficult after that, especially if there were children involved. The research results differ from Lane and DiStefano's (1992) three-phase findings of elation, distress, and adjustment. The interviewees noted that because they were given very short notice from their home-country organisations before moving internationally, the first phase (i.e., before moving abroad) was one of apprehension, and not elation as suggested by Lane and DiStefano, especially for those interviewees who were the first females to represent their organisations abroad. These interviewees reported that because of the lack of training and often having the responsibility for organising a spouse and family it was a very stressful phase. The interviewees categorised the beginning of the second phase of their move (arriving in their new location) as generally being more stressful personally than professionally. The respondents stated that balancing work and home life was particularly difficult for them during this phase, especially when young children had to be settled into new schools, and arrangements for childcare had to be organised. One of the interviewees who moved to Japan found the early stages of adjusting to working in her new environment particularly difficult. Lane and DiStefano also suggested that the average adjusting period for international managers was three to nine months; however, the interviewees in this research reported that it took one to two years for them to adjust to their new situations. Interestingly, previous literature did not record if the ability of female managers to cope with other demands, such as their 'second career' at home, was an influence on adjustment. The respondents reported that the lack of networking facilities and the lack of female role models were contributory factors to their longer adjustment period. The interviewees believed that in some cases social adjustment was more difficult than organisational adjustment, as in most countries it is not the norm for females to socialise alone, consequently females needed a longer adjusting period than that of their male counterparts.

Borg and Harzing (1995) noted that the first six months abroad are perceived by most expatriates in a similar way. At the beginning of the assignment many things are new and exciting, but after about three months difficulties begin to emerge as the expatriate experiences what has been described as 'culture shock'. Lane and DiStefano (1992) defined culture shock experienced by expatriates as a behavioural pattern associated with powerlessness. These authors identified symptoms of culture shock as fatigue, tension, anxiety, excessive concern about hygiene, hostility, an obsession about being cheated, withdrawal into work, family, or the expatriate community, or in extreme cases, excessive use of drugs and alcohol. After about five or six months the expatriate starts to adapt to the foreign culture and gradually moves to a more neutral state. In this research, the twenty-eight managers from dual career couples, that relocated to facilitate the careers of the female partner, expressed that their male trailing spouses experienced greater culture shock than themselves. Eight of the managers spoke of the exclusion their partners experienced, for example, one of the managers who relocated to the United States and was the first female manager to represent her organisation there, recalled an incident where her partner was deliberately not invited to a social gathering organised by her organisation for the (female) partners of the other managers. She believed that, as her partner was the only male trailing spouse, the organisation did not know how to deal with this situation. The manager also noted that the organisation also experienced difficulty in coping with having a female in a very senior position for the first time.

As thirty of the managers were the first females to represent their companies internationally, they did not know if their international experience would be considered valuable by home-country senior management, therefore, they perceived their international assignment as a risk to their future careers. All the managers believed that they have succeeded in their international assignments, but believed, because of their additional autonomy and global experience, that returning to their home organisations would be very difficult. The interviewees believed that a possible solution to this would be to partake in another international move. Some of the interviewees who wished to partake in another international assignment, outlined the difficulties this involved:

I am from Canada originally. I moved from Canada to Belgium and I found this an extremely big change. It was a huge change both from a work standpoint and from a personal standpoint. From a work standpoint my goal was the same, but I was dealing with a different set of players and a different set of politics and also a different support group. Coming over here, I started cold. I didn't know what the procedures were in this country. I didn't know what the challenges were, and it was really only after a year and a half that I learned enough to be able to set my goal clearly. The hours and the travel were also very difficult, because I travel about four days a week. I am coming up on three years here soon, and in my particular area it is only in the last year that I have really been making headway, because with the learning curve and what is expected of me I will definitely need four years. I feel good about that, but my husband is iffy about it. Before I leave I want to achieve what I set out to achieve, and I can't achieve that in three years. At this stage my husband and I are negotiating. My initial assignment was for three years, so I want to extend it for another year. At this point, for me, returning to Canada is not an option as there is nothing there for me. So, I would like to go on to another region where they need my talents. I think it is going to be difficult to get back into another position in the company. Once you take an expatriate assignment your future has a question mark, and it seems to have a question mark regardless of how well you do. So, it is a big risk for me to take an international career assignment (Manager, Freight Carrier Company).

When I talk to people who move internationally they always say that you really don't adjust to the country until you have been there two years, because you are still finding new things that were not in your former country. I have been here in Ireland just two years and I still find that I haven't adjusted to it. This was my second international move, so I was more aware of what goes on. My first move from the United States to England was much more difficult, more of a culture shock. When I moved to Ireland from England I found that they are very different countries, as the cultures and the people are very different again. Moving is very hard at the very beginning and it is also very lonely for a woman, even more so than for a man. Part of that is that men can go out and do things by themselves socially, women cannot (Financial Controller, Pharmaceutical Company).

An international assignment should be for at least three years, because one needs a year to adapt and to understand and to feel welcome, so three years is good. I have been moving around now seven years, to Prague, Tokyo, and Dublin, and when I move I know it is always more difficult for a woman. This is the case everywhere. Because of historical background, it is an exception to have women expatriate managers. You cannot afford to make a mistake as a woman, because a mistake by a woman is more visible, so a woman has to be extra good. When I go to meetings for the first time with all other men it takes extra time to get accepted, then it is all right, but the difficult thing is getting established (Bank Manager).

The findings on *senior* female international managers make comparisons with other research rather difficult, as the available data regarding the international transfer cycle are generally based on the experiences of the male expatriate manager, since approximately 97 per cent of expatriate managers are male. Adler's research in North American (1988) identified that the three per cent of female managers in her study were fairly *junior* within their organisations and careers. She reported that, on average, the female expatriate assignments lasted two and a half years, while the individual assignments ranged from six months to six years. Adler's female interviewees believed that their international assignments were of shorter duration and were in more junior positions than those of their male counterparts. The female managers believed that this was because home-country management perceived female expatriates as more of a risk and were unsure of their abilities to succeed internationally.

Overall, this research indicates that the adjustment period for female international managers takes longer than for their male counterparts because of additional family and home responsibilities. The managers, however, believed that when their families and themselves have adjusted to their new locations, female international managers can be as successful or even more successful than their male counterparts. All the interviewed managers perceived their first international assignment as successes, with many of the managers partaking in subsequent international assignments. The managers also believed that home-country senior management judged their performance as successful, because in many cases they were offered another international assignment, following completion of the first one.

4.4.3   Re–entry

According to Handler and Lane (1997), the repatriation process can often be problematic for returning expatriates, their families, and their companies. The research confirms Handler and Lane's work, as thirty-one of the thirty-two interviewees who re-entered their home countries experienced difficulties after returning. The views of these interviewees concur with Torrington (1994) who noted that, despite the problems associated with repatriation, coming back from an international assignment seldom receives the organisational attention it requires. Torrington suggested that the main reason for this is because repatriation is not expected to be problematic, as all the problems are expected to be connected with going on assignment and getting settled.

The returning managers in this research experienced similar difficulties to those encountered by the returning managers in Scullion's (1992) research, for example, finding suitable posts and feeling undervalued. Two interviewees stated that they are considering going on another international assignment but that they would not return to their home organisations after that period. These interviewees believed that at that stage, they would need a new challenge. The findings from this research confirm Johnston's (1991) study, which suggested that little appears to be done by companies to facilitate returning managers. The findings revealed that in some cases the readjustment to the home-country organisation often took between six and twelve months.

Eighteen of the fifty managers have not yet experienced the repatriation process, as they are still on their first international assignments. Four of these eighteen managers have decided to turn their international assignment into a permanent move and not to return to their home countries. These four managers (three American and one French) have chosen Ireland as a permanent location for their careers and families. All four managers are married. The three American managers have young children and the French manager has grown-up children now living in the United States. These managers believed that their careers and families would be too disrupted if they had to make another international move. Thirty-two interviewees had experienced re–entry to their home organisations, but only one interviewee perceived that she had no problem with the re–entry process. The remaining thirty-one managers believed that re–entry to their home organisations and reintegration socially were more difficult than the original move. The main difficulties which the interviewees experienced in the re–entry process were:

- failure to receive credit from home-country management for their achievements internationally
- not having a suitable position to return to
- outgrowing their home organisations
- problems of social readjustment for themselves and their families
- missed promotional opportunities due to home-country senior management overlooking them while abroad.

When one comes back one starts to outgrow the organisation and the local issues. It is not that one feels above it, but one starts to find the home organisation restrictive from a more global perspective. When I came back from the States I moved to another organisation, and now I feel that if I take another international assignment I would not be able to come back into this organisation. It is the re–entry stage that I would worry about. At the end of this year if I decide that I want to go overseas again I really don't know if I would come back in here when my assignment was over. I don't know if I would come back doing what I was doing before I left. I would probably have to come back to a whole new, different challenge. One tends to outgrow one's former situation. Except for changing companies or maybe coming back into a start-up environment or coming back into major new challenges it would be difficult (Purchasing Manager, Manufacturing Company).

Coming back is as bad if not worse. Going abroad is difficult in that one doesn't know what they are facing, whereas when one is coming back they have a fair idea of what they are coming back to. Then there is the readjustment period when one returns. When I came back from New York it took me about six months to settle down again. I could not believe, for example, how long it took the local delicatessen to make a sandwich, it flabbergasted me. In New York things were just so fast, no sooner were the words out of one's mouth than the sandwich was wrapped. The slowness used to drive me crazy. I actually started to bring my own sandwiches in on occasions because I just couldn't bear it. After about six months one settles down again. One's personal life with one's family and friends are also disrupted. It is very difficult to maintain long-term friendships and one has to be very lucky to slot back into friendships when one returns (Counsellor, Government Department).

If you sever your ties with your home organisation for too long you have nothing to come back to. When I came back it was hard to get credit for the work that I had done. I will be perfectly honest: people thought because I worked in Paris that I had a great holiday. I was given a job very easily and very quickly, because I had the skills that the company wanted. What I do wonder about is, if I had not gone away and stayed in the home organisation, would I have moved up the organisation in those four years. I might have moved up a little. At the same time, I don't think that I got credit for what I did while I was abroad, therefore I don't think it was beneficial for my career here at home, in Britain. Was it beneficial to me in terms of what I learned and in terms of what I can contribute with my experience?   Yes, it was a terrific experience (Account Executive, Technology Company).

When I came back from my assignment in France after two years, some of my social network of friends had gone away. But, work was my main problem. There was not really a place for me when I first came back. Nobody really knew what to do with me, so I used to come in to work and they would try to find things for me to do. But, I used to think to myself that nobody would notice if I was not here. And then the whole cultural behaviour at work was different from France. Nobody says good morning when they come into work here, whereas the French go around to everybody and shake hands with everybody. I began to notice that people here seemed very unfriendly. People were just sitting there and they would not even look up from their computers when one came in. But, there was one guy here who had remembered going through the same thing a few years previously, since he had spent some time with his family in Thailand, and he was very supportive and friendly. So, it took me a while to feel that I fitted in again. I felt awkward. One would think that it would be easy coming back to one's own country (Senior Engineer, Manufacturing Company).

The problem is when one comes back from an international assignment it may happen that there is no position for the person to return to. Sometimes it is necessary to be a supplementary person in a department and one has to wait for a job. That is not very nice to come back to (Bank Manager).

The interviewees suggested that the readjustment period usually takes six months and in some cases it could take up to nine months, particularly if families or spouses are involved. Only two organisations in this research prepared expatriates for re-entry, one German company and one American company. The two interviewees in these companies reported that preparation for re-entry facilitated the process and eliminated many of the problems which are normally associated with repatriation. These interviewees stated that the re-entry process began six months before the employee was due to return to their home organisation:

Regular contact with employees is needed while they are overseas. When people come for their home trips once a year it is mandatory that they call in here and present reviews of their work abroad. The main idea is to let the expatriates know that people are not forgetting about them, that we still care about them. Then when it comes closer to the point of finishing their assignment we can start planning for their return to the organisation (Head of International Personnel Management, Manufacturing Company).

Our home-company career manager is responsible for facilitating the expatriate's integration back into the workplace. Six months before expatriates come back, they start the process of establishing their next role and the actual job they are coming back to. So, there is a six months preparatory period. It is a difficult period for people coming back, because if people have played a bigger role during their assignment than the role the played before they left, their expectation would be to return to a higher level post. In the meantime, while they were away, other people have progressed as well, so that can be difficult for them. They would sometimes expect a job waiting for them, but that is often difficult because we don't keep jobs open for them.   So, six months should be a minimum period which a company would have for sorting this out before the assignee comes back (Human Resources Manager, Computer Company).

The participants believed that not enough attention from home-country senior management is given to the problems experienced by the returning expatriates.   The interviewees suggested that the re-entry stage should be built in as part of an overall career plan before the expatriates initially leave their home organisations.   This plan should be developed to identify the probable length of stay, the projected responsibilities while abroad, and subsequent job position upon repatriation.   The interviewees believed that if they had the support of mentors or networks during their international assignment the re-entry process might have been easier, as they would have been informed of developments in their home organisations while abroad.   In conclusion, the thirty-two repatriated managers reported that the re–entry phase is usually haphazard and ill-planned.   Thirty-one of the managers had experienced difficulties in readjusting, both in terms of their careers and socially.   They had to cope with readjusting to the culture of the home organisation, after losing the status and responsibilities which the international assignment provided for them.   They noted that they went through stages similar to those of culture shock — the first being an excited mood which lasted only a short time, then descending to a low mood, and finally returning to their normal mood.   They believed that the difficulties with re–entry are underestimated at present, and that the re–entry process should receive more attention in the future.

4.5   Do Female Managers *Want* International Careers?

From the discussion above, it is clear that female international managers experience greater barriers than their male counterparts.   Given the additional strains that coping with these difficulties involve, especially for married female managers, the thirty-one married interviewees believed that the perceptions of home-country senior management were that they would not be interested in pursuing an international career.   The data in this section, however, challenge this perception and provide an answer to the question of whether female managers want international careers or not.

Career theories have largely been built on male models of success and work.   Those models are supported by psychoanalytic conceptions of the centrality of work to identity (Levinson et al., 1978; Erikson, 1968). The interviewees in this research believed that in many organisations commitment to work is measured by the number of hours managers spend at their organisations in the evening time and at weekends and also on social networking. The thirty-one married interviewees believed that the majority of female managers choose between a career and family. They noted that societal and organisational perceptions of mothers expected them to devote themselves primarily to their family responsibilities. The following quotations typify some of the existing societal perceptions:

> If my husband had the high-powered job I would be expected by society to take second place. Here in Ireland people cannot get over the concept that my husband is a trailing spouse. People in Ireland find this harder to accept than people do in the United States, for example, our friend's cleaning lady was appalled that I didn't come home and do my husband's ironing. I might have just flown in from Brussels and be catching up on mail before heading to Moscow the next morning, and even though my husband was at home, she was appalled (Director, Computer Company).

> Here in Belgium the people have a very old-fashioned attitude. They believe that women should still be at home with the children. Society is still very male dominated in Belgium. And in the organisation here, they have very different opinions of men and women. I believe that because I am a woman I am seen as a threat to men (Partner, Management Consultancy Company).

Twenty-eight of the thirty-one married managers considered themselves rather unusual in pursuing an international career. They believed that, as many females choose marriage and child rearing in their early adult years, these traditional roles are considered more important for women's identity than for the identity of their male counterparts. Five of the ten unmarried interviewees reported that their pursuit of an international career caused their personal relationships to suffer. They also stated that they have to make difficult choices regarding personal relationships, even more difficult than for their international careers, choices that their male counterparts rarely have to make. The unmarried managers suggested that it is not yet the norm for females to be internationally mobile:

> Women are less likely to apply for an expatriate move. I applied for it because I was single at the time, and I am still single, and it didn't really make any difference because there wasn't anybody to bring along and there

weren't any children. I don't notice a lot of married women applying for international moves. I found that when I went to Texas it put a real strain on my relationship because my boyfriend wasn't going to move out, and I didn't see him for four months. The strain is more so than if he had to move abroad. There is always this 'problem' that I am always the one that is going away, because I also do a lot of travel for my job (Senior Engineer, Software Company).

I went overseas alone, because I am single. I was based in Sydney, but my area included north east Asia, south east Asia, Japan, the Middle East, Africa, and India. There were one or two individuals that I met who wondered what skills I as a female brought, as it is not the norm for single women to go overseas alone. But, by listening and showing sensitivity to their culture and by positioning quite clearly what I was trying to do, they recognised me for my capabilities rather than my gender (Human Resources Manager, Telecommunications Company).

Research by Gallos (1989) established that professional women are capable of aggressively competing and succeeding in the male corporate world, but that they are prepared to sacrifice their own careers and personal needs in order to support their spouses and to assume more of the accommodative role in order to avoid confrontations. The sentiments expressed by the eight divorced or separated interviewees resonate with the research of Gallos. Seven of these interviewees, however, believed that they sacrificed their own careers for the sake of their marriages, but realised that they were then unhappy both in their careers and their marriages. Five of these interviewees stated that they would have liked an international career at earlier stages in their careers, but that their former husbands would not agree to them moving abroad, and this dissuaded them from applying for an international transfer until they were divorced. These interviewees stated that their divorces now gave them the opportunity to concentrate on their careers.

The married managers asserted, because of family commitments, that female managers frequently have to reduce career involvement by cutting back on job-related travel, and also that women managers may be unwilling to relocate internationally. The interviewees suggested that women's careers almost inevitably suffer when they curtail work schedules. The managers suggested that the attitudes and behaviour of their spouses can have substantial positive or negative effects on the ways in which they balance their careers and family activities. The participants believed that many female managers reduce their own career involvement in order to facilitate the career needs of their husbands. All the married managers believed that having supportive husbands was essential for their international careers:

> Some women managers may not choose an international assignment, not because of their children, but because of their husbands. I consider my situation to be quite unique as my husband decided to retire. He is fifty-eight and I am forty-two and we have an agreement that he is now the home focused person and it is my turn to have a career. And that is why the STUDS group is so important for him (Partner, Management Consultancy Company).

> In my industry, which is mining, there are not many women. It is heavy industry. I am the first woman expatriate, but I hope over a period of time women will be as equally regarded as men and more will be offered international assignments. The only question is whether their personal circumstances will allow them. That is a problem that may arise. In order for an international career move to work, the biggest problem may be the spouse. I have two little children, one fifteen months and the other is three and a half, and the main obstacle is not childcare (Managing Director, Manufacturing Company).

> When a woman chooses an international career it puts a lot of pressure on her. It is more difficult for a woman if she has a partner with her because she is trying to find work for him also. I am very fortunate in that regard because my partner works for a humanitarian organisation, so professionally he is a lot more flexible than I am. He tends to do a lot more of the housework and he takes the kids to school. We try to balance things. But, balancing two careers is very difficult. My partner is very, very good regarding my career having priority. Our circumstances are unusual in that my career takes priority, and also unusual because my partner has been very supportive. He has probably pushed me on to do more than I would have otherwise done which is good, and so we are very, very unusual. In my own social circle and here at work there is nobody I know in that situation (Vice-president, Computer Company).

All fifty interviewees stated that they wanted an international career, but that they often had to persuade home-country senior management to 'take the risk' and give them the opportunity to work abroad. Thirteen of the thirty-one married interviewees considered themselves to be 'lucky' to be married to spouses who agreed to them pursuing international careers.

These interviewees believed that due to societal and cultural norms, it is not yet widely acceptable for female managers to have the main career. Each of these interviewees stressed that in their social networks, they did not know any other females who had spouses that facilitated their international career moves. The interviewees spoke of being 'eternally grateful' to their spouses for their career opportunities. These interviewees also acknowledged that they have never heard any male colleague considering himself 'lucky' when his partner facilitated his careers. Where top managers presume that married women do not want international careers, all the interviewees believed that it was unlikely that these organisations will invest in the development of their women managers and provide assignments that provide power and opportunity. Thirty-nine of the participants, as female international managers, believed that they have had to base their lifestyle decisions on factors that men generally do not have to consider:

> Sometimes companies automatically assume that women will not go on an international assignment. With this assumption they don't give them the opportunity. I know of a woman in an office here, who has a husband and kids, and it was just assumed that she wouldn't go, so she wasn't offered the job. But, she went and said 'I want to be thought of'. They said 'Oh, you would be great, but . . . ', and they reminded her that she's got a husband and kids to think of before that, and they also know that her husband has a good job, so they thought she wouldn't move. But, they don't do that with men. They might know that the wife has a good job, but they assume that she will go. They don't consider that maybe the man might do the same thing (Financial Controller, Pharmaceutical Company).

> In our organisation here, it is clear that we would not be considering women who have children for an international assignment. I was surprised last week when a woman who is a senior manger on my team told me that she is available for an international transfer. I asked her if it was with or without her children and spouse, and she said it was without the children. I was surprised with this. It is more difficult for a woman with children to make this decision rather than men. People have to decide for themselves what they want, and if they want to live in the same place there are some compromises to be made. At the time I left for Thailand by myself, it was a good time for my husband and myself to make that kind of decision. We would not have been ready for that type of transfer a few years before, so the timing of the transfer is very important   (Head of Corporate Communications, Pharmaceutical Company).

I believe that an international career is particularly difficult when there are children involved. My children are aged eleven and thirteen, and they are studying for exams, so I thought it would have been quite disruptive for them to move to France. Usually, women would hesitate about taking on an international assignment on that basis, but my situation is a little unusual in that the children live with their father, so I left them at home. In my experience though, when I was at home and still married most of the responsibility for child rearing was mine, and that is the case with most of the other women I know. So, the fact that I haven't got these ties now has helped me in that I just pursued the direction that I wanted in my career. It definitely was the case with my international career move   (Senior Engineer, Manufacturing Company).

The views of the interviewees also confirm the findings of Hewlett (1986) and Giele (1982) who maintained that there are obvious and logical reasons to expect that women would have their own values for interpreting the world. These include their capacities for childbirth, early-life socialisation differences, and social or political pressures for maintaining the traditional feminine role. As a result, women have generally been employed in service and care-giving positions, for example, teachers, social workers, nurses and secretaries. The interviewees talked about their early socialisation experiences, where typically their mothers were at home, and their fathers went out to work. The interviewees believed that they are the first generation to have to fight many battles and break through the glass ceiling. They added that some of the younger female employees do not realise how difficult it had been for them, especially at the early stages of their careers.

Three of the interviewees spoke of the difficulty of finding time 'for themselves', for example, going to the hairdressers, shopping for clothes for work, or having their nails manicured, all of which they believed were necessary for senior female managers. These managers also pointed out that when male managers move internationally, they generally need 'only two suits, and a few shirts', as the interviewees believed that their male colleagues are not judged by their appearances as much as female managers. The interviewees believed that as they are in a minority group, they feel more visible and responsible for representing all females, therefore it was necessary for them to establish a suitable dress code. The respondents also stated that they did not want to dress 'in an overly feminine' manner, as this could attract unwanted attention to themselves as females.   These interviewees also stated that in the early stages of their careers they attempted to wear hairstyles and clothes which 'made them look older', in order to reduce the amount of attention being paid to them as females rather than as managers.

The managers also suggested that as it is not yet possible for women to 'have it all', they believed that female managers are generally forced to choose between an international career and a family.   Three of the interviewees who perceived that they 'had it all' — a successful marriage, career, and children — considered themselves to be 'very, very, unusual and very lucky'. The interviewees believed that they were unusual because until recently international careers were largely reserved for male married managers. These interviewees also remarked that they have never heard any of their male colleagues considering themselves to be lucky when 'having it all'. These three interviewees also believed that as they 'had it all', younger female managers might be encouraged by this, and also aim to have successful marriages, careers and children.

The participants believed that the thirties age-group was particularly difficult for female international managers, as they believed at this stage many female managers want an international career, but they also want marriage and children. The managers in their thirties who did not have children spoke of their biological clock 'ticking loudly' for them. For those who have children, the exhaustion of balancing multiple roles meant cutting back on either career or parenting, which inevitably increased stress and role conflict. The managers in their thirties who have achieved professional success wondered what they might have sacrificed:

> I often wonder if I had kids would I be able to take an international career move. I suppose I would find it very difficult in my career to be in a situation where I could commit to a family, because it is hard to manage both. I would be concerned about its affect on my career, as up to now I haven't had any restrictions or anybody imposing that on me. I am thirty-four now and if I were going to have kids I would want to be starting to have them in a couple of years. The company might then say 'Well, she has one, and she will probably have another one in twelve months'. Would that then hamper my progress? I can't say that it would not, because one is not supposed to discriminate, but men being men, I suspect that is the way they would think. When you work in this environment it is hard to manage both. If you had children then it would be more difficult and especially when you are travelling. But, that does not mean that that is not something that I will never do. We were actually talking about it in the U.S. the last time I was over and we were laughing about it. I said to one of my friends 'Could you

imagine me coming into the lobby here with a baby and putting it into the day-care centre for two weeks!, and then me coming back to pick it up?' — and that is just a caricature of a very real problem. And then I wonder if it is totally selfish to go and have kids if I couldn't guarantee to be there all the time. I love my job and I love what I do and I enjoy the whole travel element of it and being out and about and meeting people. All of these decisions are more difficult for women, without a doubt, and being a mother is very definitely much more difficult. In the back of my mind I am always wondering if I had kids would I have a successful career (Purchasing Manager, Manufacturing Company).

In most cases the reason why women don't go on international assignments is because of family circumstances. Women tend to choose between career and family. It also has to do with the individual development of the woman, where they come from and what kind of picture has been painted for them. For example, is it dutiful for a woman to follow a career? A lot of women learn that it is good to have a good education and career, but next they find themselves with a husband and children. How many women are really encouraged to go for international assignments? When I talk to some of the younger women who are still independent, they feel they might want to take an international assignment, but then they wait and when the time comes they will have a husband, and a lot of things change because the husband's career will have priority. It is a big decision for women to make, but we lose a lot of women because their careers do not have priority. This is a pity because women can offer a lot of special skills (Head of International Personnel Management, Manufacturing Company).

Parasuraman and Greenhaus (1993) suggested that women are often forced to make difficult and complex decisions regarding what lifestyle to adopt. Hewlett (1986) and Catalyst (1982) also observed that, because women hold primary responsibility for home and family life, they often feel forced to make major career sacrifices for the welfare of their children. The interviewees in this research believed that for women in international management, lifestyle choices are even more difficult, especially when there are children involved. Ten of the interviewees with children believed that they adopted a 'superwoman' strategy. This strategy has been defined by Parasuraman and Greenhaus (1993, p. 196) as 'extensive career involvement with a frenzy of activity at home, including extraordinary efforts to spend more time with children'. Cross-cultural research has established that these 'superwomen' who have young children spend more time with their children than male managers do; they find themselves less able to relax at the end of the day; and are more susceptible to feelings of guilt, role conflict and work overload. The ten interviewees in this research who had adopted a 'superwoman' strategy also spoke of feelings of guilt when away from their children for long periods of time, which they believed their male counterparts do not experience. The interviewees also reported that their husbands did not spend as much time with their children as they did, and believed that men did not experience feelings of guilt when away on work trips. These interviewees also spoke of work overload which they asserted created additional strain for them, and one interviewee admitted that she would like to 'bail out' of corporate life, but then wondered if she would be able to 'live with herself'

The married participants with young children believed that sometimes it was necessary for them to adopt a 'superwoman' strategy in order to convince their organisations that they are still serious about their commitments to their careers. These participants added that adopting a 'superwoman' strategy is extra difficult while partaking in an international assignment. Disadvantages which the managers highlighted included: role conflict; the upheaval of moving and settling family members into a new environment; not having enough time for their new career; feelings of guilt about not being a good wife or mother; lack of emotional and domestic support from their spouses; and, work overload. The managers perceived that female managers may prefer not to choose an international career because of the difficulties involved in successfully balancing an international career with home and family:

> Women more than men have to choose between career and family. I have found myself at different crossroads in my life in the last twelve years and whenever I felt that the children were upset I asked myself 'Should I keep going or not?' — and I don't think men would ask themselves if they should give up their careers for the sake of their children. I wonder at least once a year if I should continue working. It is a balancing act managing everything, and some times are better than others (Chief Accountant, Computer Company).

> There are not many women that I know who are in the same situation as I am in, where they had taken a career like mine and also decided to have a family. A lot of women that I know got married when I got married and their careers tended to stop or slow down after marriage and being pregnant. Having children slows down your career, but we can't get away from the biological fact that men can't have children. While it might slow down your

career advancement, on the other hand, it enriches you in ways that you would not be enriched through work. It brings out another aspect of you that might not have been brought out. It is very difficult for women to balance a demanding career and a family, and I have done a lot of thinking about this. I have three children, and you have to be very organised. I am not saying that I am very good at it, because we have our tensions like everybody else. When it comes to finding and replacing babysitters, organising school runs, and looking after illness, that always falls to me. I am not blaming my husband for that. I see myself doing that because that is what my mother did and it is very hard to get out of that cycle. Anyway, I wouldn't trust my husband to look after all of those things! My husband works as a financial lawyer, but I am paid more than he is and that does cause tensions. I don't think he likes me earning more than him, but we have managed to work it out. The decision that I made regarding my choice of career had nothing to do with more or less responsibility because of child rearing. It was based on my chosen career path. I wanted to do this. I wanted to have this senior position (Medical Consultant).

The participants suggested that organisations could do more to help female managers to cope with the additional difficulties of balancing a 'high-powered career' with family responsibilities. The managers also predicted that the number of female international managers will increase in the future, and organisations that will pay attention to them will benefit. From this work, it is evident that more research needs to be undertaken in order to understand women's careers more fully and in particular the interdependencies of their families with their careers. The fifty interviewees believed that senior female managers want international careers, but many females also want marriage and children. The participants expressed that career success is still based on men's traditional work experiences and assumptions about the importance of work to identity. The findings suggested that female career perspectives, choices, and priorities do not imply that women's career achievements are any less important than those of men, but that some women do not fit the male model of work and careers. The interviewees believed, because female managers do not always fit the dominant male career model, that they are often forced to choose between an international career and family. In choosing an acceptable lifestyle, the interviewees believed that women face a number of dilemmas, and their choices are more difficult than for their male counterparts because of women's typically stronger linkages to both career and family roles.

4.6   The Impact of Gender on Female Managers' International Careers

It is clear from the discussion that female managers experience many more obstacles to their career advancement than their male counterparts do. Despite these obstacles, which they reported to be overt and covert, the participants asserted that female managers are available, suitable and motivated to partake in international management. The discussions reveal that presumptive but erroneous attitudes are adopted by top management about female managers' potential abilities, willingness, and availability for international assignments. In contrast, the findings show that top managers offer more assignment opportunities to their male colleagues, for whom they do not hold the same presumptions on their availability, willingness, and potential for international assignments. The interviewees also perceived that home-country top managers make gender-based value generalisations, for example, that all women are generally alike and they are all very different from men. This section addresses the question raised in the first chapter on the impact gender has on the international careers of female managers.

Forty-six of the interviewees in this research stated that they were very conscious of their gender as they believed they were occupying positions 'in a man's world'. The interviewees believed that two overt examples of discrimination against them based on gender grounds were relative salary scales and educational qualifications. The participants noted that they generally were on lower salaries than their male counterparts even though they were as experienced and as skilled as their male counterparts. This finding confirms the earlier studies which have established that managers are initially differentiated on gender grounds. This study also confirms that after initially differentiating managers on grounds of gender, further prejudgements are made on their overall managerial qualities and, in turn, these preconceptions inform decisions on career prospects and management choices for these managers, which are made by top management. Other studies confirm that organisations treat men and women differently in terms of managerial and pay opportunities (Powell, 1990; Rosener, 1990; Heilman et al., 1989).

Forty-six interviewees had third level qualifications, with the MBA degree representing the most widely held qualification. The interviewees considered the MBA to be an important part of their management development programmes, adding, however, that male managers with MBA degrees were more likely to be promoted to senior positions and to higher salary scales than female managers. This finding concurs with Simpson's (1995) and Sinclair's (1995) research.

The views expressed on gender differences by the fifty participants can best be described as the 'complementary contributions approach' (defined by Adler and Izraeli, 1988), which recognises the equal contributions made by male and female managers. According to Adler and Izraeli, the complementary contributions approach to gender acknowledges that differences are gender based, but it does not suggest that women or men are inherently better managers, but better at certain managerial tasks. The participants, however, noted that the contributions made by female managers are not always valued by senior male management. Many of the interviewees believed that their suggestions by female managers at meetings are more frequently dismissed or not heeded than those tendered by their male colleagues. One interviewee mentioned a case where her idea was rejected, only to be immediately accepted when a male colleague made a very similar suggestion at a later stage — as if other males assume authority was more inherent in a contribution from a fellow-male manager. Grant (1988) suggested that differences which female managers bring to organisations have, for the most part, been ignored, discounted, suppressed, or have not been valued. These differences resonated in the interviewees' claims that their contributions to collective management are frequently ignored. One of the interviewees summarised this by stating 'there is sometimes in the stereotypical image that if you are young and female that you have no brain':

> Because of my gender I had to fight hard for certain assignments. I had to fight hard for my first business development project — where I actually led the team as opposed to supporting the team. I am never given the high priority deals to do, but when I am, somebody else gets the credit. Recently I made a very important deal, the most important deal for the company here in Europe. We were very successful and I am extremely proud of the job I did, and yet the credit is not pointed in my direction. And this is definitely gender related. Men are given promotions and opportunities much more easily. There is no question about it. It is much harder for a woman. I am at the level now where the next promotion requires consensus from the top management team of the company, because it is all about whether you fit in the slot or not. There are very few women at my level, not to mention the next level up. But, I will make sure that I will get the next promotion. I *will* get there, even it will take a lot longer (Managing Director, Telephone Company).

Thirty-one of the fifty participants expressed that gender was a definite ongoing obstacle to their career progression, while another sixteen participants believed that their gender had created difficulties for them occasionally. Only three participants believed that gender was not a barrier, and one of these three participants believed that gender was an advantage for her career progression:

> Overall, my gender has been an advantage to me in my career. I have been very fortunate. I felt there was a real period of opportunity for me during the 1980s. The company was looking for female managers to promote. I was the third female ever at senior manager level in the company. So, it was probably easier for me at the beginning, because I was different and I stood out more. We now have 130,000 employees, but at my level there are only about twenty females. I am also very lucky that my husband has been so supportive. I find it interesting when I stop to think about these things because I don't think about being a woman, I just get on with it (Manager, Retailing Company).

Twenty-eight of the interviewees believed that gender was certainly an obstacle, particularly in the early years of their managerial careers:

> The hardest time of all for a woman to be taken seriously is in her twenties. If a woman is reasonably attractive, and most women in their twenties can make themselves presentable, she is seen as a woman first, and a professional second. When she is giving a presentation, for the first twenty minutes she is looked at because she is female, and is seen out of context. That is a terrific barrier. There are always slow-downs for women because of gender, for example, when women take time out to have a child, and unless they come back and prove themselves quickly they are never taken seriously, and they are considered part-time workers (Accountant Executive, Technology Company).

> At the beginning of my career I came up against obstacles because of my gender. When I asked for a salary increase it was difficult because I was a woman. When I was in my twenties, people did not like being told things by a woman. I always tried to look very professional and dressed accordingly, so that people would think of me as a lawyer rather than as a female. When I began working as a company lawyer I was trying to look twenty years older, even wearing my hair in a bun. Certainly, there are invisible barriers today, because if you look at senior management you will find very few women, and there is no real reason why women should not be there. When

I moved from France to England there were also some social barriers because of my gender, e.g., when I came to England I had a neighbour who was an American and she thought that I was a threat to her husband, and she told me so. It took me six months to overcome that, and then I wanted to invite them to my house, but I never did, because after that I never knew how to behave. I do not think that would happen if I had been a man (Legal Director, Manufacturing Company).

I have come up against barriers in my career, but that is just part of being a woman in management. I had an experience when I was in middle management where a chief executive sexually propositioned me two or three times. I made it very clear to him it would have to stop and at the time I was only about twenty-nine, so he began to let me out of meetings. But, there was no way that he was going to change, so I left the organisation. You are always a woman and they are always men, it is not balanced. The dialogue is not balanced, the power is not balanced. When I was interviewed for the position that I am now in, the chairman was a lovely man, very proper, from a Protestant public school, and he said 'we have never had a woman as an executive here at all. It is not that we don't want women, but it is just that women don't want these jobs, they want to be able to get home on time'. And then he said 'we have a lot of problems here in this company, and you are going to have a lot of responsibility and you are going to be working late into the night with male colleagues and you are the only woman, are you going to be able for that?' If I said what I thought at the time I would never have got the job (Director, Health Insurance Company).

The research results indicate that the respondents believed that they had to work harder at the beginning of their careers in order to prove that as women they were not there because of a quota system. Another interviewee noted that when a woman is promoted to top management she has to be 'very, very, good' and, because of bias based on gender difference, she has to be better than men to get to the top. The findings indicate that most gender barriers are covert as it is illegal to have explicit barriers, as one interviewee expressed it: 'most barriers are under the guise of something else'. The female interviewees believed that power was central to much of the discussions regarding gender in organisations. The participants believed that male managers reinforce their power in organisations by promoting people most similar to themselves. The interviewees believed that senior male managers frequently felt threatened by them, as all fifty managers had successfully reached senior managerial positions, many at a very young age, and while balancing home and family demands:

I am the only woman in senior management and the first woman at this level, and being the first woman is probably the most remarkable part of this. So when I arrived, I joined what was a very small and under-developed management team of guys who were directors. The whole environment had traditionally been male. It was not only difficult to break into this male domain, it was murder! I was not prepared for it in this country, because I had fought so many battles mostly at home in Britain, but I thought that internationally we might have made a lot of progress and that we had achieved acceptance, whereby a woman would be given the support that she would expect once she was recruited. I have found the situation totally otherwise. When I came here first, there was abusive language used about me and in front of me, and for the first year two of the directors developed a strategy of interrupting my work and undermining anything I said, or turning down whatever proposals I put forward . I came here with a superb track record, but they expected a man to be appointed to this position. They were additionally threatened by a woman because they had never had a woman before, so I realised that a lot of their behaviour was based on fear (Manager, Standardisation Organisation).

I worked in Portugal for a year where I had a lot of trouble working with men. For women it is very difficult to work in Portugal. It is very difficult for Portuguese men having a woman telling them what to do. I was educated a Catholic and so were those Portuguese men, whose Catholic education supported the tradition of women having to submit to men. It was very difficult, therefore, for men who were educated in this way to accept a woman boss. The reason I first went was that I was divorced at that time, so I had no husband or children to worry about. I was chosen because of that. Working with Portuguese men at the head of the bank was not easy. They just could not accept that women had their own ideas and that I was able to defend my ideas. They asked to have a woman in the position because they thought that a woman would say yes to everything. I think that men are driven more by power for themselves and I think that women in general look at the broader picture while men look more at their own interests (Bank Manager).

At the moment, I am a production manager in the pharmaceutical industry and this is a very unusual job for a woman. I am unaware of any other female production manager in any of the countries we operate in. It is tough for women in industry and there are not many women working in the production area of industry. I have worked in Germany, I have worked in the States, I have worked in Switzerland and I have worked in start-up jobs in Puerto Rico, Mexico, Brazil and of course here in Ireland, and I can honestly say the most prejudice that I found was in the States. But, it is couched there, they have their regulatory quota of what personnel mix they have to have. They have to have women and blacks and minority groups in various managerial positions, but I would have been a lot more aware of prejudice there than in any of the other countries. I was a bad statistic for them, I was a woman. In the field that I have chosen they found it particularly difficult to accept a woman. They certainly did not expect women to reach senior positions. I was more conscious of being a woman in the States than in any other country I worked in. People said thing like: 'What? — a woman in production?' My biggest triumph was when I was promoted in the States, because there was very much that anti-women culture there, in fact it was very, very strong there. I was promoted on my ability and I would say that the feeling was that they knew I was ambitious and they knew that I wouldn't stay if I had not been promoted, and they knew that I knew I was capable of doing the job (Production Manager, Pharmaceutical Company).

I have twenty years experience of working in the United States and it is clear that different generations exhibit different behaviours towards women in management. While gender discrimination is not overt, it is apparent that women always meet resistance. On a logical level you are not sure what the reasons are, but there are underlying cultural feelings that the resistance is because I am a woman. What has repeatedly happened in my case is that when I am sitting around a table with all males, and my European boss is there, and he does not like women being in senior positions, he will not say my name or even look at me, or ask me to produce anything. He will ask a male colleague of mine, who is less capable, to draw information from me to produce something, so my work is repeatedly plagiarised. So, really, my gender is my problem. I believe this man feels threatened by me because I know I am competent and capable of executing my work, and there is very little that shakes me in that sense (European Technical Support Manager, Computer Company).

The interviewees believed that they are still judged on the male model of career development regarding the appropriateness or their fit in organisations. They are assessed overtly or covertly on the male model with respect to selection, promotion, and career development. They suggested that despite European Union legislation on sex discrimination and equal opportunities, in recent years, there is little evidence that much has improved. The interviewees believed that they do not lack personal skills, experience or educational qualifications, but they are not yet given equal opportunities in their organisations:

In our organisation we have about 7,000 employees and I am the only female at my level. The biggest problem is that there are double standards still in place for evaluating and promoting. In most cases the person at the top, usually the man, needs to establish the culture and the standards that are acceptable. There is no question that there is a dual standard in place. Men are much more easily forgiven for mistakes, and women are expected to achieve far more than their male counterparts. I am a Stanford MBA graduate with fifteen years. Ten years ago we had a reunion, where a woman in my class reported that she established her own market research business. She put together a survey which asked all kinds of funny questions, like 'How grey is your hair since graduation?', and so on. It also asked 'What was your annual earnings, including bonuses? and 'What is your title'. The average earnings of the women were 40 per cent less than the men; this is Stanford MBAs! The average earnings for women was $100,000 and it was $140,000 for the men. It was that kind of a staggering gap. Achievements were almost directly correlated to title: women were managers and a few of us were directors, whereas the men were directors and a few were vice-presidents and CEOs. A couple of years later they did the same survey and got the same results. It is staggering (Managing Director, Telephone Company).

The interviewees suggested, from their experiences during the past twenty years, that the promotion of females to senior international managerial positions has grown at a very slow rate. Many of the interviewees considered themselves to be unusual in reaching senior management positions and particularly in pursuing international careers. They perceived that the barriers to women in management appear to be strong internationally. They believed that embedded in all cultures are traditions, practices, and views that impede women's economic equality and, instead, reinforce patriarchal systems and male operating procedures. Sixteen interviewees considered that gender is still a disadvantage to them, even in countries which are popularly portrayed as being more enlightened:

Sweden is one of the countries where equality of men and women is widely supposed to be highly developed, but of course equality is not there at all. I worked in a big international company there, where I was the only woman belonging to the board of directors, and when I left there was a man appointed again. In Sweden, especially in the big international companies, there is no equality at all. They have very, very few women managers and I found this difficult at board meetings because I don't accept the behaviour and structure that men have created (Director, European Commission).

Many of the interviewees believed that, because of the gender disadvantages they experienced, they often worked much harder and gained personal satisfaction in overcoming these obstacles during their international assignments:

> When I got to Japan there was only one woman in management in the whole company, and she was an international assignee from Scotland. It was a very, very difficult environment to work in. You had to adopt a completely different approach to management. That is not to say that you can't achieve. You can achieve, but you have got to go about achieving in a completely different way to the way that you would here in England. And you have an isolation factor, as firstly you have a language barrier, secondly the culture, and then, thirdly, being a woman. If you were male you would go in with a totally different air of respect. You gain respect simply because of gender in Japan, so it means that you have to work twice as hard. I saw it as a personal challenge and the reward for me was great, but you go through pain, but the reward at the end was great (International Assignment and Repatriation Manager, Telecommunications Company).

> The attitude of men in the business world was a big obstacle for me because it made me lack confidence in myself. Because of my gender it is much more difficult to establish working relationships with people whom you can share things with. As a woman I am not part of the game or part of the gang. I always had to work harder and this is difficult because it requires more energy (Human Resources Manager, Financial Services Company).

The research indicates that the interviewees believed that changing many male managers' negative attitudes towards female managers will take a long time. Forty-six of the interviewees stated that they experienced negative male attitudes towards them, but suggested that there will always be attitudinal barriers when people are in a minority. In conclusion, the findings report that senior female managers perceived gender difference to be an obstacle to their career progression. While female managers have the educational, technical and personal skills to achieve success in their domestic organisations and internationally, they were promoted to senior managerial positions, but in much smaller numbers than their male colleagues. Despite the difficulties discussed above, pertaining to their gender, it is clear from all fifty managers that their determination and commitment ensured that they successfully overcame many of these barriers and succeeded in their international assignments. A commonly shared sentiment of the fifty interviewees reflects the following finding of McGee-Calvert and Ramsey (1992, p. 82): 'until we admit to the fact that most organisations, as they currently exist, are seriously flawed, the glass ceiling will remain firmly in place, while being polished assiduously by those above it'.

5 A Model and Propositions for the Female International Managerial Career Move

The overall purpose of this research was to increase understanding of the international career move made by *senior* female managers in a European context. More specifically, the empirical research aimed to gather women's perceptions of the costs and benefits, difficulties and satisfactions involved in their own experiences or choices with respect to an international career and family in order to develop a comprehensive model of the senior female international career move.

The grounded theory approach adopted in this research offers a way of attending in detail to the large amounts of qualitative data collected, in order to systematically develop theories about the phenomena observed. This approach allows the discovery of theory from data, from which a number of propositions emerged concerning the relationships between a number of key determinants of the senior female international career move. The propositions are based on the perceptions of the fifty interviewees and relate to circumstances surrounding each of the three phases of the senior female international managerial career move. These propositions which can henceforth be tested are aimed at generating further research in the field of women in international management.

This new research contributes to the primary research domain of international human resource management literature — an area which has given very little attention to women as expatriates in Europe. An explanation for the scarcity of research in this field might be attributable to (i) the lack of appropriate theoretical structures, as a field of research, and (ii) the lack of a universal model of human resource management.

A theoretical model of the senior female international career move, which was developed from the interviews, provides an understanding of the career moves made by senior female international managers in Europe. The model details the expatriation process and highlights the influencing factors, many of which are barriers, at each of three phases in the senior female international career move. The model of the senior female international career move presented in this chapter has three constituent elements:

- Phase One, circumstances antecedent to expatriation
- Phase Two, circumstances during expatriation
- Phase Three, post-expatriation circumstances.

5.1   A Model of the Senior Female International Career Move

It is evident from the research that the female international manager has to overcome far more obstacles than her male counterpart has to contend with. The interview data indicates that the three stages of the international career move differ for male and female managers. The findings confirm that, in all three stages, the persistent stereotypical characteristics of a successful international manager are those characteristics which are typically associated with male management. Organisational assumptions and policies regarding the suitability of an individual as an international manager are based on societal assumptions about men and women. Beliefs, such as, that successful managers must prove their worth by their early thirties, that career breaks to care for family members indicate a lack of organisational commitment, and that being the last person to leave at night demonstrates organisational commitment.   The participants believed that the view generally held by home-country managers — that typically male characteristics are necessary for effective management — means that management itself is typically equated with masculinity. Home-country male managers perceive women as being different and not like themselves, so they tend not to select women for international positions. The findings suggest that female managers would have to be much more determined than men if they want international managerial positions, and must be prepared to ask for these positions because females are rarely offered such opportunities. In particular, senior home-country male managers believe that entry into a new job requires total involvement and longer than usual hours of work, therefore, the married expatriate manager is likely to be even less available to her family than when working in her home organisation.

It is apparent from the managers that the wishes and desires of female managers to partake in international managerial positions are equal to those of male managers. The career paths of female managers, however, are still compared with those of their male counterparts, despite women in dual-career marriages inevitably having to face more difficulties when partaking in overseas positions. Home-country senior management may assume that because of these barriers women may not want to partake in international managerial positions. An analysis of the views gathered from participating managers suggests that these obstacles can be subdivided into three distinct stages, thus contributing to the development of a model of the senior female international managerial career move.

Figure 5.1
Three-Phase Model of the Senior Female International Managerial Career Move

PHASE 1: CIRCUMSTANCES ANTECEDENT TO EXPATRIATION ASSIGNMENT

STAGE 1: NECESSITY OF PRIOR SENIOR MANAGERIAL CAREER EXPERIENCE IN HOME ORGANISATION

⇒

STAGE 2: DECISION TO APPLY FOR INTERNATIONAL CAREER MOVE

| Glass ceiling | Exclusion from networks | High visibility | Test cases for future female managers | Stress resulting from conflicting managerial styles | Gender identity | Lack of female career path | Mentoring relationships can contribute to success |

⇒

STAGE 3: PREPARATION

Necessity for personal life to be in order

| Limited provision of organisational training | Little or no help with dual-career or trailing spouse issues | Decision to go with partner: additional difficulty of *male* trailing spouse | Decision to go alone: personal relationships suffer |

⇒

PHASE 2: CIRCUMSTANCES DURING EXPATRIATION

| Additional home vs. work conflicts | No support for dual-career issues | Longer adjustment period | Uncertainty regarding re-entry | Inflexible organisational policies, particularly at early stages | Tokenism, isolation, exclusion | Test cases for future women managers | Lack of networks | Stress from conflicting managerial styles |

⇒

PHASE 3: POST-EXPATRIATION CIRCUMSTANCES

| Pioneering role causes difficulties for reintegration | Missed promotional opportunities due to lack of networks | Role models for future managers | Mentoring role |

The data from the interviews can be structured in outline using the three phases of the senior female international managerial career-move model as follows:

Phase 1: Antecedent Circumstances Of Expatriation

The model in Figure 5.1 helps to illustrate how the circumstances which surround each of the three phases of the international move affect the senior female international manager. The first phase of the model of the senior female international career move can be further divided into three stages, based on the perceptions of the participants. These stages are: (i) the requirement to have senior managerial career experience in one's home organisation; (ii) the decision to apply for an international career move; and (iii) the preparation for the international career move.

Phase 1, Stage 1: Necessity of Prior Senior Managerial Experience in Home-Country Organisation

The research suggests that during phase one, i.e., prior to the international career move, female managers face far more difficulties than their male counterparts. The interviewees perceived that there were more difficulties for them during this phase than during the other two phases. First, the findings suggest that female managers tend to require senior managerial career experience in their home countries before being considered for an international career move, as female managers may be perceived to be a greater risk than their male counterparts for their companies while abroad. The interviewees believed that home-country senior managers may be prepared to risk sending junior male managers abroad, but from the experiences of the interviewees, female managers need to 'first prove themselves in their home organisations'. The research establishes that many covert and overt barriers still prevent female managers from progressing to senior management. The interviewees believed that, from their experiences, these barriers are gender related, as male managers who were less educated and less qualified than themselves were promoted to senior management positions in their organisations.

The interviewees perceived that gaining the necessary senior managerial experience in their home organisations was the most difficult of all stages, since many overt and covert barriers still prevent female managers from breaking through the glass ceiling in their home organisations. The participants perceived that it appears easy for women to gain employment at the lower levels of the organisation, but it can prove very difficult for them to reach upper, middle, and senior management positions.   Research conducted in North American by Adler similarly suggested that corporate barriers to women, especially to women entering top management, persist (Adler, 1986-1987, p. 23).

The findings in this study established that, despite these additional obstacles, female managers are capable of reaching senior managerial positions, but that in comparison with their male colleagues they often have to make decisions about the importance of their careers relative to their personal lives.   The interview participants believed that these gender obstacles contribute to the glass ceiling which still exists in Europe, and that it is extremely difficult, though possible, to break through the glass ceiling, but unlike their male counterparts, it is not yet the norm for female managers to 'have it all', that is, to have a successful career, marriage and children. Therefore,

> Proposition 1:   Female managers require senior managerial career experience in their home organisations before being considered for an international career move.

Phase 1, Stage 2: The Decision to Apply for an International Career Move

The second stage of phase one of the model, based on the interview data, suggests that the next element is a decision to apply for an international career move.   The model indicates that, after gaining the necessary managerial experience in their home organisations, the fifty interviewees decided to apply for international career moves. The research suggests that when female managers decide to apply for an international career move they again face far more obstacles than those of their male counterparts. The interviewees believed that there is still a resistance to women's growing involvement in a 'man's world'. The interviewees further believed that the reluctance of home-country male managers to send female managers on international assignments illustrates how female managers may be systematically excluded from these career options because of sex biases and not because of their managerial abilities.

The interviewees believed that female managers are offered international assignments 'only in rare circumstances'. The interviewees perceived that this finding contrasts with the career experiences of their male counterparts for whom offers of international assignments are made. All thirty-one married interviewees reported difficulties in persuading home-country senior managers that they would be available for international assignments. These managers experienced that home-country top managers were reluctant to appoint females to *senior* positions internationally.

Scullion (1992, p. 65) suggested that 'the lack of willingness to recruit and develop women as international managers is worrying as recent research suggests that, in many ways, women are well suited to international management'. All fifty participants in this study believed that they were as interested and as suited as their male counterparts in pursuing an international managerial career. The various obstacles which the interviewees experienced at this stage of their careers are detailed below.

The Glass Ceiling

After deciding to apply for their international career moves the interviewees perceived that the covert barriers of tokenism, exclusion, and isolation, which contribute to the glass ceiling, are still very prevalent at this stage of their careers. The interviewees suggested that because female managers are frequently the sole female in an otherwise all-male environment, they face increased stereotyping, visibility, and performance pressure. The findings suggest that the sex labelling of occupations which involves the expectation that an occupation will and ought to be filled by one sex rather than the other is also problematic for female managers. The paucity of women in executive roles and the lack of visible role models reconfirms the traditional view and keeps sex labelling intact. Izraeli et al. (1980) similarly suggested that once an occupation acquires a sex label, each sex tends to self-select itself as an 'appropriate' candidate, thus precipitating selection for particular jobs. There is, for example, a strong expectation that managers are men and nurses are women. Consequently, women are not even considered for promotion to top positions in complex organisations. According to the International Labour Office, about half the world's workers are in sex-stereotyped occupations. Men still dominate the technical and managerial tasks, while women are concentrated mainly in caring and nurturing occupations and support roles (The Economist, 1998). The interviewees suggested that organisations may choose to either address or ignore these problems — by ignoring them, however, the interviewees believed that organisations lose valuable managerial talent. Thus,

> Proposition 2: Female managers who have gained senior managerial experience in their home organisations are likely to experience the effects of the glass ceiling again when applying for international career moves.

Networking

The interviewees believed that the exclusion of female managers from formal and informal networks compounds professional isolation, restricting the availability of peer support, which in turn benefits the promotional prospects of their male colleagues. The interviewees believed that women experience additional difficulties when they are excluded from 'old boy networks'. The respondents believed that networks are useful at all three stages of the international career move. The managers, however, stated that women frequently found themselves between two networks: a women's network which provided social support and a male-dominated network which provided assistance in career progression. The respondents also believed that networking relationships in international management are even more important in the absence of family and friends. The interviewees perceived that their careers should have benefited from the support they would have received from peers — particularly in the absence of mentors — if they had been better integrated in organisational networks. The research suggests that in addition to providing the much needed professional support for the international move, networking provides many other advantages, such as psychological support, during all stages of the female career. The interviewees added that exclusively male networks can nurture negative male attitudes towards female managers, thus continuing to promote male managers as the dominant power holders in organisations. Therefore,

> Proposition 3: Female managers who are members of influential networks are likely to be more successful in gaining international assignments.

High Visibility and Test Cases for Future Female Managers

The respondents suggested that another source of stress for them is their high visibility in a largely male environment which focuses inordinate attention, including critical attention, on female managers. This is a burden which can provide additional strain for female managers. The interviewees believed that male managers do not experience such stress, as males generally belong to the majority group in organisations. The interviewees further believed that a high percentage of one gender in a job category leads to the expectation that people in that job should behave in a manner consistent with the gender role of the dominant number of that group, which can cause further stress for the minority members. Similarly, Powell (1993) suggested that female managers may enact a 'masculine' role to lessen the apparent differences between token women managers and men managers, as women in this situation may conform to their male colleagues' style of management in order to reduce their gender visibility.

The interviewees also perceived that being considered test cases for future international managerial women adds a burden to the development of the personal potential of female managers. The managers reported 'feeling responsible for representing all female managers', a strain which they believed their male counterparts did not experience. As only three per cent of female managers move internationally, the participants believed that their token positions increases their isolation and that their high visibility intensifies their performance pressures. Thus,

> Proposition 4: For pioneering female managers, being highly visible and being considered 'test cases' increases performance pressure.

Managerial Styles

The interviewees perceived that a further source of stress which female managers experience results from alternating between feminine managerial styles and efforts to adopt the more readily accepted male styles of management. Some of the managers believe that because of a sense of alienation arising from working in a masculine environment, they have to behave in an entirely 'unnatural' way in order to succeed, and this means adopting characteristics of male colleagues. The interviewees believed that if women choose to adopt the masculine role or the traditional female 'mother' role, there are problems associated with either role. Many of the interviewees believed that the persistent stereotypical attitude from male senior managers caused problems for them regarding their choice of managerial style, particularly at the earlier stages of their career advancement,. The managers suggested that organisations should move away from their dependence on gender as a means of classifying people, and develop a working environment where everyone is free to be themselves.

The interviewees also stated that the managerial style which they had adopted in their home organisations is sometimes not acceptable in their host organisations, and this was another source of apprehension for them. The thirty-nine interviewees who had adopted individual styles of management perceived that this was a contributory factor in helping them to break through the glass ceiling. These managers suggested that they combined the best of both male and female managerial traits to develop a style with which they felt most comfortable. The managers also suggested that the experience they gained from international assignments helped them to change from their original male style of management. The interviewees noted that this style evolved over time as they became more confident. Therefore,

> Proposition 5: Female managers who adopt individualistic styles of management are more likely to have successful managerial careers.

The Impact of Gender

It is clear that the comparative number of females in senior management positions remains very low, and in particular the comparative number of female international managers remains even lower, at approximately only three per cent. The research results indicate that gender is a major barrier to the progression of female managers to senior management positions while in their home countries, which in turn affects their prospects for senior international management appointments. A large majority, ninety-four per cent, of the participants stated that gender bias was a barrier for them at a number of times in their career progression. The participants suggested that gender bias was evident in the selection methods used by organisations when they initially attempted to gain entry, and gender bias still continued when they moved through the hierarchy of the organisation.

Forty-six of the interviewees believed that gender was their main obstacle to obtaining international managerial assignments. These interviewees spoke of having to convince many male home-country senior managers of their willingness and desire to participate in international career moves. The findings indicate that the interviewees experienced greater gender difficulties in traditional industry sectors. The sentiments of the interviewees concur with Fisher's (1987) research which suggested that newer industries, such as computer firms, are not in existence long enough to have developed a view that equates manager with male, and these industries tend to rely on ability rather than gender for progression to senior management. The findings establish that, even though gender was a barrier in all of the countries which the participants worked in, the participants believed that they had to overcome greater gender barriers in their home organisations to reach senior management positions before partaking in international management. Thirteen of the participants quoted examples of less qualified and less experienced male colleagues achieving considerably faster promotions. The interviewees believed that, in most countries, and as Schein (1989) suggested, to think manager is to think male. The interviewees also perceived that female managers have to strive harder than their male colleagues to prove their worth and have an ongoing burden of managing their gender identity in the male-dominated environment of organisational management. The findings suggest that the most significant barrier to women in management is the unnecessary differentiation based on gender and the male bias against this differentiation. Thus,

Proposition 6: Gender will negatively affect the opportunities of female managers in obtaining international career moves.

Female Career Planning

The research results indicate that the image of the successful manager as a male predominates throughout Europe. This is based on theories of the life cycle which take the lives of men as their model. The interviewees, therefore, suggested that when female managers are measured against the male norm, any difference in career development is perceived as a deficiency since career theories are largely based on male models. The participants suggested that there are little or no differences between the abilities, education and motivations of managerial men and women, but competing home and family demands mean that career development for women is different from career development for men.

The twenty-six interviewees with children stated that the traditional male linear model of career progression, which does not cater for the option of childbearing and child rearing created extra problems for them. These interviewees found difficulties in convincing home-country senior managers that they are capable of balancing their managerial careers with motherhood. The interviewees stated that they have often been referred to as 'part-time workers' by male senior managers. These interviewees also perceived that in the organisations in which they are employed managerial commitment is still measured by 'being in the office first in the morning, and last to leave in the evening'. The interviewees suggested that as females generally assume greater responsibility for home and family commitments, organisational norms still favour the male lifestyle. Thus,

> Proposition 7:   Use of the traditional male linear career model by organisations will negatively impinge on the career prospects of female managers

Mentors

From the model it is apparent that mentoring relationships developed in home-country organisations can contribute to the success of the female international career. Given the glass ceiling and the current male-dominated composition of most organisations, the forty respondents who had experience of mentors believed that their career successes could be attributed in part to their mentors. This finding suggests that females who develop mentoring relationships should have better promotional prospects than those who do not. Mentors can increase the self-confidence of protégées by counteracting the effects of negative stereotypical sex-role socialisation in organisations, which can otherwise lead female managers to doubt their own abilities. Mentors were recognised by the respondents as being particularly beneficial at the early stages of career development, for providing challenging assignments, personal support, and friendship. Mentors were also perceived as being instrumental in helping women to overcome gender-related obstacles in organisations. The interviewees stated that having a mentor in their home organisations, while on an international assignment, is beneficial in terms of receiving social support and providing information on repatriation assignments. Because of the scarcity of senior female managers as sources of mentoring support, organisations might develop more female mentors at middle management level, thus reducing the burden placed upon the few senior managers. Based on the interview findings, this increase in the availability of mentors should develop the career prospects of more women managers. None of the ten managers who now provide mentoring support to junior managers reported any difficulties with their roles. These ten managers believed that mentoring relationships may be most effective for junior female managers at early career stages where, in addition to the general mentoring support they provided, they also acted as role models. This finding contrasts with Bowers's (1984) research which suggested that female executives are discouraged from becoming mentors to others in organisations because of non-supportive environments and time pressures. Thus,

> Proposition 8: Female managers with mentors in their home organisations are more likely to have successful international careers than those without mentors.

Phase 1, Stage 3: Preparation for the International Career Move

The final stage before going on an international assignment, i.e., the preparation stage, was considered by the participants to be a crucial stage for the success or failure of the assignment. The preparatory stage of the international career move, was considered by respondents to be often 'haphazard and ill-planned' and overlooked by many organisations. The interviewees pointed out that there is often a very short interval between the announcement of the international transfer and the actual move. The various obstacles which surround this stage of the international career move are detailed below.

Organisational Training

The interviewees reported that organisational training was generally very limited, superficial, or non-existent. The findings indicate that only ten per cent of the participants received any form of training or formal preparation for the international assignment, a figure which is significantly lower than for similar training provided for male expatriates. Previous research studies were critical of the lack of training for male expatriates, as the studies established that, on average, only twenty-five per cent of aspirant expatriates received preparatory training (Baumgarten, 1995; Borg and Harzing, 1995). Of the cases where training was provided for male expatriates, twenty per cent included partners on the training programme. In contrast, however, despite the acknowledged additional difficulties when the trailing spouse is male, none of the ten per cent of participants who received training had their partners included on the programmes. The respondents perceived that each country presents the international manager, and the international manager's family, with a unique set of adjustment problems, even when transferring to countries which are perceived to be similar to their home countries. Previous research studies have tended to concentrate on international managers who have moved to cultures very different from their home country. The research confirms that the more divergent an international assignment and location are from the home country, the greater is the potential for experiencing culture shock. The respondents also asserted that pre-departure training is even more important for female international managers because of their largely pioneering roles. Therefore,

> Proposition 9: Organisations that prepare in a planned and rigorous manner for the career moves of their international female managers will improve the likelihood of success of these moves.

Trailing Spouses and Dual Careers

The managers also reported that female managers are further disadvantaged because of the additional problems associated with male trailing spouses. Twenty-eight couples moved internationally to facilitate the careers of the female partner. These interviewees perceived that their male partners experienced many more difficulties in adjusting to the move than they anticipated. The interviewees also suggested that their spouses were looked upon as 'oddities' in their new neighbourhoods, and they believed that it was not yet socially acceptable for males to be 'house husbands'. The interviewees noted that their spouses were often excluded from organisational functions which had been arranged for (female) trailing spouses. The interviewees perceived that there was little or no organisational help available with dual-career or trailing-spouse concerns. The interviewees believed that the expatriate community and informal groups, such as the STUDS group in Brussels, were important for providing social networks and support for male trailing spouses.

The thirty-one married interviewees are all married to professional partners, therefore a number of possible solutions — such as commuter marriages, the male partner putting his career on hold, or retiring — had to be availed of in order to facilitate the international career move. These interviewees noted that a major obstacle for them was convincing many home-country male managers of their availability for international careers. All the interviewees, however, asserted that it was very important for the success of the move to have the dual-career professional issues agreed on for both partners before applying for an international career move. The interviewees also suggested that many home-country male managers need to realise that female managers who are part of a dual-career couple actively want to be considered for international management positions. Thus,

> Proposition 10: Married female managers who move internationally with their partners are likely to experience additional stress because of the difficulties associated with having a male trailing spouse.

Necessity for Personal Life to be in Order

The model highlights that for managers it is essential to have their personal lives in order before going abroad. Previous research with male expatriates has indicated that the main cause of expatriate failures is the inability of spouses to adapt to their new surroundings (Scullion, 1993; Tung, 1982). As suggested above, the interviewees believed that because of the additional difficulties involved when the trailing spouse is male, female managers have to make extra efforts to ensure that their personal lives are in order before partaking in international management. The interviewees reported, from their experiences, that female managers tend to consider the position of their spouses to a greater extent than their male counterparts do, and that this in turn could help explain the success of the female international managerial assignment. Ensuring that one's personal life is in order, however, created additional difficulties for the married managers, as they are all married to professional spouses, and there was little or no organisational help for dual-career issues.

The interviewees perceived that home-country managers contend that marriage has a stabilising effect on male expatriates. They also perceived that, for female international managers, home-country managers contend that marriage increases the risk of the assignment failing due to the additional difficulties associated with the male trailing spouse. The interviewees predicted that because of an increasing number of females pursuing managerial careers, and the difficulties associated with male trailing spouses, the number of commuter marriages will increase. They also believed that as the prevalence of commuter marriage is a relatively recent phenomenon, few senior home-country managers may be directly acquainted with couples having such an arrangement, and therefore may view such an arrangement as a threat to the longevity prospects of an assignment. The interviewees believed that personal relationships of unmarried female managers tend to suffer, particularly because of the difficulties involved in maintaining long-distance relationships, as many of their partners perceive that it is not the norm for female managers to move internationally. Unmarried female managers also experienced loneliness and isolation due to societal and organisational norms, norms which are not applicable to their male counterparts. Thus,

> Proposition 11:   Spousal satisfaction with female international managers' career moves will significantly affect the success of expatriation.

> Proposition 12: Unmarried female managers who move internationally without their partners are likely to experience difficulties in maintaining personal relationships while abroad.

For most organisations, the women expatriates were 'firsts'. This meant that neither the women nor the companies had the benefit of role models or established patterns. Despite these additional difficulties, however, both married and single female managers have expressed a willingness to relocate internationally. Difficulties regarding their marital status, however, still persist in their home countries, as senior managers continue to be sceptical about a woman's ability to function effectively in a foreign country. As seen from the successes of the fifty interviewees, women have proved that they can be successful in other national cultures, regardless of their marital status. Home-country senior managers should, therefore, reconsider their traditional bias of relying only on male international managers.

Figure 5.2

Phase One of Model of the Senior Female International Managerial Career Move

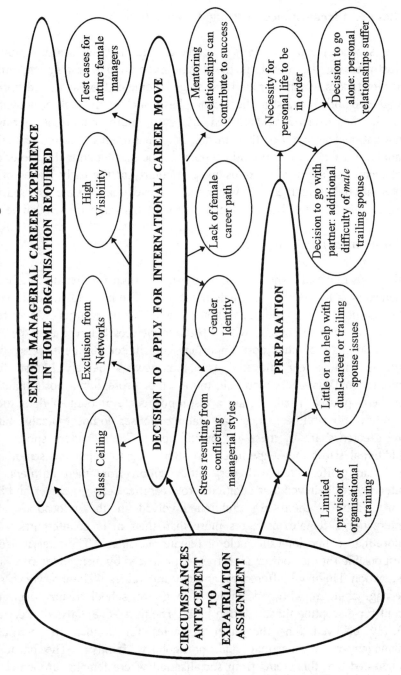

Phase 2: Circumstances During Expatriation

The second phase of the senior female international career move, as illustrated by the model, is the actual international assignment, and the circumstances which surround this stage. Some of the barriers identified in stage one above persist in the second phase, such as the lack of networking, which the research established as even more important during an international assignment than in domestic management, when networks of family and friends can provide support. The participants also experienced tokenism, isolation, and exclusion, particularly at the early stages of their international assignments — which they believed their male counterparts did not encounter. The obstacles which surround this stage are detailed below.

Home versus Work Conflicts

The research establishes that the adjustment time for female international managers is longer than for male managers. The participants believed that this is due to the additional home versus work conflict which female managers have to contend with. The interviewees believed that the family situation may be the most important contributor to the success of the international career move.   The interviewees perceived that female international managers who hold more senior professional posts than those of their spouses usually retain a disproportionate amount of domestic and family responsibilities, since male trailing spouses do not, typically, take up the greater share of these responsibilities.   The managers spoke of the additional stress they experienced in attempting to balance a senior career and family life, often with very little support from their partners.   The interviewees believed that additional role conflict between career and home, particularly if there are children involved in the relocation, affects international female managers more than their male counterparts — and more than either domestic male or female managers. The interviewees felt responsible for the conflict and stress experienced by their children regarding education, language differences, and cultural values. The interviewees with teenage children, who had developed long-term school friends, experienced guilt for disrupting those relationships. The thirty-one married interviewees firmly believed that the main obstacles for women in international management are marriage and, particularly, family.   The participants suggested that this stems from socialisation where females are expected to balance a number of roles simultaneously. The participants also suggested that they experienced additional stress, at the early stage of this phase, due to inflexible organisational policies. The fairly recent phenomenon of the male trailing spouse also caused additional difficulties as, at present, it is not the norm for the male partner to give priority to the female career. This difficulty was again compounded by the lack of support for dual-career issues from home-country organisations. Thus,

> Proposition 13: Role conflict between career and home will be greater for female international managers with children than for childless women.

Dual-Career Issues

As noted in the preparation stage, home-country organisations do not provide support to assist managers in coping with dual-career issues. Similarly, host-country organisations do not provide any support for dual-career concerns. Eighteen of the fifty interviewees were the main careerists, a situation which they believed was still 'very unusual' in all countries where they had worked. These interviewees also suggested that it is more difficult for the male partner to adjust to the secondary careerist role, as this role is still more socially acceptable for females. The managers believed that society judges men, more than women, by their career advancement and, by extension, when men become the secondary careerist this can be especially troublesome for many males as they can be understood to undertake a 'negative' career move.

The experiences of the divorced or separated interviewees suggest that another problem facing dual-career couples is when a woman chooses a more 'high flying' career. This can be interpreted as relative demotion for the partner's image, or as prioritising career over one's partner, and thus can lead to a destabilising of the former interpersonal balance or to an undermining of the partner's self image and confidence in the relationship. These non-traditional career women may also experience external pressures which make life choices difficult for them, as they receive little or no organisational or societal support.

The managers also believed that senior home-country managers show lack of understanding for the concerns of dual-career couples or how to deal with these concerns. In the past it was considered a personal matter and not of concern to the organisation. The interviewees believed that because of the lack of interest and concern shown in the management of dual-career issues this was a further contributory factor in explaining the scarcity of female international managers. Therefore,

> Proposition 14:   Female managers in dual-career relationships are likely to receive little organisational support for dual-career issues.

Adjustment Period

The participants believed that the adjustment period for female expatriates takes longer because of lack of networking and scarcity of female role models, together with stereotypical attitudes and social and cultural norms which still associate successful management with male characteristics. The participants suggested that their own particular international career moves were more difficult, as they did not have female role models to follow. As a result, these individuals were considered test cases for future female international managers. The interviewees perceived that these difficulties could be further reduced at this stage if there was a female career path that they could follow. The participants suggested that the managerial career is still based on a male linear model of progression, which they now considered to be out of date. The findings reveal that the average length of international assignments for the participants was three years, and if a female career plan existed, female managers would be able to include their international assignment at a time which would also suit their personal plans regarding childbearing and child rearing.

Additionally, if there is a trailing spouse and children involved, the female usually takes responsibility for settling them into their new environment, which inevitably places more strain on the female, and consequently increases the adjustment period. The participants, however, believed that expatriate males are solely focused on their new jobs, but because of the extra responsibilities typically assumed by females, women have to develop the capabilities of balancing home and work. The twenty-six interviewees with children also believed that female managers tend to take the responsibilities of ensuring that family members adjust to their new surroundings, as well as taking on the responsibilities of their own 'new high-powered assignment'.

The participants believed that feelings of isolation were compounded due to the lack of networks and lack of female role models, which consequently increased their adjustment period to their new surroundings. Because of the longer adjustment period, the interviewees believed that an overseas move should be at least three years in duration. Previous research by Adler (1988) indicated that North American female expatriate assignments, averaging two and a half years, were of shorter duration than those of their male counterparts. The findings from this research, however, indicate that female expatriate assignments were equal in length to their male counterparts, averaging three years. An explanation for these longer assignments might be that the managers occupied more senior positions, and consequently had more responsibilities and therefore required longer time to achieve their goals. Despite the additional difficulties associated with longer adjusting time, however, the managers believed that the overall female expatriation experience was very successful. The managers, therefore, suggested that home-country senior management could no longer afford to ignore female managers for international assignments. Thus,

---

Proposition 15: The lack of networks and lack of female role models are likely to increase the adjustment periods for female international managers.

Uncertainty of Re-entry

The managers suggested that the uncertainty surrounding re-entry is problematic for both male and female managers. The interviewees, however, perceived that as many female international managers are in a pioneering role, this increases their uncertainty regarding re-entry. The participants believed that examples of gender discrimination which they had experienced at the re-entry phase included lower salaries and fewer promotions than those of their male counterparts. The interviewees also expressed concern about the opportunities or lack of opportunities to get desirable assignments on their return.

Many of the repatriated interviewees returned to positions that did not utilise the skills and experiences they acquired overseas. Thirty-one of the thirty-two repatriated interviewees believed that they experienced a loss of status, loss of autonomy, and had to cope with major changes in their personal and professional lives when they returned to their home countries. These interviewees believed that planning for repatriation is a very important element in the international career move. The interviewees also believed that not enough attention is paid to long-range career planning when arranging international assignments. The participants also believed that home-country management did not always recognise the difficulties associated with re-entry. The managers believed that re-entry is often overlooked and their views echo those of Solomon (1995) who suggested that when expatriates return home they face an organisation that does not know or care what they have done for the past number of years. The managers suggested that preparation for re-entry to the home organisation should begin at least six months before the return date, and that re-entry should be seen as the final stage of the international career move. The interviewees further suggested that uncertainty could be reduced if re-entry was included as part of an overall career plan. Therefore,

> Proposition 16: Female international managers who know what their repatriation employment will be are more likely to be successful while abroad.

Inflexible Organisational Policies

The model, from the interview data, also suggests that organisations are too inflexible regarding the additional demands of balancing home and work, for example, while settling children into new schools, or on occasions when children are ill, or when child-minders are ill. The interviewees believed that they experienced the additional strains associated with inflexible organisational policies particularly during the early stages of relocation, and they also expressed that this affects females more than males. The twenty-six interviewees with children experienced high levels of career–family conflict because of the opposing pressures arising from these two concerns. These interviewees believed that female managers have to base their lifestyle decisions regarding career and children on factors that male managers have generally not had to consider, and consequently their career achievements have been limited by factors that generally have not impaired men's achievements.

The interviewees asserted that unless human resource management policies are re-examined and reassessed women will remain a small minority in international management. The sentiments of the interviewees resonate with the findings of Burrell and Hearn (1989), which suggested that human resource management practices primarily reflect the interests of the dominant group in the organisation, and that organisations generally have not succeeded in introducing training and development strategies that effectively meets the needs of women. The interviewees also believed that organisations should seek information about the individual requirements and career aspirations of women managers who may be interested in a career in international management. Thus,

> Proposition 17: Female international managers will experience additional stress associated with home and work conflict, particularly at the early stages of their international career, if their organisational policies are inflexible.

The remaining circumstances, as outlined in the model for this second stage of expatriation, are common to female managers both in their home-country and host-country organisations. The interviewees perceived that tokenism, isolation, and exclusion are often more pronounced for female international managers than for female *domestic* managers, due to even more male-dominated cultural and societal norms in many host countries.

As specified in the first phase of the international career move, most female international managers are treated as test cases by home-country managers, since they play a pioneering role in what was until recently an exclusively male pattern. Being test cases for future international female managers continues from the first stage into the second stage of the assignment, monitored by both home-country and host-country managers, especially as females are seen as test cases for other female managers more than males are for future male managers.

Networks, which are more available and accessible to male managers, help to substitute for the lack of family and friends while abroad. The managers believed that there are considerable benefits from informal and formal networking, particularly in an international context. Exclusion from organisational networks, however, compounds the isolation experienced by managers within the minority gender, which is usually female. This suggests that one of the most significant problems facing women seeking international careers can be found within the organisational culture. Some of the managers further reported that an additional burden was that of developing a managerial style to fit in with local cultural and societal norms, which is more difficult for women as they generally have to adopt a style to fit the tradition of male dominated management. Other participants noted that where they might have adopted a macho management style in their home organisations that this might be unacceptable in some host countries, also necessitating a change in their managerial behaviour when they moved abroad. Despite the additional difficulties experienced by female managers at this stage, the findings establish that female managers *do* want international careers, and in some cases marriage and children.

Figure 5.3

Phase Two of Model of the Senior Female International Managerial Career Move

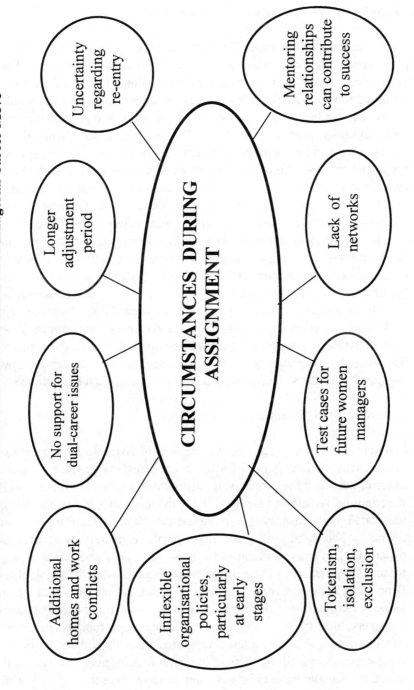

Phase 3: Post-Expatriation Circumstances

The third stage of the senior female international career move refers to the post-expatriation circumstances. The research establishes that the participants found many difficulties, both professional and personal, on returning to their home countries. Lack of networking was again highlighted as an obstacle by the participants at this stage, as the participants believed that networks provide means of 'keeping in touch' with the home organisation and help with promotional opportunities. The respondents also suggested that two important factors at this stage were the clarity of the repatriation process and the repatriation training received prior to returning to their home countries. The interviewees expressed that clearer repatriation policies would have a positive impact on work adjustment. The interviewees also perceived that training for international managers and their families for the re-entry process, and for any likely problems related to repatriation, should reduce the uncertainty normally associated with re-entry. Overall, the interviewees believed that three years was an appropriate length of time for an international career move. The interviewees believed that the difficulties experienced at this stage are frequently overlooked by home-country senior managers, as problems are not anticipated when returning to home-country organisations. The experiences of the respondents, however, suggest that repatriation can often be more stressful than expatriation.

Difficulties With Re-entry

Scullion (1994) suggested that the problem of ensuring an adequate supply of international managers is further exacerbated by growing resistance to international mobility which was attributable to several factors including uncertainties regarding re-entry. The managers believed that the difficulties associated with re-entry are more serious than home-country managers realise. The return of pioneering female managers with international experience can cause difficulties for home managers when redeploying them to suitable positions. Outgrowing home organisations is a risk shared by female and male expatriates. Missed promotional opportunities because of being overlooked is, however, a greater risk for female international managers, due to a scarcity of networking opportunities and mentoring relationships. The participants suggested that, in additional to technical competence acquired by both male and female managers in their host countries, females have to be more independent and self-sufficient in finding suitable employment on their return because of the lack of support available to them from networks and mentors. The interviewees believed that many repatriates report feelings of impatience with colleagues while they wait to be redeployed. Effective support systems and repatriation policies are particularly important for female expatriate managers, and yet there is very little empirical research specifically on the issues associated with the repatriation of female expatriate managers. Peltonen (1999) suggested that repatriation should be situated in the context of career development, and that an understanding of the organisational logic behind repatriation career outcomes should be helpful for designing human resource strategies which would be more sensitive to the structure and culture in which international careers evolve. Therefore,

> Proposition 18: Well structured repatriation policies and pre-return training for female international managers and their families will increase the likelihood of successful repatriation.

Role Models

As mentioned above, female managers are still in a pioneering role, and as they do not have female role models or established female career paths to follow, this further increases the uncertainties regarding re-entry to their home organisations. The research establishes that, arising from their international careers, the participants who have re-entered their organisations are now considered role models for future female international managers. These managers are also providing mentoring relationships and thus encouraging younger female managers to take part in international careers.

All the participants perceived themselves to be successful international managers, and they predicted that the participation rate of female international managers will increase in future years. The interviewees believed that if they can show junior female managers that it is possible to combine a successful international career with family life, more female managers may be encouraged to apply for international career moves. The managers believed that role models should also help to develop informal communication channels, mutual credibility and respect, together with good-companionship and friendship for more junior female managers. The managers also believed that as role models they can also help with the provision of formal information, advice, influence, and power which are important for international career success. These managers further believed that role models are particularly relevant, given the difficulties of breaking into organisational networks and the lack of available female mentors. While the negative effects from the lack of mentors, networks, and role models for females in *domestic* managerial positions have been well documented, these areas have not, however, been the subject of much research attention for females in *international* management. Thus,

> Proposition 19: Female managers who have female international role models to follow are more likely to be successful in their international careers.

Mentoring Benefits

Many potential protégée international managers are denied career-development support from fellow women mentors, because of the scarcity of women with senior international management experience. To redress this situation, organisations might introduce formal and informal mentoring strategies specifically designed to promote the participation of women managers in international management. As identified in the research, female managers can have different mentoring needs than those of men, and they are likely to be assisted in their career development in different ways by female colleagues than by male colleagues.

Managers with international experience bring advantages to other managers by establishing mentoring relationships which provide support for junior managers. The majority of respondents (forty out of fifty) attribute their success in part to mentoring relationships, which were established in their home organisations and which they maintained throughout their international careers. Ten of the interviewees reported that in their senior managerial positions they now attempted to help junior managers deal with barriers to advancement, and to provide psychosocial support and role modelling functions. The interviewees reported that they received a sense of satisfaction and fulfilment from fostering the development of junior managers.

Because of the severe shortage of female mentors, organisations urgently need to address the question of how to encourage female managers to take on mentoring roles. Organisations need to develop a pool of senior female mentors who can advise, support, and sponsor the new generation of female managers seeking to break into careers in international management. Therefore,

> Proposition 20: Repatriated senior female managers who provide mentoring relationships for junior managers are likely to increase the career successes of junior managers.

Finally, the research establishes that female managers are capable of succeeding internationally. The findings also show that many of the desired qualities for international management are common to males and females. Despite the difficulties highlighted throughout the research, the findings suggest that, overall, international management is a positive experience for female managers.

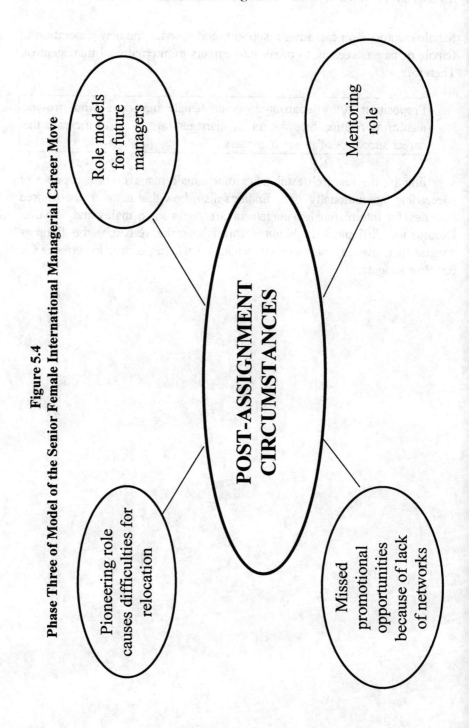

Figure 5.4
Phase Three of Model of the Senior Female International Managerial Career Move

Role models for future managers

Mentoring role

POST-ASSIGNMENT CIRCUMSTANCES

Pioneering role causes difficulties for relocation

Missed promotional opportunities because of lack of networks

5.2 Recommendations for Practice

The interviewees in this research suggested that because of their qualifications and ambitions, home-country senior management can no longer assume that the male career will have priority, and they predict that the likely trend is for more female managers to take part in international management. It is apparent, therefore, that organisations now need to develop policies to provide more flexibility for managers to relieve the additional strains of balancing home and work conflicts in an international setting.

It is clear from this research that, in addition to organisations developing flexible working policies, the inclusion in these policies of support issues for dual-career couples, and specifically addressing the needs of the spouse in these transfers, would benefit both dual-career couples and organisations. Home-country senior management should develop policies to assist dual-career couples, based on the three phases of the international career move outlined in the model. First, organisations should allow longer preparation time for the move in order to assist the trailing spouse, e.g., with visas and work permits. A pre-assignment trip should also be arranged to allow the trailing spouse to make employment contacts. The plan should also specify the duration of the assignment, and outline any assistance for the male partner to be provided by the organisation.

Second, during the overseas phase, as the trailing spouse needs to engage in activities which are meaningful to them, organisations might provide funds for further education of the partner, particularly where it is not permissible for him to work. The plan should also ensure that the female manager keeps in regular contact with the home organisation. This might be facilitated through mentoring and networks in order to make repatriation less stressful. Preparation for return to the home organisation should begin well in advance of the return date.

Third, the repatriation process, as confirmed by the findings, can often be problematic. It is clear that the manner in which home-country management chooses to deal with international managers *after* their return can define the success or failure of the assignment. This emphasises that long-range career planning is needed when making international arrangements for dual career couples.

A further perception by home-country senior management, highlighted by Berthoin-Antal and Izraeli (1993) and Adler (1988), revealed that female international managers are considered to be additional risks for their organisations. As the results of previous studies have shown, organisations can attempt to reduce risks for both personal safety and organisational involvement by limiting female expatriate manager's professional contacts to corporate personnel, by defining her assignment as temporary, and by not offering her the most senior position in the host country. The findings from the current research question these measures for reducing risk, particularly in countries which treat women in a manner similar to that in the home country, e.g., in North America and Europe, and suggest that these strategies may instead increase the organisational risks involved, as the managers may be restricted by such constraints. All fifty managers successfully occupied *senior* managerial positions in their host countries, seven of the participants held their respective company's number one position in the country, with the length of international postings being equivalent to those of their male counterparts. It is clear from this research, therefore, that organisations in Europe no longer need to employ these risk-reducing strategies for female managers and that senior international positions should now be offered to managers regardless of gender considerations.

The participants suggested that these traditional home-country perceptions are usually based on men's apprehensions about the possibility of female managers being more successful than male managers. The participants also suggested that many home-country senior male managers frequently feel threatened by female managers, and to reduce this threat they often promote people most similar to themselves (i.e., other males) to international management positions. This research suggests that organisations can no longer afford to ignore their female managers, especially in the area of international management where shortages of managers have been reported, because of misjudged perceptions such as these.

Given the many benefits provided by mentors, as outlined by the forty interviewees who had mentoring relationships, perhaps organisations should now consider formalising mentoring relationships in order to help more female managers to break through the glass ceiling and glass border. Ten of the interviewees are now acting as mentors in their organisations, mostly for younger female managers. They believed that as more women reach senior management positions, despite having less gross professional time than their male colleagues, due to family commitments, they will be able to provide the necessary support for other females, which in turn, could increase the number of female managers partaking in international management. The research results have indicated that mentors, role models, and networks can be powerful contributors to women in international management. The participants believed that as more female managers reach senior management positions, they will be prepared to act as mentors and role models and be in stronger positions to break into the old boy networks, all of which should encourage more females to partake in international management.

The research reveals that the stages of career development for female managers do not have the predictable phases that male life patterns tend to have. The participants confirmed that evaluating many life choices, for example, whether or not to have children, is more difficult and complex for female international managers. The participants believed that their careers would have benefited from a model of career development which acknowledged different life paths and which placed positive values on a variety of experiences, both inside and outside their organisations. The findings recommend that organisations develop career plans for male and female international managers, which would include: substantial training and preparation time before an individual assignment; a projection of the likely length of the international assignment; an outline of the responsibilities; regular contact and support from mentors and networks while abroad; preparation for personal repatriation; and preparation for job deployment after return. The participants believed that the re-entry stage is often overlooked by home-country senior management, and in some cases repatriation proves even more difficult than expatriation.

The managers stated that negative male attitudes, sexual harassment, and stereotypical attitudes — which associate successful management with males — were additional encumbrances to career advancement. The participants, from the varied industry sectors, believed that discrimination and prejudice against them solely on gender grounds affected their promotional prospects. Organisations should benefit from a wider cross-gender resource of international managers if efforts were made by them to reduce or eliminate these negative and dated attitudes, which in turn should enable female managers to achieve their full potential.

5.3   Agenda for Further Research

This research provides opportunities for further research with senior female international managers. As international management is relatively new for female managers, very little empirical research outside of North America has been conducted with this management sector. This research investigates some of the findings put forward in the international human resource management literature, and it empirically assesses these findings in a European context to add to the corpus of knowledge on the senior female international career move. The model presented is largely based on a number of propositions which might be tested in future research, while the findings can contribute to the literature field of international human resource management. The model focuses attention, in a structured manner, on the senior female international career move and invites new research on the topic. The model and propositions developed in this study provide research guidelines that should offer researchers a better understanding of the determinants of the senior female international career move. Arising from the interviews, a number of specific themes emerged, each of which can be further developed in future research.

The findings highlight the additional difficulties that dual-career couples have to overcome when international relocation is necessary — as it is rare that both partners are employed by the same organisation, and it would be very exceptional for such a couple to be offered geographically shared international assignments.   Dual-career appointments almost invariably have to cope with the outcome of one career having to suffer for the career advancement of the partner who receives the international reassignment. In addition to the propositions, outlined in this chapter, relating to dual-career couples and trailing spouses, future research might also investigate the decision-making practices used by both dual-career couples and home-country senior management in relation to international transfers. The findings indicate that home-country senior management should no longer assume that the male partner's career will maintain priority among couples, despite the additional obstacles that have to be overcome when the male partner adopts the role of trailing spouse. The failure of organisations to respond to dual-career issues results in costs, not only to the couple, but also to their organisations. The willingness of organisations to address dual-career issues may be important for achieving competitive advantage in the future. Future research, therefore, might investigate if organisations formulate policies to accommodate trailing spouses and if these policies influence the decision-making process used by dual-career couples. As indicated in the research findings, only one organisation was found to provide assistance for trailing spouses. Regarding the career development of individuals who are from dual-career couples and the attendant difficulties outlined above for dual-career couples, the question of whether relocation is really necessary and, if so, to what extent, needs to be addressed.

Alternatively, if dual-career couples are unable to reach a decision to relocate in the same geographical location, then further research should explore the advantages and disadvantages of commuter marriages from both the viewpoint of the couple and that of the organisation. The participants predicted that the proportion of commuter marriages is likely to increase among dual-career couples, as prior work and the findings of this research establish that females do want to participate in international management. Further research is needed to investigate: the arrangements for children if they are part of commuter marriages, the geographical distances between the couples, the time span between couples meeting, and the overall anticipated duration of the commuting arrangement of the marriage.

Further research might usefully focus on the trailing spouse phenomenon. Studies might investigate the implications of one partner putting his or her career on hold, as previous studies have generally concentrated on other difficulties experienced by the trailing spouse while abroad. Traditionally, the trailing spouse tended not to have a career and was female. Now, as more women move into management positions, it is increasingly likely that many male partners may have to put their careers on hold. Research might investigate the implications for both males and females who put their careers on hold. Questions arise regarding the financial, personal, and emotional costs experienced by the trailing spouse in an international move. Such research might also assess the overall advantages and disadvantages of putting a career on hold from the individual's perspective and from the perspective of the organisation. Adding to the findings of this research, new research on careers which are put on hold should contribute to a relatively new area in career-theory literature, as studies on international management careers have largely been based on the mainly linear progression of male managers' careers.

Arising from discussions with the fifty participants, and from previous research, other specific barriers which prevent female managers from partaking in international careers include the lack of mentors, lack of networking opportunities, and lack of female role models. These three areas merit further investigation. With regard to mentoring, for example, the extent of the use of mentoring in organisations outside the United States, and the advantages and disadvantages of same-gender and cross-gender mentoring might be assessed. The research findings in the mentoring literature, particularly on the gender mix of mentoring relationships, are inconclusive and further empirical investigation with female managers who had mentoring relationships should help to clarify this area. Finally, as proposition 8 suggests, further research might also investigate the impact of mentors in home organisations on the career successes of female international managers.

The participants also highlighted the benefits of formal and informal support networks for career advancement, particularly during their international assignment. Very little empirical research, however, has been conducted on networks. Future research might investigate the similarities and differences of male networks, female networks, and mixed gender networks. The research might also examine the entry barriers to these networks, and report on the personal and career benefits these groups provide. As suggested in proposition 3, future research might also usefully investigate the likelihood of more successful international careers for female managers who are members of influential networks.

The research findings highlight the lack of available role models for female international managers. The participants reported that, because of the relative scarcity of female international managers, they were more visible and yet more isolated than their male colleagues. The majority of interviewees were the first female senior managers to represent their organisations internationally. The participants believed that, if there had been previous female managers, they would have learned and benefited from their experiences. They also believed that it was necessary for them to adopt individualistic management styles, as in some instances the male style of management which they might have used in the home organisation was not deemed appropriate within the culture of the host organisation. A question which arises from this is: If more women reach senior management positions, would this lessen the widespread dominance of the male managerial style of management? This new inquiry might also be revisited.

As suggested in proposition 5, future research might examine the career successes of international female managers who adopt individualistic styles of management. Additionally, as suggested in proposition 19, further research might investigate the benefits that role models are deemed to provide in the career development of female managers, and this in tandem with empirical evidence from managers who already consider themselves to be role models for junior staff members should add new evidence in this important area.

Bibliography

Adler, N.J. (1994), 'Competitive Frontiers: Women Managing Across Borders', in N.J. Adler and D.N. Izraeli (eds), *Competitive Frontiers: Women Managers in a Global Economy*, Basil Blackwell, Oxford, pp. 22-40.

Adler, N.J. (1993a), 'Competitive Frontiers: Women Managers in the Triad', *International Studies of Management and Organization*, vol. 23, no. 2, pp. 3-23.

Adler, N.J. (1993b), 'Women Managers in a Global Economy', *HR Magazine*, (September), pp. 52-5.

Adler, N.J. (1991), *International Dimensions of Organizational Behavior*, PWS-Kent Publishing, Boston.

Adler, N.J. (1987), 'Pacific Basin Managers: A Gaijin, Not a Woman', *Human Resource Management*, vol. 26, no. 2, pp. 169-92.

Adler, N.J. (1986-7), 'Women in Management Worldwide', *International Studies of Management and Organization*, vol. 16, no. 3-4, pp. 3-32.

Adler, N.J. (1984c), 'Expecting International Success: Female Managers Overseas', *Columbia Journal of World Business*, vol. 19, no. 3, pp. 79-85.

Adler, N.J. and Ghadar, F. (1990), 'International Business Research for the Twenty First Century: Canada's New Research Agenda', in A. Rugman (ed), *Research in Global Strategic Management: A Canadian Perspective*, JAI Press, Greenwich, Conn., pp. 179-205.

Adler, N.J. and Izraeli, D.N. (eds) (1988), *Women in Management Worldwide*, M. E. Sharpe, New York.

Albert, F.J. (1989), *Les Ressources Humanies, Atout Stratégique*, Editions L'harmattan, Paris, p. 75.

Albertsen, J. and Christensen, B. (1993), 'Women in Business and Management: Denmark', in M.J. Davidson and C.L. Cooper (eds), *European Women in Business and Management*, Paul Chapman Publishing, London, pp. 58-78.

Alimo-Metcalfe, B. (1995), 'Leadership and Assessment', in *The Essence of Women in Management*, S. Vinnicombe and N.L. Colwill (eds), Prentice Hall, London, pp. 92-109.

Alimo-Metcalfe, B. (1994), 'Gender Bias in the Selection and Assessment of Women in Management', in M.J. Davidson and R.J. Burke (eds), *Women in Management: Current Research Issues*, Paul Chapman Publishing, London, pp. 93-109.

Alimo-Metcalfe, B. and Wedderburn-Tate, C. (1993), 'Women in Business and Management: the United Kingdom', in M.J. Davidson and C.L. Cooper (eds),. *European Women in Business and Management*, Paul Chapman, London, pp 16-42.

Aptheker, B. (1989), *Tapestries of Life: Women's Work, Women's Consciousness, and the Meaning of Daily Experience*, University of Massachusetts Press, Amherst.

Arnold, V. and Davidson M.J. (1990), 'Adopt a Mentor: The New Way Ahead for Women Managers?', *Women in Management Review and Abstracts*, vol. 5, no. 1, pp. 10-18.

Astin, H.S. (1985), 'The Meaning of Work in Women's Lives: A Sociopsychological Model of Career Choice and Work Behaviour', *The Counselling Psychologist*, vol. 12, pp. 117-26.

Australian Bureau of Statistics. (1994), *The Labour force Australia*, Cat. 6203.0, AGPS, Canberra.

Australian Bureau of Statistics. (1993), *Women in Australia*, Cat. 4113.0. AGPS, Canberra.

Barclay, L. (1982), 'Social Learning Theory: A Framework for Discrimination Research', *Academy of Management Review*, vol. 7, pp. 587-94.

Bardwick, J. (1980), 'The Seasons of a Woman's Life', in D. McGuigan (ed), *Women's Lives: New Theory, Research, and Policy*, University of Michigan Centre for Continuing Education of Women, Ann Arbor.

Barham, K. and Devine, M. (1990), *The Quest for the International Manager: A Survey of Global Human Resource Strategies*, Ashridge Management Guide/Economist Intelligence Unit, London.

Barham, K. and Rassam, C. (1989), *Shaping the Corporate Future*, Unwin Hyman, London.

Baumgarten, K. (1995), 'Training and Development of International Staff', in A.W. Harzing and J Van Ruysseveldt (eds), *International Human Resource Management*, Sage, London, pp. 205-28.

Berthoin-Antal, A. and Izraeli, D.N. (1993), 'A Global Comparison of Women in Management: Women Managers in their Homelands and as Expatriates', in E.A. Fagenson (ed), *Women in Management: Trends, Issues and Challenges in Managerial Diversity*, Sage, London, pp. 52-96.

Black, J.S. (1988), 'Work Role Transitions: A Study of American Expatriate Managers in Japan', *Journal of International Business Studies*, vol. 19, pp. 277-94.

Black, J., Stephens, G.K., and Rosener, J.B. (1992), 'Women in Management around the World: Some Glimpses', in U. Sekaran and F.T. Leong (eds), *Womanpower: Managing in Times of Demographic Turbulence*, Sage, London, pp. 223-21.

Borg, M. and Harzing, A.W. (1995), 'Composing an International Staff', in A.W. Harzing and J. Van Ruysseveldt (eds), *International Human Resource Management,* Sage, London, pp. 179-204.

Bowers, A. G. (1984), Mentors and Protégés in Male-dominated Cultures: The Experience of Top-level Women Executives, *Dissertation Abstracts International,* vol. 45, no. 9, p. 3103B.

Brett, J.M., Stroh, L.K., and Reilly, A.H. (1992), 'What is it like being a Dual Career Manager in the 1990s?', in S. Zedeck (ed), *Work, Families and Organizations,* Jossey-Bass, California.

Brewster, C. (1993), 'The Paradox of Adjustment: UK and Swedish Expatriates in Sweden and the UK', *Human Resource Management Journal,* vol. 4, no. 1, pp. 49-62.

Brewster, C. (1991), *The Management of Expatriates,* Kogan Page, London.

Brewster, C. and. Bournois, F. (1991), 'Human Resource Management: A European Perspective', *Personnel Review,* vol. 20, no. 6, pp. 4-13.

Brewster, C. and Hegewisch, A. (1994), 'Human Resource Management in Europe: Issues and Opportunities', in C. Brewster and A. Hegewisch (eds), *Policy and Practice in European Human Resource Management: The Price Waterhouse Cranfield Survey,* Routledge, London, pp. 1-21.

Brewster, C., Hegewisch, A., and Lockhart, J.T. (1991), 'Researching Human Resource Management: Methodology of the Price Waterhouse Cranfield Project on European trends', *Personnel Review,* vol. 20, no. 6, pp. 36-40.

Brewster, C. and. Scullion, H. (1997), 'A Review and Agenda for Expatriate HRM', *Human Resource Management Journal,* vol. 7, no. 3, pp. 32-41.

Brewster, C. and Tyson, S (eds) (1991), *International Comparisons in Human Resource Management,* Pitman, London.

Burke, R.J. and Davidson, M.J. (1994), 'Women in Management: Current Research Issues', in M.J. Davidson and R.J. Burke (eds), *Women in Management: Current Research Issues,* Paul Chapman, London, pp. 1-8.

Burke, R.J. and McKeen, C.A. (1994), 'Career Development Among Managerial and Professional Women', in M.J. Davidson and R.J. Burke (eds), *Women in Management: Current Research Issues,* Paul Chapman, London, pp. 65-79.

Calori, R. and De Woot, P. (eds) (1994), *A European Management Model: Beyond Diversity,* Prentice Hall, London.

Carmody, H. (1989), *Work and Family,* Paper presented to Australian Family Research Conference, 27 November, Ballarat, Victoria.

Catalyst. (1996), *Census of Women Corporate Officers and Top Earners,* Catalyst, New York.

Catalyst. (1990), *Women in Corporate Management: Survey,* Catalyst, New York.

Catalyst Career and Family Centre Staff. (1982*),* 'Corporations and Two-Career Families: Directions for the Future — *A Report on the Findings of Two National Surveys',* Catalyst, New York.

Cleveland, J.N. (1994), 'Women and Sexual Harassment: Work and Well-being in US Organizations', in M.J. Davidson and R.J. Burke (eds), *Women in Management: Current Research Issues*, Paul Chapman, London, pp. 168-91.

Cleveland, J.N. and Kerst, M.E. (1993), 'Sexual Harassment and Perceptions of Power: An Under-articulated Relationship, *Journal of Vocational Behaviour*, vol. 42, pp. 49-67.

Clutterbuck, D. (1993), *Everyone Needs a Mentor: Fostering Talent at Work*, Institute of Personnel Management, London.

Clutterbuck, D. and Devine, M. (1987), 'Having a Mentor: A Help or a Hindrance?', in D. Clutterbuck and M. Devine (eds), *Business-Women: Present and Future*, Macmillan, London.

Cockburn, C. (1991), *In the Way of Women: Men's Resistance to Sex Equality in Organisations*, Macmillan Education, Basingstoke.

Connelly, A. (ed) (1993), *Gender and the Law in Ireland*, Oak Tree Press, Dublin.

Cooper, C.L. and Davidson, M.J. (1982), *Executive Families Under Stress*, Prentice-Hall, Englewood Cliffs.

Cooper, C.L. and Hingley, P. (1983), *The Change Makers*, Harper & Row, London.

Cooper, C., and. Lewis, S. (1993), *The Workplace Revolution: Managing Today's Dual Career Families*, Kogan Page, London.

Dallalfar, A. and Movahedi, S. (1996), 'Women in Multinational Corporations: Old Myths, New Constructions and Some Deconstruction', *Organization*, vol. 3, no. 4, pp. 546-59.

Davidson, M.J. (1987), 'Women and Employment', in P. Warr (ed), *Psychology at Work*, Penguin, London.

Davidson, M.J. and Cooper, C.L. (eds) (1993), *European Women in Business and Management*, Paul Chapman, London.

Davidson, M.J. and Cooper, C.L. (1992), *Shattering the Glass Ceiling: The Woman Manager*, Paul Chapman, London.

Davidson, M.J. and Cooper, C.L. (1987), Female Managers in Britain: Comparative Review, *Human Resource Management*, vol. 26, pp. 217-42.

Davidson, M.J. and. Earnshaw, J. (1990), 'Policies, Practices and Attitudes Towards Sexual Harassment in UK Organizations', *Personnel Review*, vol. 19, no. 3, pp. 23-7.

Davison, E.D. and Punnett, B.J. (1995), 'International Assignments: Is there a Role for Gender and Race in Decisions, *The International Journal of Human Resource Management*, vol. 6, no. 2, pp. 411-41.

De Cieri, H., Dowling, P.J., and Taylor, K.F. (1991), 'The Psychological Impact of Expatriate Relocation on Partners', *International Journal of Human Resource Management*, vol. 2, no. 3, pp. 377-414.

de Woot, P. (1994), 'Towards a European Model of Management', in A R. Calori and P. de Woot (eds), *European Management Model,* Prentice Hall, London, pp. 261-77.

Diamond, E.E. (1989), 'Theories of Career Development and the Reality of Women at Work', in B.A. Gutek and L. Larwood (eds), *Women's Career Development,* Sage, Beverly Hills, California, pp. 15-27.

Dickens, L. (1994), 'Wasted Resources?: Equal Opportunities in Employment', in K. Sisson (ed), *Personnel Management: A Comprehensive Guide to Theory and Practice in Britain,* Blackwell, Oxford, pp. 253-96.

Dickens, L. (1992), *Whose Flexibility?: Discrimination and Equality Issues in Atypical Work,* Institute of Employment Rights, London.

DiTomaso, N. (1989), 'Sexuality in the Workplace: Discrimination and Harassment', in J. Hearn, D.L. Sheppard, P. Tancred-Sheriff, and G. Burrell (eds), *The Sexuality of Organization,* Sage, Newbury Park, California, pp. 71-90.

Dix, C. (1990), *A Chance for the Top: The Lives of Women Business Graduates,* Bantam Press, London.

Dowling, P.J. (1988), 'International and Domestic Personnel/Human Resource Management: Similarities and Differences', in R.S. Schuler (ed), *Readings in Personnel and Human Resource Management,* West Publishing Co, St Paul, MN.

Dreher, G. and Ash, R. (1990), 'A Comparative Study of Mentoring Among Men and Women in Managerial Professional and Technical Positions', *Journal of Applied Psychology,* vol. 75, no. 5, pp. 539-46.

Economist (1998), 'Women and Work: For Better, for Worse', *The Economist,* 18 July, pp. 3-16.

Edström, A. and Galbraith, J. (1977), Transfer of Managers as a Coordination and Control Strategy in Multinational Organizations, *Administrative Science Quarterly,* vol. 22, no. 2, pp. 248-63.

Erikson, E. (1968), *Identity: Youth and Crisis,* Norton, New York.

European Commission (1999a), *Employment in Europe 1998: Jobs for People — People for Jobs: Turning Policy Guidelines into Action,* Office for Official Publications of the European Communities, Luxembourg.

European Commission (1999b), *Employment Performance in the Member States: Employment Rates Report 1998,* Office for Official Publications of the European Communities, Luxembourg.

European Commission (1998), *Equal Opportunities for Women and Men in the European Union, Annual Report 1997,* Office for Official Publications of the European Communities, Luxembourg.

Eurostat (1996), *Basic Statistics of the European Union, Comparison with the Principal Partners of the Union,* 33rd ed., Office for Official Publications of the European Communities, Luxembourg.

Fagenson, E.A. (1989), 'The Mentor Advantage: Perceived Career/Job Experiences of Protégés Versus Non-protégés', *Journal of Organizational Behaviour,* vol. 10, pp. 309-20.

Feldman, D.C. and Thomas, D.C. (1992), 'Career Management Issues Facing Expatriates', *Journal of International Business Studies,* vol. 23, no. 2, pp. 271-293.

Fernández, M. V. (1993), 'Women in Business and Management: Spain', in M.J. Davidson and C.L. Cooper (eds), *European Women in Business and Management,* Paul Chapman Publishing, London, pp. 185-99.

Fierman, J. (1990), 'Why Women Still Don't Hit the Top', *Fortune,* July 30, pp. 40-42.

Fisher, A.B. (1987), 'Where Women are Succeeding', *Fortune,* 3 August, pp. 78-86.

Fitt, L.W. and Newton, D.A. (1981), 'When the Mentor is a Man and the Protégée is a Woman, *Harvard Business Review,* vol. 59, pp. 56-60.

Fitzgerald, L.F. and Crites, J.O. (1980), Towards a Career Psychology of Women: What do we Know? What do we Need to Know?, *Journal of Counselling Psychology,* vol. 27, no. 1, pp. 44-62.

Flanders, M.L. (1994), *Breakthrough: The Career Woman's Guide to Shattering the Glass Ceiling,* Paul Chapman, London.

Forrest, A. (1989), 'Women in a Man's World: Developing Women in Management', *Journal of Management Development,* vol. 8, no. 6, pp. 61-8.

Forster, N. (1992), 'International Managers and Mobile Families: The Professional and Personal Dynamics of Trans-National Career Pathing and Job Mobility in the 1990s', *International Journal of Human Resource Management,* vol. 3, no. 3, pp. 605-24.

Freeman, S.J.M. (1990), *Managing Lives: Corporate Women and Social Change,* University of Massachusetts Press, Amherst.

Fuchs, V.R. (1989), 'Women's Gains on the Job: Not Without a Heavy Toll', *The New York Times,* 21 August, pp. A13-4.

Gallos, J.V. (1989) 'Exploring Women's Development: Implications for Career Theory, Practice, and Research', in M.B. Arthur, D.T. Hall, and B.S. Lawrence (eds) *Handbook of Career Theory,* Cambridge University Press, New York, p.110-32.

Giele, J. (1982), 'Women's Work and Family Roles', in J. Giele (ed), *Women in the Middle Years,* Wiley, New York.

Gilligan, C. (1982), *In a Different Voice: Psychological Theory and Women's Development,* Harvard University Press, Cambridge.

Gilligan, C. (1979), 'Woman's Place in Man's Life Cycle', *Harvard Educational Review,* vol. 49, pp. 431-46.

Ginzberg, E. (1984), 'Career Development', in *Career Choice and Development,* D. Brown and L. Brooks (eds), Jossey-Bass, San Francisco, pp. 169-91.

Ginzberg, E., Ginsberg, S.W., Atelrad, S., and Herma, J.L. (1951), *Occupational Choice: An Approach to a General Theory*, Columbia University Press, New York.

Glaser, B.G. and Strauss, A.L. (1967), *The Discovery of Grounded Theory: Strategies for Qualitative Research*, Weidenfeld and Nicolson, London.

Glick, P., Zion, C. and Nelson, C. (1988), 'What Mediates Sex Discrimination in Hiring Decisions?', *Journal of Personality and Social Psychology*, vol. 55, no. 2, pp. 178-86.

Gordon, J.R. and Whelan, K.S. (1998), 'Successful Professional Women in Midlife: How Organizations Can More Effectively Understand and Respond to the Challenges', *The Academy of Management Executive*, vol. 22, no 1, pp. 8-27.

Grant, J. (1988), 'Women as Managers: What Can They Offer to Organizations?', *Organizational Dynamics*, Winter, pp. 56-63.

Gutek, B. A. and Larwood, L. (1989), 'Women's Careers are Important and Different', in B.A. Gutek and L. Larwood (eds), *Women's Career Development*, Sage, London, pp. 7-14.

Hackett, G., and Betz, N.E. (1981), 'A Self Efficacy Approach to the Career Development of Women', *Journal of Vocational Behaviour*, vol. 18, pp. 326-39.

Hall, D.T. (1990), 'Promoting Work/Family Balance: An Organizational Change Approach', *Organizational Dynamics*, vol. 18, pp. 5-18.

Hammond, V. and Holton, V. (1991), *A Balanced Workforce: Achieving Cultural Change for Women: A Comparative Study*, Ashridge Management College, London.

Handler, C.A. and Lane, I.M. (1997), 'Career Planning and Expatriate Couples', *Human Resource Management Journal*, vol. 7, no. 3, pp. 67-78.

Harris, H. (1995a), 'Organizational Influences on Women's Career Opportunities in International Management', *Women in Management Review*, vol. 10, no. 3, pp. 26-31.

Harris, H. (1995b), 'Women's Role in (International) Management', in A.W. Harzing and J Van Ruysseveldt (eds), *International Human Resource Management*, Sage, London, pp. 229-51.

Harris, P.R. and Moran, R.T. (1987), *Managing Cultural Differences*, Gulf, Houston, Texas.

Harvey, M. (1985), 'The Expatriate Family: An Overlooked Variable in International Assignments', *Columbia Journal of World Business*, Spring, pp. 84-92.

Hegewisch, A. and. Mayne, L. (1994), 'Equal Opportunities Policies in Europe', in C. Brewster and A. Hegewisch (eds), *Policy and Practice in European Human Resource Management*, Routledge, London, pp. 194-215.

Heilman, M., Block, E.C., Martell, C., Simon, R., and Simon, M. (1989), 'Has anything Changed?: Current Characteristics of Men, Women and Managers', *Journal of Applied Psychology*, vol. 74, no. 6, pp. 935-42.

Henning, M. and Jardim, A. (1977), *The Managerial Woman*, Pan Books, London.

Herbert, T.T. and Daitchman, J. (1986), 'The Canadian Dual-career Couple: Relocation and the Corporate Response', *Business Quarterly* vol. 51, no. 2, pp. 54-60.

Hewlett, S. (1986), *A Lesser Life: The Myth of Women's Liberation in America*, Morrow, New York.

Ho, S. (1984), 'Women Managers in Hong Kong: Traditional Barriers and Emerging Trends', *Equal Opportunities International*, vol. 3, no. 4, pp. 7-29.

Hochschild, A. (1989), *The Second Shift*, Viking, New York.

Hoskyns, C. (1985), 'Women's Equality and the European Community', vol. 20, no. 70, p. 72.

Hunt, A. (1981), 'Women and Underachievement at Work', *EOC Research Bulletin*, Spring, no. 5.

Hunt, A. (1975), *Survey of Management Attitudes and Practices Towards Women at Work*, HMSO, London.

Ibarra, H. (1993), 'Personal Networks of Women and Minorities in Management: A Conceptual Framework', *Academy of Management Review*, vol. 18, no. 1, pp. 56-87.

International Labor Organization. (1993), 'Unequal Race to the Top', *World of Work: US*, no. 2, pp. 6-7.

Izraeili, D.N. and Adler, N.J (eds) (1994), *Competitive Frontiers: Women Managers in a Global Economy*, Basil Blackwell, Oxford.

Izraeli, D.N., Banai, M and Zeira, Y. (1980), 'Women Executives in MNC Subsidiaries', *California Management Review*, vol. 23, no. 1, pp. 53-63.

Izraeli, D.N. and Izraeli, D. (1985), 'Sex Effects in Evaluating Leaders', *Journal of Applied Psychology*, vol. 70, no. 1, pp. 148-156.

Johnston, J. (1991), 'An Empirical Study of the Repatriation of Managers in UK Multinationals', *Human Resource Management Journal*, vol. 4, no. 1, Summer, pp. 102-9.

Kanter, R.M. (1977a), *Men and Women of the Corporation*, Basic Books, New York.

Kanter, R.M. (1977b), 'Some Effects of Proportions of Group Life: Skewed Sex Ratios and Responses to Token Women', *American Journal of Sociology*, vol. 82, pp. 965-90.

Kirkham, K. (1985), *Managing Diversity in Organizations: Teaching About Majority Group Behavior*, presentation at the 12th Annual Organizational Behavior Teaching Conference, University of Virginia.

Kleiman, C. (1992), 'Right Stuff Can Bump Against the Glass Ceiling', *Chicago Tribune*, 6 January, p. 6.

Knight, J. (1994), 'Motherhood and Management', in M. Tanton (ed), *Women in Management: A Developing Presence,* Routledge, London, pp. 141-61.

Kochan, T., Batt, R., and Dyer, L. (1992), 'International Human Resource Studies: A Framework for Future Research', in D. Lewin (ed), *Research Frontiers in Industrial Relations and Human Resources,* Industrial Relations Research Association, Madison, WI.

Korn/Ferry International in conjunction with Australian Institute of Company Directors. (1993), *Twelfth Study of Boards of Directors in Australia,* Korn/Ferry International, Sydney.

Korabik, K. (1988), *Is the Ideal Manager Masculine?: The Contribution of Femininity to Managerial Effectiveness,* Paper presented at the annual meetings of the Academy of Management, Anaheim, California.

Lach, D.H. and Gwartney-Gibbs, P.A. (1993), 'Sociological Perspectives on Sexual Harassment and Workplace Dispute Resolution', *Journal of Vocational Behaviour,* vol. 42, pp. 102-15.

Lane, H.W. and DiStefano, J.J. (1992), *International Management Behavior: From Policy to Practice,* PWS-Kent Publishing Company, Boston.

Larwood, L. and Gattiker, U.E. (1986), A Comparison of the Career Paths Used by Successful Women and Men, in B.A. Gutek, and L. Larwood (eds) *Women's Career Development,* Sage, Newbury Park.

Laufer, J. (1993), 'Women in Business and Management: France', in M.J. Davidson and C.L. Cooper (eds), *European Women in Business and Management,* Paul Chapman, London, pp. 107-32.

Laurent, A. (1986), 'The Cross-Cultural Puzzle of International Human Resource Management', *Human Resource Management,* vol. 25, no. 1, pp. 91-102.

Lawrence, P. (1993), 'Management Development in Europe: A Study in Cultural Contrast', *Human Resource Management Journal,* vol. 3, no. 1, pp. 11-23.

Leeming, A. (1994), 'Climbing Up The Ladder', *Proceedings of the British Academy of Management Conference,* Lancaster University, 14-16 September.

Legge, K. (1995), 'HRM: Rhetoric, Reality and Hidden Agendas', in J. Storey (ed), *Human Resource Management: A Critical Text,* Routledge, London, pp. 33-59.

Levinson, D., Darrow, D., Klein, E., Levinson, M., and McKee, B. (1978), *The Seasons of a Man's Life,* Knopf, New York.

Lewis, S. (1994), 'Role Tensions and Dual-Career Couples', in M.J. Davidson and R.J. Burke (eds), *Women in Management: Current Research Issues,* Paul Chapman London, pp. 230-41.

Lewis, S. and Cooper, C.L. (1987), 'Stress in Dual Earner Couples and Stage in the Life Cycle', *Journal of Occupational Psychology,* vol. 60, pp. 289-303.

McCracken, G. (1988), *The Long Interview: Qualitative Research Methods,* Sage, Beverly Hills.

McDonald, L.M. and Korabik, K. (1991), 'Work Stress and Social Support Among Male and Female Managers', *Canadian Journal of Administrative Sciences*, vol. 8, no. 2, pp. 231-8.

McGee-Calvert, L. and Ramsey, V.J. (1992), 'Bringing Women's Voice to Research on Women in Management: A Feminist Perspective', *Journal of Management Inquiry*, vol. 1, no. 1, pp. 79-88.

MacKinnon, K. (1979), *Sexual Harassment of Working Women*, Yale University Press, New Haven.

Mandelker, J. (1994), 'Breaking the Glass Border', *Working Woman*, vol. 19, no. 1, p. 16.

Marshall, J. (1995), 'Gender and Management: A Critical Review of Research', *British Journal of Management*, vol. 6, December, pp. 53-62.

Marshall, J. (1984), *Women Managers: Travellers in a Male World*, Wiley, Chichester.

Mason, J. (1996), *Qualitative Researching*, Sage, London.

Mendenhall, M., Dunbar, E, and Oddou, G. (1987), 'Expatriate Selection, Training and Career-Pathing: A Review and Critique', *Human Resource Management*, vol. 26, no. 3, pp. 331-45.

Mintzberg, H. (1979), 'An Emerging Strategy of Direct Research', *Administrative Science Quarterly*, vol. 24, December, pp. 582-89.

Monks, K. (1998), 'Employment Equality: Rhetoric and Reality in Irish Organisations', J.S. Walsh, K. Monks, and B.R. Roche (eds), *Human Resource Strategies: Policy and Practice in Ireland*, Oak Tree Press, Dublin.

Morrison, A.M. and Von Glinow, M.A. (1990), 'Women and Minorities in Management', *American Psychologist*, vol. 45, no. 2, pp. 200-8.

Morrison, A.M., White, R.P., and Van Velsor, E. (1987), *Breaking the Glass Ceiling: Can Women Reach The Top Of America's Largest Corporations?*, Addison-Wesley, Reading, MA.

Nielsen, R. (1983), *Equality Legislation in a Comparative Perspective: Towards State Feminism*, Kvinderidenskabelight Forlag, Copenhagen.

Noe, R. (1988), 'An Investigation of the Determinants of Successfully Assigned Mentoring Relationships', *Personnel Psychology*, vol. 41, pp. 457-79.

O'Donovan, K. and Szyszczak, E. (1988), *Equality and Sex Discrimination Law*, Basil Blackwell, Oxford.

O'Leary, V.E. and Johnson, J.L. (1991), 'Steep Ladder, Lonely Climb', *Women in Management Review and Abstracts*, vol. 6, no. 5, pp. 10-16.

Olivares, F. (1993), 'Women in Business and Management: Italy', in M. J. Davidson and C.L. Cooper (eds), *European Women in Business and Management*, Paul Chapman, London, pp. 161-73.

Parasuraman, S.J. and Greenhaus, J.H. (1993), 'Personal Portrait: The Life-Style of the Woman Manager', in E.A. Fagenson (ed), *Women in Management: Trends, Issues and Challenges in Management Diversity*, Sage, London, pp. 186-211.

Perun, P.J. and Bielby, D.D.V.   (1981), 'Towards a Model of Female Occupational Behaviour: A Human Development Approach', *Psychology of Women Quarterly,* vol. 6, pp. 234-52.

Peters, T. and Waterman, R.   (1982), *In Search of Excellence,* Harper & Row, New York.

Pieper, R. (ed)   (1990), *Human Resource Management: An International Comparison,* Walter de Gruyter, New York.

Pierce, J. and Delahaye, B.L.   (1996), 'Human Resource Management Implications of Dual-Career Couples', *The International Journal of Human Resource Management,* vol. 7, no. 4, pp. 905-23.

Pleck, J.H.   (1985), *Working Wives/Working Husbands,* Sage, Newbury Park, California.

Peltonen, T. (1999),   'Repatriation and career systems' in C. Brewster and H. Harris (eds), *International HRM: Contemporary Issues in Europe,* Routledge, London.

Potter, J.M.   (1989), 'Family-Related Programs: Strategic Issues', *Canadian Business Review,* pp. 27-30.

Powell, G.N. (1993), *Women and Men in Management,* Sage, Beverly Hills.

Powell, G.N. (1990), 'One More Time: Do Female and Male Managers Differ?', *Academy of Management Executive,* vol. 4, no. 3, pp. 68-75.

Pryor, J. B. (1987), 'Sexual Harassment Proclivities in Men', *Sex Roles,* vol. 17, pp. 269-90.

Punnett, B.J., Crocker, O.l., and Stevens, M.A.   (1992), 'The Challenge for Women Expatriates and Spouses: Some Empirical Evidence', *The International Journal of Human Resource Management,* vol. 3, no. 3, pp. 585-92.

Ragins, B.R.   (1989), 'Barriers to Mentoring: The Female Manager's Dilemma', *Human Relations,* vol. 42, no. 1, pp. 1-22.

Remer, A.   (1986), 'Personnel Management in Western Europe: Development, Situation and Concepts', in K. Macharzina and W.H. Staehle (eds), *European Approaches to International Management,* Walter de Gruyter, Berlin.

Reynolds, C. and. Bennett, R.   (1991), 'The Career Couple Challenge', *Personnel Journal,* vol. 70, pp. 46-9.

Roobeek, A.J.M.   (1989), 'Women, Management and Technology', in *Proceedings of the 5th Annual Conference of the European Women's Management Development Network,* Amsterdam, 25-27 October, pp. 12-22.

Rosener, J. (1990), 'Ways Women Lead', *Harvard Business Review,* November-December, pp. 119-225.

Rothwell, S.   (1984), 'Positive Action on Women's Career Development: An Overview Of The Issues for Individuals and Organizations', in C.L. Cooper and M.J. Davidson (eds), *Women in Management: Career Development for Managerial Success,* Heinemann, London, pp. 3-31.

Scase, R. and. Goffee, R. (1990), 'Women in Management: Towards A Research Agenda', *The International Journal of Human Resource Management,* vol. 1, no. 1, pp. 107-225.

Scase, R. and Goffee, R. (1989), *Reluctant Managers: Their Work And Lifestyles,* Unwin Hyman, London.

Schein, V.E. (1994), 'Managerial Sex Typing: A Persistent and Pervasive Barrier to Women's Opportunities', in M.J. Davidson and R.J. Burke (eds), *Women in Management: Current Research Issues,* Paul Chapman, London, pp. 41-52.

Schein, V.E. (1989), *Sex Role Stereotyping and Requisite Management Characteristics, Past, Present And Future,* Working paper series, no. WC 98-26, University of Western Ontario, National Centre for Management Research and Development.

Schein, V.E. and Mueller, R. (1990), *Sex-Role Stereotyping and Requisite Management Characteristics: A Cross-Cultural Look,* Paper presented at the 22nd International Congress of Applied Psychology, 22-27 July, Kyoto, Japan.

Schein, V.E., Mueller, R., Lituchy, T., and Liu, J. (1994), *Think Manager — Think Male: A Global Phenomenon?,* Gettysburg College Management Dept. Working Papers, Gettysbury, PA.

Schwartz, F.N. (1989), 'Management Women And The Facts Of Life', *Harvard Business Review,* vol. 67, no. 1, pp. 65-76.

Scullion, H. (1995), 'International Human Resource Management', in J. Storey (ed), *Human Resource Management: A Critical Text,* Routledge London, pp. 352-82.

Scullion, H. (1994), 'Staffing Policies and Strategic Control in British Multinationals', *International Studies of Management and Organization,* vol. 3, no., pp. 86-104.

Scullion, H. (1992), 'Strategic Recruitment and Development of the 'International Manager': Some European Considerations', *Human Resource Management Journal,* vol. 3, no. 1, pp. 57-69.

Seidman, I.E. (1991), *Interviewing As Qualitative Research,* Teachers College Press, London.

Serdjénian. E. (1988), *L'égalité Des Chances Ou Les Enjeux de la Mixité,* Les Editions d'Organization, Paris.

Shellenbarger, S. (1992), 'Lessons From the Workplace: How Corporate Policies and Attitudes Lag Behind Workers' Changing Needs', *Human Resource Management,* vol. 31, no. 3, pp. 157-69.

Simpson, R. (1995), 'Is Management Education On The Right Track for Women?', *Women in Management Review,* vol. 10, no. 6, pp. 3-8.

Sinclair, A. (1995), 'Sex and The MBA', *Organization,* vol. 2, no. 2, pp. 295-317.

Smith, C.R. and Hutchinson, J. (1995), *Gender: A Strategic Management Issue,* Business & Professional Publishing, Sydney.

Smith, C.R. and Still, L. (1996), *Breaking The Glass Border: Barriers To Global Careers For Women Managers in Australia*, Paper presented at 5th International Human Resource Management Conference, San Diego, California, 24-28 June.

Solomon, C. (1995), 'Repatriation, Up, Down, Or Out?', *Personnel Journal*, vol. 74, no. 1, pp. 28-30.

Storey, J. (ed) (1989), *New Perspectives On Human Resource Management*, Routledge, London.

Super, D.E. (1984), 'Career and Life Development', in D. Brown and L. Brooks (eds), *Career Choice And Development*, Jossey-Bass, San Francisco, pp. 192-234.

Super, D.E. (1957), *The Psychology Of Careers*, Harper & Row, New York.

Tangri, S.S., Burt, M.R., and Johnson, L.V. (1982), Sexual Harassment at Work: Three Explanatory Models, *Journal of Social Issues*, vol. 38, pp. 33-54.

Tanton, M. (1994), 'Developing women's presence', in M. Tanton (ed) *Women in Management: A Developing Presence*, Routledge, London, pp. 7-26.

Taylor, A.S. and Lounsbury, J.W. (1988), 'Dual-Career Couples and Geographic Transfer: Executives' Reactions to Commuter Marriage and Attitude Toward the Move', *Human Relations*, vol. 41, no. 5, pp. 407-24.

Thurley, K. (1990), 'Towards a European Approach to Personnel Management', *Personnel Management*, vol. 22, no. 9, pp. 54-7.

Thurley, K. and Wirdenius, H. (1991), 'Will Management Become "European"?: Strategic Choices for Organisations', *European Management Journal*, vol. 9, no. 2, pp. 127-34.

Tijdens, K. (1993), 'Women in Business and Management: The Netherlands', in M.J. Davidson and C.L. Cooper, (eds), *European Women in Business and Management*, Paul Chapman, London, pp. 79-92.

Torrington, D. (1994), *International Human Resource Management: Think Globally, Act Locally*, Prentice Hall, London.

Tung, R.L. (1984), 'Strategic Management Of Human Resources in the Multinational Enterprise', *Human Resource Management*, vol. 23, no. 2, pp. 129-43.

Tung, R.L. (1982), 'Selection and Training Procedures of US, European and Japanese multinationals', *California Management Review*, vol. 25, no. 1, pp. 57-71.

Tung, R.L. (1981), 'Selecting and Training of Personnel for Overseas Assignments', *Columbia Journal of World Business*, vol. 16, no. 1, pp. 68-78.

United Nations. (1993), *The Human Development Report*, Oxford University Press, Oxford.

United States Department of Labor. (1996), '*Employed Persons By Occupation, Race And Sex, Employment and Earnings*', Department of Labor, Washington, DC.

Vinnicombe, S. and Colwill, N.L.   (1995), *The Essence of Women in Management*, Prentice Hall, London.

Vinnicombe, S. and Sturges, J. (1995), 'European Women in Management', in S. Vinnicombe and N.L. Colwill (eds), *The Essence of Women in Management*, Prentice Hall, London, pp. 1-19.

Webb, J. (1987), 'Gendering Selection Psychology', *Occupational Psychology*, vol. 3, pp. 4-5.

White, B., Cox, C. and Cooper, C. (1992), *Women's Career Development: A Study Of High Flyers*, Blackwell, Oxford.

Whitley, R. (1992), *European Business Systems, Firms and Markets in their National Contexts*, Sage, London.

Woodall, J. and Winstanley, D. (1998), *Management Development: Strategy and Practice*, Blackwell, Oxford.

Index